A Photographic
Garden History

Quinta dos Azulejos, Portugal.

For Phoebe & Amy
who trekked around the world uncomplainingly
(well, almost!)

A Photographic Garden History

Roger Phillips & Nicky Foy

Layout Jill Bryan

The Generalife, Granada, Spain.

MACMILLAN

Acknowledgements

First and foremost we wish to thank the owners, gardeners and managers of the gardens we visited world-wide as it is their work that has given us all the privilege of enjoying this great inheritance.

Secondly Brent Elliot and the staff of the The Royal Horticultural Society's Lindley Library at Vicent Square. Thanks also to Martyn Rix, Gillian Barlow, Bill Bokatis and Leslie Land, who very generously photographed some gardens for us; their work has been credited on the pictures as they occur in the book.

Many thanks, also, to the hundreds of individuals who helped us in numerous ways. We would especially like to thank the following: Brenda and Nicholas Cravens McAdoo, Peglyn Faber, Vivien Perkins, Martyn and Alison Rix, Gillian Stokoe, Anne Thatcher, Junko Uno, Abe Kyoko, Mr. and Mrs. Sagamoto, Gail Zawaki, Zheng Jianming, Zhou Jiangxia. Last, but not least, thanks to our ever-patient editor, Catherine Hurley.

Powis Castle Gardens, Wales.

The main cover picture is Chenies Manor Garden, Buckinghamshire, England.

First published 1995 by Macmillan Reference Books

This edition published 1997 by Macmillan
an imprint of Macmillan Publishers Ltd
25 Eccleston Place, London SW1W 9NF
and Basingstoke

Associated companies throughout the world

ISBN 0 333 71101 7

Copyright © Roger Phillips and Nicky Foy 1995

The right of Roger Phillips and Nicky Foy to be identified as the authors of this work has been asserted by them in accordance with the Copyright, Designs and Patents Act 1988.

1 3 5 7 9 8 6 4 2

A CIP catalogue record for this book is available from the British Library.

Typeset by Parker Typesetting Service, Leicester
Printed by Toppan Printing Co. (Singapore) Pte. Ltd

Contents

Drummond Castle Gardens, Tayside, Scotland.

Introduction

This book is a record in pictures and words of a personal journey of discovery into the history of gardens and the great movements that have influenced that history. Although it has taken more than six years to complete, it doesn't purport to be a definitive history of gardens nor, practically, could it be because the ensuing book would have been too large and expensive to produce. The Middle East, India and South America were (and still are) crying out to be visited but time and finance dictated the parameters we had to set ourselves.

However, what we have attempted to do in this book is trace the history of gardens from the earliest times to the present day using extant gardens to show the representative features of particular garden styles, periods or movements. To do this, we have concentrated on three main areas: firstly, the Western European tradition of gardening and its influence on the established gardens of North America; secondly, the Eastern tradition of garden making in China and Japan and, thirdly, the gardening developments of the twentieth century which have stressed the importance of native plant conservation and wild flower gardening.

To this end, we travelled extensively in Britain and Europe from where the most seminal and influential garden movements have sprung and photographed gardens on the east and west of the United States, tracing links and parallels as well as recognizing and admiring differences. We also visited the huge Chinese Imperial Gardens and the small private scholar gardens of Wuxi and Suzhou together with the Japanese Imperial Palaces and Zen gardens of Kyoto, which enabled us to observe how ancient Chinese culture influenced the Japanese philosophy of landscape design. It also made us realize that despite enormous differences in the overall style and feel of Chinese and Japanese gardens when compared to European gardens, there were certain points of similarity (both in philosophy and design)

Mount Emei San in Sichuan, China. An archetypal landscape.

between the Eastern and Western gardening traditions. We were particularly struck by the parallels between the Imperial Gardens and the English Landscape gardens of the eighteenth century. Finally, the English Natural movement of the early twentieth century has culminated in a worldwide upsurge of interest in wild flowers and the preservation of native plant ecology that has given rise to a number of specialist gardens with some, as in The Living Desert Reserve in Palm Springs, developing the use of a new landscape technique – xeriscaping – to protect endangered species.

We had great difficulty in deciding which gardens to visit and feature as there are so many beautiful and famous ones that people expect to read about in a book on garden history. In the end, we decided that our overriding principle would be to try to select gardens that illustrated a particular period, movement or style that we were trying to elucidate rather than predominantly choose gardens that everyone had heard about or which are renowned for their general loveliness. Sometimes, of

Garden of the Gods in Colorado, North America. Rocks and plants so perfectly arranged in nature gives man an infinity of ideas to interpret.

Boscawen-un Standing Stones in Cornwall, Britain. Is this an example of man's early structural work?

course, the most famous gardens are the ones that quintessentially illustrate a specific style and so they have been included, but there are many well-known and interesting gardens that either haven't been included or have a short entry only because they didn't fulfil our primary criteria.

Although numerous excellent books on the history of gardens and gardening exist we felt that there was a need for a practical, photographic guide to garden history. In the majority of books the preponderance of text over pictures means that there is a shortage of visual evidence to back up or illustrate the points being discussed. Often, the gardens described as representative of a particular period or style are no longer in existence so they cannot be visited and it is hard for the reader to imagine what the garden was like.

This book aims, as its title suggests, to trace the history of gardens first and foremost in photographs and, by visiting the gardens during public opening hours, we have tried to give an account that while being personal and, we hope, informative, can be substantiated (or refuted!) by any reader visiting the garden themselves.

How To Use The Book

The book is organized in three main sections. The first section covers the European Tradition and within that the gardens are arranged chronologically with pictures and accompanying descriptions linked in time and/or style, following on logically from one period to the next, over the centuries. The second section covers Chinese gardens and the third section Japanese gardens which are also organized on a chronological basis. Interspersed throughout are sections on specific garden details such as grottoes, fountains, statuary, water, sculpture, etc., which cut across chronological boundaries and draw on examples from all periods to illustrate the diversity of a particular feature. Thus the book starts with the Roman peristyle gardens, then moves on over the centuries to the Italian Renaissance Gardens, the French Formal movement, the Baroque German Gardens, the English Landscape movement, on through the Rococo, the Picturesque and the Gardenesque, to the Natural movement and the Native Plant movement.

Each featured garden is introduced in a rubric with its date, name and a couple of sentences that try to

encapsulate its significance either within its period or to garden history as a whole. This is followed by more detailed text which gives the historical background to the garden before describing its main features and explaining how it is important in the spectrum of garden history.

Garden history is full of terms that refer to certain styles and movements and, over the centuries, the meaning of these terms has often shifted or changed slightly which can be rather confusing for the amateur garden historian. What we have tried to do in the text is explain terms when we come to them but as no reader is likely to sit down and read the book chronologically from cover to cover we have drawn up an extensive glossary, with definitions of gardening terms and styles.

The Photographs

All the photographs were taken during normal, public opening hours with an ordinary, hand-held 35 millimetre camera and no step-ladders or other unnatural means of gaining height were used. We took the weather as we found it so some gardens are shot in glorious sunshine while others are photographed with thunderclouds gathering overhead. The result is: *what you see is what you get.*

All the photographs were taken on a Nikon FM2 camera using Kodak Ektachrome 64 professional film. Three prime lenses were used: 28mm, 50mm, 105mm.

Roger Phillips and Nicky Foy
Eccleston Square, March 1995

Bermudan jungle as it might have been 10,000 years ago.

100 BC–AD 100 THE HOUSE OF THE WATER JETS A Roman peristyle garden at Conimbriga in which the entire garden is a pool containing raised flower beds embedded with 400 water jets and surrounded by a mosaic walkway.

The unique peristyle garden at Conimbriga has 400 water jets; sadly out of action when we photographed it. Visited March 26.

One of the many geometric mosaics at the site.

Conimbriga is a large, deserted Roman town built between the first century BC and the first century AD, and further developed around the end of the third and the beginning of the fourth centuries AD, which is now undergoing extensive archaeological investigation.

A large area in the centre of the town has been excavated revealing a number of palatial villas with peristyle gardens (see page 10). The most impressive and interesting from an historical point of view is known as the House of the Water Jets or the House of the Fountains. Unlike the majority of Roman gardens, which simply feature one large or perhaps several small fountains set within an enclosed space containing pots of plants or shrubs and statues, this garden is surrounded by a colonnaded mosaic walkway and the entire peristyle is a pool. Raised above the water are six geometrically patterned stone flower beds to match those in the surrounding colonnade, in the walls of which are embedded pipes that supply 400 jets with cool, tinkling, water.

Unfortunately the water pressure was not turned on the day we were there and we weren't able to speak Portuguese with sufficient proficiency to establish when the fountains would be functioning.

Address: Museo Monografico de Conimbriga, 3150 Condeixa, Portugal.

Another peristyle garden on the site with symmetrical, raised flower beds surrounded by an early geometric mosaic.

Note the 'slice-of-cake' bricks used to construct the pillars of the colonnaded walkway round this small peristyle garden.

AD 79 POMPEII Roman peristyle gardens were enclosed areas in the middle of the house with no external views except to the sky above. Frescoes, statues, small fountains or canals and trees, shrubs and flowers create the mood of calm tranquillity so essential in a town garden.

The ruins of Pompeii are alive with the flowers of oleander during the summer. Visited July 20.

Pompeii was totally buried by volcanic ash and tiny pumice stones when Vesuvius erupted in AD 79. A terrible tragedy for its citizens who tried, in vain, to flee but were suffocated in their houses. This natural catastrophe has, however, proved an irreplaceable source of information about every conceivable aspect of Roman life, including gardens.

The remains of Hadrian's Villa (see pages 12–13) and the letters of Pliny the Younger (AD 61–113) provide a wealth of information about the countryside gardens of the élite but the excavations at Pompeii give a unique insight into the town dwellers' gardens.

In marked contrast to Pliny's Laurentian or Tuscan Villas, the town dweller had no views and no open landscape to look out on. In fact the houses had no external windows onto the noisy streets and the garden was an enclosed area in the centre of the house surrounded by a portico or colonnaded walkway. These enclosed areas were known as peristyle gardens. Originally this *hortus* (garden) had been used for growing vegetables and was approached from the *atrium*, which was the centre of family activities. Gradually the *atrium* served more as a kind of hallway or foyer and the peristyle garden that led off from it was transformed from a utilitarian garden to a pleasure garden. The porticoes around the peristyle garden were often painted with frescoes depicting landscapes, seascapes, statues,

flowers, birds and animals. These paintings appeared to increase the spatial dimension of the house and gardens, creating an impression of looking out onto a landscape and symbolically providing the views that Pliny extolled in country gardens.

Water was, as always in hot countries, an important feature providing both coolness and sound so the peristyle garden would have one or more fountains and sometimes a small canal or pond or series of ponds. There would also be statues or herms, usually representing ancestors or gods of the house. Priapus, the god of fertility, almost always had a place somewhere, even in the smallest garden. Trees, shrubs and flowers provided shade and perfume.

One of the most delightful peristyle gardens in Pompeii is that at Casa Vetti, the house of two brothers who were wealthy merchants. The peristyle has an elegant, open, rectangular court with a painted colonnade and a number of statuettes which serve as little fountains. Priapus is in the hallway as one enters the house, placed there to banish envy.

The whole complex is enormous and you need to allow yourselves at least four to six hours to walk around and preferably **not** in the middle of the day.

Address: Pompeii, Salerno, Italy.

The House of the Faun.

House of Loreius Tiburtinus, showing the marble impluvium.

The garden behind the restaurant.

The peristyle garden of The House of the Two Brothers, Casa Vetti, has a cool, elegant colonnade surrounding the courtyard garden.

AD 118–138 HADRIAN'S VILLA A Roman villa garden with open views across the surrounding countryside as advocated by Pliny the Younger, and dramatic expanses of water that foreshadow the ideals of the Italian Renaissance garden.

The Canopus was named after Hadrian's favourite town on the Nile. The Serapeum at the far end commemorates Antinous, his favourite.
Visited July 16.

Hadrian's Villa (Villa Adriana), a huge complex of buildings covering 760 acres and exceeding in magnitude even such great royal palaces as those at Versailles or at Escurial, was built continuously by the Emperor Hadrian from AD 118 until his death in AD 138.

According to historical accounts Hadrian was an extraordinary man: soldier, conqueror, administrator, architect and patron of the arts. His travels and conquests had brought him into contact with many different cultures, ideas and styles, and numerous influences are reflected and commemorated at his villa complex in Tivoli. Contemporary writings name no

The Canopus looking north from the Serapeum.

architects connected with the building of the Villa which either substantiates the claim that Hadrian himself both planned and oversaw the execution of the works or, at least, suggests that he was instrumental at every stage of the proceedings.

An eclectic and compulsive acquirer of beautiful objects, Hadrian filled his villa and the surrounding spaces with a wonderful collection of statues, mosaics, paintings, reliefs and friezes. Sadly, the Villa has been mercilessly plundered over the centuries but a few objects remain to suggest what it must once have been like.

We learn from the contemporary writer Spartian that Hadrian specifically constructed his domain to resemble provinces and areas of great renown such as Academia, Temple, Lyceum, Poccile (now Pecile) and Canopus.

The Pecile was designed to resemble the Stoa Poikile (literally 'painted colonnade') in Athens but Hadrian's version is much larger than the original and its purpose was primarily that of an *ambulatio* or *gestatio*: a place to take slow walks after large meals to aid digestion, as advocated by the best medical practitioners in ancient Rome. The design of the Pecile was that of a double portico – a colonnaded walkway – on either side of the Pecile wall which provided a shady walk and a sunny walk depending on the time of day and inclination of the walker. The holes which held the beams for the roofing can be seen in some sections of the wall.

The Canopus (a long rectangular lake or canal lined

The Pecile, a vast colonnaded canal based on the original Stoa Poikile in Athens.

There are vast additional ruins at Hadrian's Villa.

with colonnades) was named after the delightful town of that name on the Nile where wealthy tourists went in Roman times for holidays and spiritual advice. One story suggests that Hadrian's favourite, Antinous, who was drowned in the canal at the original Canopus (possibly at the Emperor's instigation or by his own hands) is commemorated in the Serapeum (temple to Serapis), a beautiful, domed building at the far end of the Canopus. Other suggestions are that the Serapeum was used as a *triclinium*, an outdoor dining room, or was an unusual *nymphaeum*, a kind of grotto with water cascading over statues and carvings of seagods and monsters.

Enough remains of Hadrian's Villa for it to be seminal in the history of gardens for it not only drew its inspiration from what had preceded it, but also exemplifies an essential aspect of the philosophy of Roman villa gardens as expounded by Pliny the Younger in his writings on his two villa gardens (AD 23 79) and (AD 61 113); namely the concept of the 'open' garden that looks out over the surrounding landscape. The position of Hadrian's Villa at the foot of the Tibur Hill and spreading out across the undulations of the land by means of terraces thus provides the panoramic vistas across the countryside so important to Pliny. Furthermore, Hadrian's Villa used large expanses of water to create dramatic effects, thus foreshadowing one of the quintessential features of the Italian Renaissance Gardens.

Address: Villa Adriana (Hadrian's Villa), Tivoli, Italy.

The Canopus showing some of the few statues that remain.

The Villa Borghese Park. Visited August 4.

The Villa Borghese gardens in Rome (Italy), now a public park, were laid out after 1605 for Cardinal Borghese; the first in the style of the great Roman villa parks in which house and garden play an equally important part in the design. The formal Renaissance gardens around the Casino were laid out *c.*1617–19 by Rainaldi.

The central pavilion, Waddesdon Manor aviary.

The Pin Mill at Bodnant.

The Gothic Temple at Painshill.

The Aviary at Waddesdon Manor. Visited May 23.

Waddesdon Manor, Buckinghamshire (England), was built for Baron Ferdinand de Rothschild between 1877 and 1889 by Destailleur. Based on the French château style, it has formal terraces with fountains and statues from Italy, France and Holland and a French Formal-style parterre bedded out with thousands of display plants in spring and summer.

Paxton's 'Conservative Wall' – a series of elegant glasshouses at Chatsworth.

The Temple of Love at Versailles.

The Gothic Alcove at Painswick.

The Pantheon at Stourhead.

Trompe l'œil rose frescoes on the intricately painted ceilings at the Villa Giulia. Visited August 1.

The Villa Giulia (1551–5), on the edge of the Villa Borghese park in Rome (Italy), was built for Pope Julius III by Vignola, Vasari and Ammanati. It originally stood in dense woods and had a long *allée* that connected it to a landing dock on the Tiber. Now all that remains are the formal courtyard and gardens at the back of the Villa.

A trompe l'œil doorway at Pompeii.

Tufa work at Villa Aldobrandini.

Trompe l'œil windows at Villa Gamberaia.

Rocaille pillar at Villa D'Este.

Rocaille work at Villa Gamberaia.

Rocaille pillar at Villa Aldobrandini.

Rocaille work at Villa Garzoni.

Rocaille work at Veitshöchheim.

Shell work birds at Veitshöchheim.

Mosaic at Villa Aldobrandini.

A water rill at Het Loo.

A simple floor at Pompeii.

A detailed floor at Conimbriga.

Crane mosaic in The Lingering Garden.

Pebblework at The Humble Administrator's Garden.

Decorative alcove at Isola Bella.

Wall mosaic at Bussaco.

Wall mosaic at Bussaco.

Geometric floor at Conimbriga.

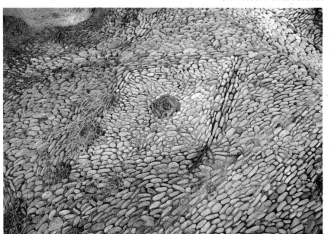

Pebblework at Stowe.

Broken china mosaic at Ballymaloe.

TEMPLA QUAM DILECTA

Decorative panel at Stowe.

13TH CENTURY THE GENERALIFE An Islamic paradise chahar-bagh garden with fountains, shrubs, trees and miradors creating an atmosphere of coolness and tranquillity and providing a retreat from the burning sun in the plains and mountains beyond the palace.

The Patio de la Acequia, the Court of the Long Pond, at the Generalife. Visited May 2.

The Generalife, meaning literally 'the garden of the architect', was built in the thirteenth century as a summer palace for the sultans of the Nazar dynasty. Set on a hill slightly above the Alhambra Palace, with a small valley in between, it can be reached either by a viaduct that spans the valley between the two gardens or from its own entrance higher up the hill.

Although the Generalife has undergone a number of changes and additions over the centuries, it still retains much of the flavour of the Islamic paradise garden. In Persia, the traditional garden layout was a chahar-bagh; literally a 'four-fold' garden in which the square or rectangular area was divided into four equal parts by intersecting water channels with a pavilion or platform at the centre.

The intimate inner garden, the Patio de la Acequia (the Court of the Long Pond), is set midway up the hill, with stunning views of the Alhambra Palace in the nearer distance on one side, and more distant views of the dry, yellowish Sierra mountains dotted with scrubby trees, on the other side. The Patio de la Acequia consists of a long, rectangular pool bordered by beds containing cypress and orange trees, hedges of myrtle and numerous shrubs of roses and magnolia. A beautifully cool colonnade walkway forms the boundary of the garden on the west side and two miradors at either end provide views over the garden and, at the north end, out over the surrounding countryside.

The pretty arching water jets that criss-cross the pond are a later, Renaissance addition. Excavations done in

1958 revealed that the original planting in the beds parallel to the pool was at least half a metre lower and would therefore, from the miradors, have created a carpet-like pattern within the chahar-bagh; the tops of the flowers being approximately on a level with the paths rather than, as now, considerably higher. Remains of column bases at the central crossing suggest that there might once have been some sort of pavilion or platform which would again fit the Islamic concept of the four-fold garden.

Above the Patio de la Acequia is another Moorish garden, the Patio de los Cipresses, with a pool, a central fountain and ancient cypress trees which can be viewed from the two storey gallery on the north side. Above this again is the Cantino de los Cascades – a stairway composed of three long, simple flights of steps, each with a landing adorned by a small basin with a fountain at the centre. Flanking the stairway are balustrades with open channels in the centre, down which water runs and tinkles musically. The whole stairway is overarched by dense foliage, creating a mysterious and magical atmosphere.

Below, and surrounding the Patio de la Acequia, a large garden containing parterres, terraces, clipped hedges, roses in profusion, patios, pools, fountains and an amphitheatre, has many delights but reflects much later planting styles than the Arab influences in the gardens surrounding the main building.

Address: The Generalife, Granada, Spain.

The Patio de los Cipreses at the Generalife.

The fountains of the Patio de la Acequia.

A verdant rill at the Generalife.

The upper garden at the Generalife.

1333–91 THE ALHAMBRA PALACE
An Islamic Persian garden recreated on European soil by the conquering Moors, with running water, shade, tranquillity and fragrance the chief components.

Looking from the Generalife to the Alhambra Palace. Visited May 3.

The Alhambra Palace or Red Castle was built predominantly in the fourteenth century by the Moorish conquerors, Yusuf I (1333–53) and his son Mohammed V (1353–91), but the earliest citadel on the site dates from the ninth century. Although the fortress complex was recaptured by the Christian monarchs Ferdinand and Isabella in 1592 and parts of it were destroyed in the early sixteenthth century by Charles V so that he could

The Court of Lions.

build an enormous, incongruous Renaissance palace in its midst, the overall feel of the palace and its gardens remains quintessentially Moorish and provides the twentieth-century visitor with a unique understanding of the traditional components of an Islamic garden.

Coolness, shade, water, tranquillity and fragrance are the elements of Islamic gardens that provide a retreat from the heat of the sun and an earthly reincarnation of the heavenly bliss that will be achieved by the faithful.

Set high on a hill overlooking Granada, above the valley of the Darro River and against the dramatic backdrop of the Sierra Nevada Mountains, the Alhambra Palace is able to recreate in its patios and courtyards the coolness and tranquillity which provide such relief to the inhabitants of hot climates and, by a complex system of irrigation, divert water from the Darro River to feed its fountains and irrigate its gardens.

The three gardens of the Palace which best capture the Islamic spirit, despite changes over the centuries, are the Patio do los Arrayianes (Court of the Myrtles), also known as the Patio de la Alberca (Court of the Pool), the Patio de los Leones (Court of the Lions) and the Patio de Daraxa (Court of the Sultana).

The Court of the Myrtles is, like most Islamic gardens, rectangular. A central, shallow pool with a fountain at

Delicate fountains abound in the Alhambra.

Islamic abstract tile work.

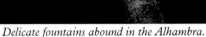

The Court of the Lions is a chahar-bagh.

each end is bordered on the long sides by two, parallel, clipped myrtle hedges which were introduced in the late nineteenth century although what form this original planting took is unknown.

The Court of the Lions is the most Islamic in feel. It follows the ancient tradition of the chahar-bagh – a rectangular garden divided into four by watercourses – in the centre of which is a twelve-sided fountain supported by the backs of twelve lions whose mouths spout water. The water flows along tunnels from fountains in four rooms that symmetrically face into the courtyard from behind arcades of alabaster arches, out into the central courtyard fountain, thus linking the interior with the exterior. The four beds which the water channels divide are now filled with gravel but originally they would have been at least a metre lower and probably planted with orange trees which would just have reached the level of the paths and which, from above, would have looked like the patterns on Persian carpets.

The Daraxa Patio also has a central fountain set in a pool with four points and four curved sides – a square on a circle which is a traditional feature of Islamic gardens. The tall cypresses and the overlooking mirador create a very romantic atmosphere of times long past, although the clipped box parterres are a much later addition not really in keeping with the original Moorish palace.

Finally, the Partal Gardens – a twentieth-century composition of terraces, parterres of clipped box and numerous potted plants – provide a marked contrast to the inner courtyard and palace and, although charming enough in themselves, have nothing to do with the tradition of the Islamic garden that is encapsulated in the Alhambra Palace itself.

Address: Alhambra Palace, Granada, Spain.

Intricate Islamic stonework.

1552 PARCO DI MOSTRI A baroque extravaganza in a sacred wood, this park with its many monstrous carvings and statues is unlike anything else of its period, and has none of the features of the other Italian Renaissance Gardens that were being built at the same time.

The Leaning House which was the original entrance to the garden. Visited August 12.

The Parco di Mostri (Monster Park), also known as the Sacro Bosco (Holy Wood), was originally part of the grounds of the Villa Orsini, Bomarzo but it is now completely separate from the Villa which is owned by the State while the Parco di Mostri is owned by the Bettini family.

Built in 1552 for Prince Vicino Orsini there seems to be considerable confusion as to who the architects were. Two very learned modern books on gardening history

The dragon.

state that Vignola (1507–73), who designed the Villa Lante (see pages 34–5), may have had a hand in it but Giovanni Bettini, the present owner of the park who has saved it from obscurity and restored it to take its rightful place in the history of Italian gardens, says quite categorically in his guide book of the garden that it was Pirro Ligorio (c.1520–85) who designed and laid out the park for Orsini. Furthermore, he says that the Temple, which Orsini commissioned in 1572 on the death of his wife and which one authority claims to be undoubtedly the work of Vignola, is far more reminiscent of the style of Ligorio.

However, like almost everything else about this garden's history, it remains a mystery.

Bomarzo is an enigma. It is like nothing else of its period and, if anything, foreshadows elements of the eighteenth-century Gothic movement. Nothing about it fits into the normal criteria of Italian Renaissance Gardens. There is no villa in the garden, nor does it appear that there ever has been. The Orsini *castello* is many hundreds of yards away on a hill in the town and presumably one could originally reach the Parco di Mostri through the villa grounds, although that no longer appears to be possible. There is no geometric basis of the classical kind in the architectural layout, no formal garden, no parterres or *allées*.

One thing there is plenty of is baroque imagination: spectacle, surprise and optical illusion greet one at every turn. Gigantic monsters, gods, sphinxes, lopsided houses, animals and mythical creatures, all carved out of the massive boulders found in the park, loom up at every corner – the meaning and purpose of which was presumably more comprehensible to Renaissance visitors than it is to modern ones.

Bettini's guide book attempts to explain the meaning behind each of the sculptures and their links with mythology and Ariosto's epic poem *Orlando Furioso* (1532) but it is difficult to find a clear pattern. Perhaps there was never supposed to be one. Perhaps the seemingly random nature and disposition of the sculptures was intended to be surprising, deliberately knocking preconceived, orderly notions on the head.

Certainly this is a wonderful place to visit with children. They will particularly enjoy the lopsided house which, according to Bettini, was where the original entrance to the park was. He says it was Orsini's plan to give his friends a surprise when they lay down for a restful siesta after a heavy lunch, only to find their heads spinning because of the topsy turvy levels.

The Park is quite hard to find so follow the signs for Parco di Mostri not Villa Orsini. Some guide books are confusing on this point and we wasted time going up to the Villa which is totally separate from the Park.

Address: Parco di Mostri, Bomarzo, Nr Viterbo, Italy.

Proteus, the son of Neptune.

The Orc, the name is a corruption of Orcus, a god of the underworld.

1628 BUSSACO A seventeenth-century reincarnation of the *sacro bosque*, a sacred wood which since earliest times had a special spiritual atmosphere that transcended that of other landscapes, and whose ancient trees were preserved by the monks who originally lived there.

A view down to the Palace Hotel from the lookout point on the top of the hill. Visited March 31.

The terrace in the formal garden.

Bussaco (Bucaco) was a piece of land originally bought by the Order of the Barefoot Carmelites in 1628 to found a monastery and provide an environment into which they could retreat from the world and live a secluded life of prayer and homage to God. On discovering the still virgin forest of Bussaco, the Head of the Order is reputed to have said: 'There are no words to hold all that the Maker has put together in this place,' and he determined that the monks who lived there should repay the forest for what it gave them in tranquillity and peace to commune with God, by protecting the trees that existed there. No tree was permitted to be cut down unless at least two-thirds of the community agreed and in this way the forest's ancient native trees were preserved. When the monks had built their monastery, refectory and infirmary, they built a wall around their land which had only one gate and thus sealed themselves into their enclosure away from all the temptations of the outside world.

Over the years, the monks moved out of their cells in the monastery and built themselves little cells in the forest where they became entirely self-sufficient for weeks or months at a time. These little hermitages can still be seen all over the forest.

When, in the nineteenth century, religious orders were disbanded, Bussaco was put up for sale but as its only treasures were its trees, there were no immediate buyers

The parterre de broderie seen from the roof of the Palace Hotel.

Tree ferns in the Vale dos Fetos.

Looking up the water staircase to the Fonte Fria in Bussaco.

Looking down from the Fonte Fria.

and the old monks were permitted to live out their lives there. Towards the end of the century King Carlos of Spain, remembering childhood holidays spent at Bussaco, gave consent for a huge palace to be built based on plans originated by his grandfather, Prince Ferdinand. However, the original concept of it as a hunting lodge was abandoned in favour of a new idea from Navarro, the Minister for Public Works, who conceived the idea of the palace as a huge hotel, in the style of those on the French Riviera and Lake Geneva, with a separate private hunting lodge in case of royal visits.

By 1909 Bussaco Palace was completed and though its incredible gothic ornateness was disapproved of by some critics, the hotel quickly became very fashionable and popular among the wealthy, travelling classes who appreciated the luxury and spaciousness of its rooms and the beauty of its setting.

Owned by the State, Bussaco Palace and forest are now preserved as a priceless example of Portugal's botanical, historical, religious and architectural heritage. Not only does the forest contain the most wonderful collection of trees and shrubs, both those that pre-date the founding of the monastery in the seventeenth century and those exotics from the New World that have been

The sunken garden of Saint Teresa in Bussaco.

planted during the last two hundred years, but the area is also an important geological site and a sanctuary for many birds and rare animals.

It is a wonderful place to stay – a haven from the crush and pollution of Lisbon – for both the fantastical gothic castle, the Bussaco Palace Hotel, and the remarkable forest with its magnificent shrubs and trees: towering pink and white camellias, deep rose red rhododendrons and thousands of arum lilies. Everywhere, little paths lead through the lush jungle-like undergrowth and unexpected little grottoes and hermitages and stations of the cross are dotted throughout the woods. Its significance to garden history lies in the most commonly accepted meaning of the word Bussaco. Although there have been many interpretations as to the origins of this word, Bussaco seems to be derived from *sacro bosque*; sacred (holy) wood. Areas of land that seemed to have a special, spiritual 'feel' about them existed thousands of years ago, according to Thacker in *The History of Gardens*, and it is precisely in this context that Bussaco should be seen. The first monks recognized it and settled there because of it and the special 'sacred' quality still seems to exist there today.

You don't have to stay at the hotel in order to visit the gardens but it takes several strenuous walks to do justice to the whole forest, so it's well worth it.

Address: Palace Hotel do Bussaco, Mata de Bussaco, Luso, 3050 Mealhada, Portugal.

A hermit's hut.

A grotto in the woods.

1559–80 VILLA D'ESTE A masterpiece of the Italian Renaissance mannerist style which drew its inspiration not only from its wonderful hill-top position but also from its use of allegory and symbolism to praise the house's owner and extol the ingenious water displays.

Looking down over the garden from the Villa d'Este. Visited August 14.

The Organ Fountain.

Villa d'Este was built between 1559 and 1580 by the architect Pirro Ligorio (*c.*1520–85) for Cardinal Ippolito d'Este (1509–72), son of the infamous Lucretia Borgia and Alfonso d'Este, a Governor of Tivoli.

Ippolito wanted to create a country retreat to outstrip that of Cardinal Alessandro Farnese at Caprarola so he commissioned a man of wide-ranging talents and interests. Ligorio was not only an architect but also an artist, garden designer, antiquary and archaeologist and all these talents were employed in the design and construction of the garden at Villa d'Este.

Familiar, no doubt, with *Del Governo della Famigha* by Leone Battista Alberti (1404–72) which extols the virtues of rural life and expounds the importance of beautiful views of the landscape achieved by siting country villas on the hillside, Ligorio exploited the hilly landscape of Tivoli to create a villa and garden that gave Ippolito (and subsequent visitors) a spectacular view over his domain and the surrounding countryside.

This commanding hilltop position not only looks out across the city and beyond but also looks down on to the most complete and varied water garden ever built.

The fundamental architectural pattern of the garden is based on the simple geometric shapes so beloved of the classical period, influenced by Ligorio's archaeological excavations at the nearby Hadrian's Villa (see pages

12–13). However, the creation of numerous water displays, fountains, statues and grottoes, often incorporating complex mechanical devices to surprise, startle and sometimes wet those who approached them, together with the numerous allegorical and iconographic references throughout the garden, put the Villa d'Este firmly in the so called Mannerist tradition of the Italian Renaissance Garden.

For example, the idea for the ingenious automata, The Fountain of the Owl, came from Hero's *Pneumatica*, a classical first-century text known but not printed in Italy until 1575. The fountain originally had metallic birds driven by a mechanism that made flute-like noises emanate from their throats until, at a certain moment, another device would make the owl screech aggressively and all the birds would fall silent or scamper away (accounts of this vary). Imagine the surprise and wonderment of contemporary visitors to this amazing contraption. Sadly, it no longer survives. Similarly, the Organ Fountain is so named because it had a water driven mechanism that reproduced the sound of an organ and it was one of the great marvels of the garden in its heyday.

The influence of classical antiquity was to be seen throughout the gardens; not only in some of the features like the 'Rometta' or Little Rome that had stone models of Roman buildings as they would have looked in ancient times and the Orato Fountain which was inspired by the Triclinium at the end of the Canopus at Hadrian's Villa (see pages 12–13), but in many of the allegorical and iconographic themes that ran throughout the garden.

Hercules symbolized the strength of the d'Este family, who claimed their ancestry back to the great hero, and was also supposed to suggest the similarity between his task of cleaning the Augean stables with the task Ippolito had set himself in redirecting the Aniene River to provide water for his magnificent garden.

There was originally a large statue of Hercules in a niche on the curving staircases on the central axis which would have been seen immediately by those entering the garden via the main entrance which used to be at the bottom of the hillside.

Diana of Ephesus.

The Neptune Fountain.

Allegorical fountain.

The Rometta (Little Rome). The stone boat symbolizes the Catholic Church in Villa d'Este.

The Fontana dell'Ovato, the Oval Fountain.

The Hundred Fountains pathway in Villa d'Este.

The Pathway of One Hundred Fountains, still a wonderfully impressive sight, used to have one hundred stucco reliefs depicting scenes from Ovid's *Metamorphoses* but, sadly, the majority of these features and the symbolic meaning that they would have imparted to a well-read and cultured Renaissance man have been largely destroyed.

However, although much of the detail has been lost or obscured over the centuries, the overall intention of Ippolito and Ligorio is unmistakable. Together they built a garden whose prime intention was to impress, amaze and overwhelm all who visited it – namely the wealthiest, most influential and powerful men of the day. Four hundred years later, it still bedazzles the visitor with its richness, spectacle and beauty but, as Thacker says in *The History of Gardens*, it seems to have lost something of the mystery and spirit to which earlier writers, painters and musicians such as Montaigne, Fragonard and Liszt pay tribute.

Address: Villa d'Este, Tivoli, Italy.

The Fountain of Dragons.

1564–86 VILLA LANTE A beautifully preserved Italian Renaissance masterpiece by Vignola, who exploited the sloping site to create a lyrical, sparkling water garden whose central axis was unbroken because of the unusual positioning of the twin villas on either side of the garden rather than in the centre.

Looking down over the formal parterres to the Isolotta in the fountain pool. Visited August 16.

The decorative, raised water-channel down the main staircase.

Villa Lante was designed by Giacomo Barozzi da Vignola (1507–73) in 1564, initially for Cardinal Riario but, subsequently, for Cardinal Gambara, who quickly succeeded him. Although Vignola died before the garden was completed, it is considered his masterpiece and it is one of the best preserved and most lovely gardens of the Renaissance period.

Villa Lante has gained a reputation as one of the quintessential Renaissance gardens. This is because, firstly, its position on a hill in Bagnaia means that even as you enter at the lower end of the property, you have a view over the town. As you ascend the long, rectangular-shaped garden, the lower parterre garden and fountains first come into view, then the surrounding countryside spreads out before you.

Secondly, the garden has a strong geometric pattern – derived originally from classical architecture but expanded and defined more strongly in the Renaissance era – which is observed as one both ascends and descends the garden.

Thirdly, the garden is above all a water garden. Not a rushing, gushing ostentatious one full of ingenious water tricks but a quieter, more contemplative garden with cooling small fountains trickling, glistening and cooling everything. The water descends from a rustic grotto at the top of the garden down through a series of fountains, pools and stairways, even disappearing underground at some points to come out in the calm fountain pool in the middle of the parterre garden below the villas.

The cascade is fed from the mouth of a crayfish, gambaro, a play on the name Cardinal Gambara.

Looking down from above the gambaro.

The Casini, the twin villas on either side of the garden, aid the symmetry but are unobtrusive, emphasizing the importance of the garden over the house; an unusual feature when you compare it with the Villa d'Este (pages 30–33) where the house is placed in the centre at the top of the garden and one is ever conscious of it as one ascends. Here, one climbs up to the grotto and looks down on the sparkling array of different water conduits and it is this view which gives the garden its individual feel and charm.

Another interesting feature of the Villa Lante is the park or *bosco* outside the formal garden. As you enter the main gates, the park spreads in front of you and away to the right while the entrance to the formal garden and villas is on the left. Although originally used as a hunting park, the *bosco* had a number of fountains (including the lovely Pegasus Fountain) and a maze (now gone) which echoed themes in the formal garden thus linking what seems like two separate entities. Unfortunately, many of these fountains and the maze were changed or destroyed by Cardinal Montalto when he took over the Villa after Cardinal Gambara's death in 1587.

Address: Villa Lante, Bagnaia, Nr Viterbo, Italy.

The fountain of Pegasus, in the bosco.

1598–1604 VILLA ALDOBRANDINI A typical Italian Renaissance garden with classical features such as a *giardino segreto*, a parterre garden, a *bosco* and a hillside setting, yet with baroque elements like the Water Spectacle foreshadowing the French Formal Movement.

The Water Theatre is cut into the hillside at the back of the house. Visited July 27.

The Villa Aldobrandini was designed by Giacomo della Porto and Carlo Maderno for Cardinal Pietro Aldobrandini between 1598 and 1604. It is the finest of a number of villas that were built in the hills at this period as the area had become a fashionable retreat for wealthy Romans trying to escape the summer heat.

While still very much a Renaissance garden in many respects with its hillside setting and panoramic views, its *giardino segreto*, its parterre garden and its *bosco*, it stands out, too, as something different because it introduces baroque elements into the classical layout and foreshadows some of the characteristics that the French Formal Movement was to take up and develop to perfection.

The first, most notable feature is the fact that the house is in the middle of the garden, not at the top as at Villa d'Este (see pages 30–33). Built halfway up the hillside, it still retains a view out over the town but, more importantly, the master of the house can, by looking in either direction from the gallery, see down the front garden *allée* of clipped ilex hedges to the main gates and, out at the back, to the Water Theatre carved into the hillside, and beyond to where the garden begins at the top of the hillside. There is the grotto from which the water descends down a series of falls, cascades and rills similar to those at the Villa Lante (see pages 34–35) but here on a much grander, more spectacular scale. The fact that those who are enjoying the statues and *giochi d'acqua* (water games, devices and automata) in the Water Theatre cannot see the descent of the water from its source while the master in his villa can, is symptomatic of the baroque obsession with optical illusion. That and the idea of the master being in authoritative control over all that he surveys are both important features later incorporated into French formal garden design.

The other leap forward in terms of garden history and design at Villa Aldobrandini was the emphasis on dramatic spectacle. This is less easy to envisage today than it was in the seventeeth century because the water is not turned on (or it certainly wasn't the day we visited) and much of the statuary and most of the automata have disappeared. But accounts by visitors in the seventeenth century highlight the overwhelming spectacle of the water devices.

John Evelyn (1620–1706), the English diarist, visited the Villa in 1654 and described with amazement 'the numerous, surprising, inventions', the water spurting out of the Atlas fountain, the Polyphemus Monster making a roaring noise with a horn, birds moving and chirping, and organ noises. But most of all he was impressed by the recreation of a stormy tempest: 'the representation of a storm is most naturall, with such fury of raine, wind and Thunder as one would imagine oneself in some extreame Tempest.'

Tickets cannot be bought at the Villa but must be obtained from Azienda di Soggiorno, Piazza Marconi 1, Frascati.

Address: Villa Aldobrandini, Frascati, Italy.

Looking back to the Villa framed by two dramatic rocaille pillars.

The Atlas statue in the Water Theatre.

Looking up the water staircase, now dry.

15TH–16TH CENTURY VILLA GAMBERAIA 'Garden rooms' perfected in this Renaissance Tuscan garden, in marked contrast to the large, spectacular spaces and baroque atmosphere in some other gardens of the period.

Looking across the water parterre and formal gardens to the Villa. Visited August 3.

The Villa Gamberaia dates back to the fifteenth century although nothing is known of its early designer and no plans exist showing its original layout. Evolving over the centuries, the most important developments took place when the Capponi family acquired the property in the eighteenth century, beginning with the quartered design of what is now the water parterre and continuing with the addition of the long bowling *allée* and grotto. At the beginning of the twentieth century the house and gardens were bought by the Serbian Princess Ghyka who laid out the rest of the garden based on Renaissance principles. After sustaining serious damage in the Second World War, meticulous restoration work has been undertaken by the Marchi family to return the gardens to

Looking down the allée to the nymphaeum.

the original eighteenth-century layout.

The gardens at the Villa Gamberaia are extolled by every eminent garden writer for encapsulating the ideal of the Tuscan garden of the Florentine Renaissance but, as little is known about how the garden evolved over the centuries, it is hard to be precise as to how much of the design was actually planned and executed during the fifteenth and sixteenth centuries and then merely worked on for the next 300 years, and how much the early layout was changed and added to by later owners working to explore ideas fashionable in their own times.

However, the fact is that the garden at the Villa Gamberaia provides an interesting and marked contrast to somewhere like the baroque garden at the Villa Garzoni (see pages 42–43). Rather than being a big spectacular garden designed to be seen as a whole, Gamberaia's design is a series of units, or 'garden rooms' as they are generally called, each having its own separate identity and purpose and only loosely interlinking to form the total garden space.

Geoffrey and Susan Jellicoe in *The Landscape of Man* feel that the gardens at Gamberaia represent some of the Mannerist principles, something halfway between the basic geometry of the classical period and the struggles of the baroque era to recognize other levels of the human mind; but Joyce's definition of the Mannerist School in *Garden Styles* which places its emphasis on iconography and *giochi d'acqua* doesn't fit the Gamberaia at all, though it does have the requisite grotto.

As espoused by Leone Battista Alberti in *De Re Aedificatoria*, the Gamberaia gardens are on a hill and make the most of the views over the Arno Valley to Florence in the distance, particularly from the balustraded south end of the long grass bowling *allée* that lies along the east side of the entrance drive, and the water garden. At the north end of the grass *allée* (parallel to the entrance drive) is a *nymphaeum* with *rocaille* decoration (a mosaic of pebbles, shells, tufa and stalactite) bordered by tall cypresses and pots of azaleas. On the left hand side as one looks down the *allée* towards Florence, two *bosci* (woods) of Ilex flank the decorated grotto and lemon garden.

The main view from the house overlooks the water parterre with beautiful hedges of clipped box and topiary and pots of orange trees. At the far end is a semicircular pond surrounded by a cypress arcade clipped into arches which alternately provides shelter from the winter wind and enjoyment of the sun in cold weather and enables one to savour the coolness and shade from the scorching sun in the summer.

Alberti would have approved of everything about the Gamberaia – its surprise views, its grotto, its enclosed areas ('garden rooms'), its geometrical outlines, its symmetrical planting and its *nymphaeum* – a perfect Renaissance Tuscan garden whose influence can be seen throughout twentieth-century British, European and American garden design.

The garden is not as easy to get into as it was but visits can be made by arrangement through Agriturist, Piazza San Firenze 3, Firenze 50100.

Address: Villa Gamberaia, Via del Rosellino, Settignano, Italy.

A detail of the nymphaeum.

The wonderful giardino segreto, secret garden.

1630–70 ISOLA BELLA An Italian baroque masterpiece conceived as a ship floating in Lake Maggiore, with its tiers of terraces now so overgrown that it conjures up images of the Hanging Gardens of Babylon.

An early morning view of Isola Bella from Stresa. Visited August 16.

Isola Bella on Lake Maggiore comprises a palace and garden whose original designs were drawn up by the architect, Angelo Crivelli, for the extremely wealthy and powerful Borromeo family who, already having built a splendid palace on the nearby Isola Madre, wanted a summer residence and garden for entertaining guests. Despite Crivelli's untimely death in 1630, the garden was laid out following his original designs although the plans for the palace were modified by the architects Morelli, Castelli and Fontana. By about 1670 work on the palace and gardens was completed.

An early engraving of the island clearly shows Crivelli's original architectural conception. The palace and garden and, in fact, the whole island were to be built in such a way as to create the impression of a huge ship majestically gliding across the waters of the lake with a fabulous back-drop of imposing, snow-clad mountains. The overall form of the island lent itself well to this conception. The wider, south end was to be the stern with ten ascending terraces culminating in the pilot bridge. The north end had the palace representing the bow and the prow by the main pointed dock which was to be the landing stage for visiting dignitaries. However, this pointed prow was never built nor did the palace

An evening shot of the boat-shaped island.

Looking through to the giardino segreto.

The Amphitheatre.

The formal parterres.

completely conform to the early plans.

The ten terraces ascending to a truncated pyramid were designed, according to some writers, to mirror The Hanging Gardens of Babylon. They were ornamented with parapets and espaliers and huge pots of citrus trees; each level had its own garden, some with pools and fountains fed by an enormous reservoir concealed under the surface structure. The placing of statues and sculpture in key positions along the terraces and balustrades all helped to create the image of a majestic galleon.

But time and nature have overpowered the original vision. Enormous trees and shrubs on the terraces have blurred the clean-cut, ship-like outline with their height and luxuriant growth, making it look more like the Hanging Gardens than they previously must have looked.

Another feature of this stunning baroque masterpiece is the rococo amphitheatre facing the house at the top end of the garden behind the 'stern' with sparkling pools, fountains, mosaic work and statues. A beautiful aviary with white doves sits on the eastern side and white peacocks parade among the exotic shrubs and trees in front of the amphitheatre. A series of elaborate grottoes, a conservatory, a *giardino segreto* (not accessible), a parterre de broderie, an English flower garden and spectacular views of the surrounding Alps in every direction combine to make this a fantastic place to visit.

Address: Isola Bella, one of the Borromean Islands, Lake Maggiore, Italy. Reached by boat from Stresa, Baveno or Pallanza.

The ten tiered terraces culminating in the balustraded Pilot Bridge.

1652 VILLA GARZONI An Italian baroque spectacle designed as a single unit that, with its emphasis on illusion and theatricality, encourages the visitor to make an imaginative leap from the familiar to the mysterious.

Looking down over the formal terraces of the Villa Garzoni. Visited August 10.

The Villa Garzoni was originally a medieval fortress on the foundations of which, in 1652, Romano Garzoni commissioned the work that was to transform it into a magnificent country villa and create gardens which would be regarded, in the twentieth century, as a perfect example of seventeenth-century Italian Baroque. Now owned by the local commune and virtually adjacent to the Pinocchio theme park, it is rather garish but, nevertheless, remains one of the great gardens of its period and place.

According to Geoffrey and Susan Jellico in *The*

An imaginative pot plant arrangement.

Landscape of Man, the Baroque movement in Italy arose out of man's changing view of himself within the universe as a result of a string of scientific discoveries from Copernicus to Newton. Renaissance thinking was moving away from the classical, finite philosophy that had dominated man's thought up this point, to a realization of the earth as a small component in a much larger universe that was a great swirling mass of unknown entities. This movement, away from the classical finite – that which could be seen – towards the baroque infinite – that which could only be grasped through imagination – is observed in the theatricality and spectacle of a garden like Garzoni where the art of illusion creates one, huge, interlocking unit of space which is not only an object in itself but, more importantly, one of many others that all interrelate to form an intricate chain.

Drawing its inspiration from two great gardens of the sixteenth century, Villa d'Este (see pages 30–33) and Villa Lante (see pages 34-35), the Villa Garzoni is built on a hillside that commands a panoramic view of the countryside yet it is, nevertheless, very different in that the garden is built to one side of the house (not behind it like at Villa d'Este or through it as is the case with Villa Lante) and is designed as a total entity in its own right. Although the formal parterre garden with its clipped box in heraldic patterns and two circular ponds sited at the bottom of the garden can be seen from the Villa, the

From the formal garden looking up to the three, grand promenade terraces with their double ramped steps.

garden is not really designed as an adjunct to the house from which the master can oversee his domain.

From the formal garden three grand, promenade terraces with double ramped steps ascend the main axis to a spectacular cascade that bursts forth from rocks made in the shape of a giant representing Fame. On either side of the steps, flanking the cascading water, *bosci* (wood) close in towards the central axis from which the statues, stone balustrades and steps seem to emerge. In the centre of the dark green shrubbery a labyrinth leads to a hidden grotto. On the upper terrace a small open air theatre lined with statues is more a conceit than an actual theatre as it is too small for practical purposes. A bath house as the top of the hill, added in the eighteenth century, was converted from what was originally, in the seventeenth century, a hermitage, according to Ethne Clarke in *The Gardens of Tuscany*.

When seen from above, the overall view of the garden seems elongated while from below the image is far more compressed: the optical illusion is deceptive from both ends.

An exceptional garden, Garzoni has certain links with the past yet it also breaks new ground, representing a marked shift in the philosophy of garden design when compared with earlier gardens, in particular the idea of 'garden rooms' that pervaded the gardens of Tuscany in the previous century.

Address: Villa Garzoni, Collodi, Tuscany, Italy.

The cascade pool.

The grotto.

Circa 1750 VILLA TORRIGIANI A perfect baroque *giochi d'acqua* in a sunken *giardino segreto* is all that remains of this seventeenth-century, formal Italian garden transformed by the influences of the English Landscape Movement which became fashionable in the nineteenth century.

The sunken giardino segreto, or Garden of Flora, looking towards the nymphaeum. Visited August 8.

The Villa Torrigiani was originally called the Villa Santini after the family that owned it in the seventeenth century and laid out the gardens, adapting the simple sixteenth-century villa to reflect the fashionable baroque manner of the period. The house, which once had a much simpler façade, was overlaid in the mid-seventeenth century with 'an intricate mask' of plaques, sculptured coats of arms and numerous statues, according to Sir Harold Acton in *Tuscan Villas*. The garden, as seen in an early plan, was laid out in formal parterres de broderie both in front and behind; shades of Villa Garzoni spring to mind (see pages 42–43). Although the house remains essentially the same, in the nineteenth century the Italian fashion for English landscape gardening resulted here in a complete uprooting of the formal beds in favour of sweeping lawns.

However, one important feature of the original garden remains intact – the sunken *giardino segreto* or Garden of Flora, which is on the right of the house as you approach it. The secret garden comprises a Grotto of the Seven Winds and a *nymphaeum* of Flora at one end with exuberantly planted box parterres on either side of a central path that leads to another hidden grotto. Flights of stone stairs on either side lead to a terrace which overlooks Flora's garden. Behind the terrace is a *bosco* with a pool ornamented with balustrades, statues and pots. This pool, or reservoir, feeds the pipes of the *giochi d'acqua*.

This water joke can be turned on in the passageway beneath the staircase so that pipes set in the stairs and balustrade soak unsuspecting visitors as they walk down into the sunken garden and then, at the far end, water spurts from the mouths of the marble statues of the Winds which stand in the niches. Water even sprays up from the floor of the *nymphaeum* and down from Flora herself on anyone who hopes to seek refuge in the cool interior decorated with shell-patterned mosaic work of stone, pebbles and tufa. Much of the *giochi d'acqua* is in working order despite the ravages it sustained in the Second World War and further restoration work is being done to return it to full working order.

Address: Villa Torrigiani, Camigliano, Italy.

Flights of stone stairs into the Garden of Flora conceal the giochi d'acqua.

View from the nymphaeum of Flora.

The reservoir which feeds the pipes of the giochi d'acqua.

Stourhead.

The Villa Gamberaia.

Wave Hill.

Hestercombe.

Gravetye Manor.

La Serre de la Madone.

Isola Bella.

Red valerian flowing over the steps at Bodnant.

Bodnant in Gwynedd (Wales) was purchased in 1874 by Henry Pochin, later the 1st Lord Aberconway, and it has been owned by the Aberconway family ever since. Although the 80 acres of garden were bequeathed to the National Trust in 1949, the Aberconway family still live in the house and, together with the three successive generations of the Puddle family that have been Head Gardeners on the estate, have made the garden into one of the most renowned in Britain. The five formal Italianate terraces overlooking the River Conway and providing glimpses of Snowdonia beyond were designed by the 2nd Lord Aberconway who also enlarged the garden and initiated numerous new plantings of trees and shrubs, particularly rhododendrons in which he took a special interest.

Villa Torrigiani.

Ling Ying Temple.

La Mortola.

The Zig-Zags at Mount Edgcumbe.

The main fountain display at Herrenhausen.

The Generalife.

Schloss Veitshöchheim.

St. James's Park.

Castle Howard.

The 276-foot water jet of the Emperor Fountain at Chatsworth, by Paxton.

Chatsworth Gardens in Derbyshire (England) have been constantly reworked since they were originally laid out in the late seventeenth century. Great designers of each epoch have had a hand in its evolution: London and Wise laid out the great parterre; Capability Brown changed the course of the river as part of his re-landscaping vision; and Paxton built the Great Stove, the largest expanse of glass in the world (destroyed in the First World War), and designed the still extant 'Conservative Wall'.

Kensington Gardens.

Chenies Manor.

Little Sparta.

Longwood.

Tatton Park with the deciduous azaleas in full flower.

The Fountain of Venus at Het Loo.

A little shell fountain at Alton Towers.

The Peacock Fountain at Het Loo.

Hestercombe.

Hidcote.

1590–93 LEIDEN BOTANIC GARDEN One of the earliest botanical gardens which under the aegis of the highly acclaimed botanist Clusius, concentrated not only on medicinal but also on ornamental plants from all over the New World.

A reconstruction of Clusius' original sixteenth-century herb garden. Visited July 20.

Leiden Botanic Garden was officially recognized in 1590 after the curators of the University of Leiden (founded 1575) requested the Lord Mayors of the city on 17 March 1587 to make available 'a vacant lot to the rear of the university' where they could create 'a courtyard to expedite the instruction of all them who study medicine'. But between the original request and the foundation of the garden the curators had decided to pursue the ideas of a revolutionary thinker of his day, the botanist Carolus Clusius (1526–1609), who was appointed Prefect of the Garden in 1593 and who established not only a medicinal garden but also a study garden which contained a survey of all plants known at that time be they medicinal, edible or ornamental, thus making

Bust of Siebold, the plant collector.

Leiden, arguably, the first truly botanical garden.

Clusius divided the garden into four main areas, each with its own series of beds containing plants that were carefully classified and listed (each bed being distinguished by a letter of the alphabet and each plant by a number) so that remembering what was what, if you did not have the printed list to hand, required extraordinary feats of memory.

The current layout of the garden is very different from the arrangement recorded in maps of the early seventeenth century but because of the great detail in the early drawings, Prefect Baas Becking was able to direct an accurate reconstruction of the original Clusius garden which now exists very near its original site. This reconstruction, which began in the 1930s and was completed in the 1980s, shows how the garden would have looked in 1594, right down to the ornamental gates and trellis work. It is absolutely charming and because it has a number of ornamental and exotic plants, it has something of a pleasure garden feel about it as well as fulfilling its scientific and scholarly function.

Under the Prefect Adriaen Van Royen, the garden was expanded to include a series of systematic order beds which followed Linnaeus's plant nomenclature – in fact, Linnaeus himself visited Leiden on several occasions around 1736 to help with their design. However, the current order beds are planted around a bust of Linnaeus but are grouped according to a system proposed by Stebbins in 1974.

Over the centuries Leiden has been famous for the number of plants it has introduced and cultivated from

Bust of Clusius, the botanist.

Giant Victoria water-lilies in the greenhouse.

all over the world. Clusius first introduced plants from his travels in Spain, Portugal, Austria and Hungary but he is most famous for cultivating exotic bulbs and tubers from western Asia, most notably tulips with which his name will be forever linked because of his observation of the phenomenon of 'breaking' (i.e. when the flower's uniform colour develops into a variegated form) now known to be caused by a virus.

Another famous plant collector associated with Leiden was the surgeon-general of Deshima Island (off Japan), Dr Philipp Franz Balthazar von Siebold (1796–1866), who collected and recorded a great number of plants unknown before then in Europe and sent them to Leiden. Plants such as hydrangea, hosta, wisteria, viburnum and Virginia creeper, all now very common throughout the Netherlands and northern Europe, can be found in the von Siebold and Japanese Memorial Garden which was designed in 1990 by Professor Nakamura, a Japanese Professor of landscape architecture, to commemorate the important role von Siebold played in seeking to unify the East and West.

Ongoing research into orchids, passion flowers and

water lilies amongst other exotic tropical plants can be seen in the greenhouses and in the recently developed fern garden at the far end of the garden.

The beautiful old orangery designed by Daniel Marot of Het Loo fame (see pages 110–113) and built between 1740 and 1744 no longer contains the 'minerals, sea plants, rare dried birds, shells, Egyptian mummy and stone idol' that used to be housed alongside the citrus plants, agaves and palms that now grow there in the winter, waiting to be distributed around the garden in the summer months when the orangery is used for exhibitions and concerts.

Leiden Botanic Garden remains as it ever was: a place for research, education, plant introduction and cultivation – an essential task in a world that seems intent on destroying so many of its natural resources without properly understanding the role each plays in the natural cycle.

Address: Leiden Botanic Gardens, Rapenburg 73, Universiteitsplein, Leiden, Holland.

The beehives are a feature of the herb garden.

Bust of Linnaeus, the botanist.

1751–71 KEW ROYAL BOTANIC GARDENS Under Sir Joseph Banks Kew made its reputation as one of the greatest botanical gardens in the world, a reputation it jealously guards with its continuing programme of development.

The ten-storeyed Chinese Pagoda beyond the heather garden at Kew. Visited March 25.

Temple of Æolus.

Chambers' ruined arch.

Kew Royal Botanic Gardens became what they are today as the result of a long and complex history.

The gardens now encompass land that was originally owned by separate members of the Royal Family: Richmond House and Gardens owned by George II and Kew House, home of his eldest son Frederick, Prince of Wales and his consort Princess Augusta. On the death of his father Frederick, only nine years after the death of his grandfather, George III inherited the Richmond estate and allowed Lancelot 'Capability' Brown to re-landscape the gardens which had formerly been laid out by Charles Bridgeman. In 1757 George's mother Princess Augusta commissioned William Chambers, architect and author of a book, *Design of Chinese Buildings*, the fruit of two visits to China, to landscape the grounds at Kew House and lay out a small botanic garden of 3.6 hectares. His designs included a ten-storeyed Chinese Pagoda, an orangery, a Roman triumphal arch (all extant) as well as an aviary, a menagerie, a mosque, about twenty classical temples and the Great Stove (which are not).

The first superintendent of the botanic garden was William Aiton, who had trained at the Chelsea Physic Garden, but it was with the appointment of Joseph Banks (1744–1820) in 1771 as horticultural and botanical adviser that Kew made its reputation as the greatest botanical garden in the world.

Sir Joseph Banks was a man fired by an insatiable academic curiosity to know, discover and explore, and he didn't lack a competitive and nationalistic edge. Under his patronage and encouragement, plant collectors such as Francis Masson, William Kerr, James Bowsie and Allan Cunningham trawled the world in their quest for

The Palm House.

Mist spray in the Palm House.

The Princess of Wales Conservatory.

new species to send back to Kew. 'Which otherwise,' said Banks, 'will have been added to the Royal Gardens at Paris (Le Jardin des Plantes) and have tended to render their collection superior to ours.' On Banks' death in 1820 the Botanic Gardens at Kew went into serious decline and it wasn't until 1841 that the Government agreed to John Lindley's recommendation that Kew should become a national horticultural and scientific institution funded by the State.

Sir William Hooker (1785–1865) became Kew's first director and, under his aegis, the botanic garden was expanded to include the neighbouring Pleasure Gardens. It was he, too, who initiated the erection of the Palm and Temperate Houses and established a herbarium, a library and a museum of economic botany. Hooker was succeeded by his son Sir Joseph Hooker (1817–1911), who had the vision to push Kew's scientific work to the fore, establishing laboratories for research into plant taxonomy, anatomy and physiology.

Covering over 300 acres, Kew Gardens provides numerous visitors with a pleasurable day in beautiful landscaped gardens with a range of interesting and exotic trees and plants to be seen in, for example, the Princess of Wales Conservatory, as well as collections of plant paintings and exhibitions on economic botany. Visitors also flock to see the Pagoda, the Orangery, Kew Palace, the botanical order beds, the Cambridge cottage gardens and much more besides. However, the historical and ongoing significance of Kew lies in the enormous body of

information about the plants of the world, both past and present, which is stored in the herbarium, the library and the seed banks; a resource that is an invaluable reference point for anyone working in the field of natural science, particularly in a world that is so carelessly consuming and plundering its natural environment. The future of some of the world's most threatened flora may only exist in the seedbanks and laboratories of botanical gardens of the world, such as Kew.

Address: Royal Botanic Gardens, Kew, Richmond, Surrey, England.

The Rockery.

16TH CENTURY CHÂTEAU DE VILLANDRY (Reconstructed 1906) French formal potager of geometric designs with fruit, flowers and vegetables creating a spectacularly colourful display from spring to late autumn.

The potager at Villandry is replanted twice a year; this is the autumn display. Visited October 5.

The terrace.

A view of the Château at sunset.

The Château de Villandry, a moated Renaissance mansion, was built in 1536 on a site that dates back to the twelfth century. The eighteenth century saw the addition of the terraces and canals but when the property was bought in 1906 by Dr Joachim Carvallo (grandfather of the present owner) all traces of the original garden had disappeared and no records of it remained. For the next eighteen years Carvallo devoted himself to reconstructing Villandry into a superb example of a sixteenth-century garden. Having no actual plans of the garden to work from he based his ideas on the designs and engravings of Du Cerceau (*c.*1515–84), an architect and engraver, who published several invaluable books on garden design including *Les Plus Excellents Bâtiments de France*.

The garden is divided into three main sections. On the lowest level is the incomparable potager. Its formal design consists of nine equal squares organized in different geometric patterns and bordered with low, clipped box hedges. Within each square a meticulous and imaginative mix of fruit, vegetables and flowers create a spectacular display of pattern, colour and texture, particularly in mid-summer and autumn when the spring and summer plantings reach their zenith.

The second level consists of four box parterres, one symbolizing tender love (hearts, flames and masks), the second fickle love (butterflies and fans), the third representing tragic love (swords and dagger blades), the fourth denoting the folly or madness of love (a maze of hearts). Symmetrically positioned clipped yews and single jets of water provide contrast to the overall flatness of the geometric design.

A view of the potager from the top of the tower.

The third section of the garden, reached by an enclosing avenue of limes, is the Jardin d'Eau which, with its ornamental basin surrounded by smaller pools, lawns and single water jets, provides an area of calm repose which contrasts effectively with the richness, complexity and exuberance of the rest of the garden. Two other areas worth mentioning are the maze and the collection of medicinal herbs.

Villandry's importance lies principally in two features: its accurate reconstruction of a period of gardening history now long gone because the amount of wealth and manpower needed to sustain such gardens is no longer readily available; and the scale of the garden and, in particular, the potager and the meticulous way it is maintained has served and continues to serve as an inspiration to numerous gardeners – Rosemary Verey and Darina Allen immediately spring to mind with their much smaller scale but delightful potagers.

The parterre planted with dahlias.

The best times of year to visit the garden are midsummer when the spring vegetables and flowers are at their best and late September/early October when the autumn fruit and vegetables create a superb display. Another tip for making the most of your visit is to go into the Château which is open to the public and climb right to the top of the tower where you can get a wonderful view across the whole garden and really appreciate the overall design which is hard to do at ground level.

Address: Château de Villandry, Villandry, Nr Tours, Indre-et-Loire, France.

Red chard, a most decorative vegetable.

The Order Beds at the the Chelsea Physic Garden.

The Chelsea Physic Garden in London (England) was founded in 1673 to train apothecaries in herbal medicine and in the eighteenth century it played a vital role in the introduction of new species from the Americas and Asia. For over 300 years it has exchanged seeds and plants with many other botanical institutions and gardens and it continues, to this day, to play a leading role in botanical and horticultural research particularly in the field of herbal medicine.

The herb garden at the Ballymaloe Cookery School.

The Ballymaloe Cookery School in Shanagarry, County Cork (Republic of Ireland), is owned and run by Timothy and Darina Allen, son and daughter-in-law of the acclaimed Irish cook Myrtle Allen of Ballymaloe House. As well as teaching and writing Darina is a keen gardener, growing much of the produce for the school in her delightful potager and small orchard. In the Victorian garden at the back of the main house a formal herb garden inspired by a visit to Villandry can be more fully appreciated from the deck of a kind of tree-house built overlooking the garden.

Thomas Jefferson's 1000-foot vegetable garden (photographed by Martyn Rix).

Monticello in Virginia (USA) was begun by Thomas Jefferson, president of the United States, in 1769 when he was only twenty-six years old. He levelled the hill after which the estate was called, not only to accommodate the classical mansion, which he designed but also to afford views over the surrounding countryside and the series of oval 'roundabouts' comprising gardens, orchards and woods which he created in the English landscape style round and below the house. The 1000-foot vegetable garden still grows many of the 250 varieties which, as a keen botanist and horticulturalist, he tested during his lifetime as recorded in his detailed Garden Book.

Arley Hall.

Barnsley House.

Wave Hill.

Chenies Manor.

1460–1530 CHENIES MANOR A Tudor manor house with medieval 'garden rooms' including a sunken garden, topiary garden, physic garden and penitential turf maze – all restored or recreated since the Second World War.

The Manor House and sunken garden seen from the west. Visited July 20.

Chenies Manor is built on a site that dates back to Saxon times, but it was not until early Tudor times that a brick house was first built (1460) and then substantially enlarged around 1530 to its present size, extending the land around it to develop the area of the present gardens as well as incorporating a substantial portion of the ground north of the house for an orchard south and north-east of the house for parkland.

Steeped in history, the house was used on at least two occasions by Henry VIII with two different wives, Anne Boleyn and Catherine Howard, and was frequently visited by Elizabeth I, after whom the 1000-year-old oak is named, it reputedly being her favourite tree.

The overall layout of the garden was substantially influenced by Lucy, 3rd Countess of Bedford – whose gardening skills are recorded in several contemporary works – when she came to Chenies in 1594. Neglect in the eighteenth century and some Victorian 'improvements' in the nineteenth century did not drastically alter the basic structure. It was purchased by the current owners, Lieutenant-Colonel and Mrs MacLeod Matthews and,

despite the inevitable neglect so many gardens suffered during the Second World War, it still largely retained its original medieval structure of a series of intimate 'garden rooms', essentially extensions of the house, that reflected the Tudor period in which the house was built.

It was with this in mind that Mrs MacLeod Matthews initiated an extensive programme of garden renovation and reconstruction based on medieval garden ideas. For example, the Sunken Garden, created in the remains of the original, is modelled on the Tudor Privy Garden at Hampton Court, with low, grassy terraces around a central pond containing aquatic plants and bordered at each end by a screen made not from hornbeam or lime but a wooden ivy-covered trellis.

The topiary garden or White Garden, which is enclosed on all sides, has a distinctly medieval feel to it but is, in fact, entirely Elizabeth MacLeod Matthews' creation. It has a statue of Cupid in the centre surrounded by a trimmed hedge and flanked in each corner by a yew hen sitting on a nest of box. All these face Cupid except one which, according to Ethne Clarke

A view across the White Garden to the Manor.

in *English Topiary Gardens*, was accidentally placed the wrong way round in the hurry and excitement of planting these large topiary shapes, which were rescued from a derelict nursery in Berkshire, having miraculously survived the war. All the shrubs, perennials and annuals in the beds bordering this garden are grey, white and green, creating a tranquil, cool and harmonious atmosphere.

Another of the 'little gardens', as the area to the west of the house was formerly called, is an entirely original creation of Mrs MacLeod Matthews. It is based on a common, late medieval feature, the Physic Garden. It contains over 200 species of herbs renowned for

medicinal, cosmetic, culinary, dyeing or poisoning properties grouped around an octagonal well-house built in the early nineteenth century over a medieval well that had, in early times, supplied the village water.

Historical records show that a Penitential turf maze once existed at Chenies so, near the orchard and kitchen garden, a new turf maze, based on a design in a late sixteenth-century painting at Woburn Abbey, was constructed in 1982 – one of the few examples of this once common feature of medieval gardens.

Address: Chenies Manor Gardens, Nr Amersham, Bucks, England.

Cupid in the White Garden.

The Tudor Ruin.

1604 EDZELL CASTLE A medieval 'pleasaunce' where the remains of a 400-year-old garden with a decorative wall of stone-carved niches initiated an authentic modern reconstruction of a seventeenth-century Scottish Renaissance garden.

The restored medieval pleasaunce looking towards the ruined Castle. Visited July 7.

Edzell Castle garden was, according to a commemorative plaque in the enclosing garden wall, laid out and presumably completed by 1604, when the castle and grounds were owned by Sir David Lindsay, Lord Edzell, and his second wife, Dame Isobel Forbes. There is little in the historical records of the time to shed light on the overall design and planting of the garden but its most striking feature, the decorative wall with stone-carved niches, still exists and indicates how closely Sir David and his chief mason must have co-operated on the design.

This wall forms three sides of the 'pleasaunce' (an enclosed garden laid out for the purposes of leisure or recreation), the other side of the garden being formed by the ruins of the castle fortress and other stone building remains. The whole garden can be viewed best either from the windows of the fortress tower or from the garden house that stands in one southern corner. In the other corner stands the bath house.

What makes this decorative wall exceptional, apart from the fact that it has survived intact for almost 500 years, is the way it has been divided into compartments. (Sadly, the free-standing pilasters are no longer there but the bases, caps and bands remain.) These have alternately, chequered recesses which provide spaces for nesting birds or flowers and above which are niches presumably once containing statues, and a single, larger, oblong recess below a sculpted stone panel with a moulded frame. These sculptures display on the east wall the Planetary Deities, on the south wall the Liberal Arts and on the west wall the Cardinal Virtues.

Little is known about the original planting or layout of the parterre. What exists today is an imaginative and historically authentic reconstruction of what an early seventeenth-century pleasance would have been like, bearing in mind that the reconstruction of the garden began in the 1930s after 150 years of neglect.

Eighty plans were made to design four triangular flower beds (one in each corner) with complicated designs based on the thistle of Scotland, the rose of England and the fleur-de-lys of France. Within these, and enclosing a central raised feature of clipped yew surrounded by four yew 'balls', are diagonally set flower beds with intricate lettering in clipped box proclaiming the Lindsay mottoes: *Dum spiro spero* 'While I breathe, I hope' and *Endure forte* 'Endure firmly'. The centres of these beds are filled with red and yellow roses. Thacker's *The History of Gardens* points out that the red *Tropaeolum speciosum* twining around the central yew wasn't introduced into Britain until the 1840s, although other *Tropolaeums* were introduced into Europe in the sixteenth century.

However, despite such minor criticisms, Edzell is greatly admired both as one of the first genuine efforts at an historically correct reconstruction of an early seventeenth-century garden and for the immaculate way it is maintained by the Scottish Department of Historic Buildings and Monuments.

Address: Edzell Castle, Edzell, Nr Brechin, Angus, Tayside, Scotland.

The formal parterre of the enclosed garden as seen from the tower, looking towards the summer house.

The decorative walls have stone-carved niches with sculptures of the Planetary Deities, the Liberal Arts and the Cardinal Virtues.

The Knot Gardens planted by Lady Salisbury's at Hatfield House are based on original Italian designs. Visited June 15.

Hatfield House Gardens in Hertfordshire (England) were originally laid out between 1607 and 1612, first by Thomas Chaundler and then by Salomon de Caus for Robert Cecil, 1st Earl of Salisbury. The park and formal gardens were planted by John Tradescant the Elder. Although changed and added to many times over the centuries, the garden still retains its seventeenth-century feel.

Impatiens in the formal parterre at Hampton Court.

Villa Lante.

Hampton Court Palace Gardens in Surrey (England) have evolved continuously since Henry VIII acquired them from Cardinal Wolsey in the mid-sixteenth century, reflecting the different tastes and interests of successive British monarchs. Charles II introduced the goose-foot plan on the east front; William and Mary initiated the Great Fountain Garden and developed the Privy Garden; and Queen Anne had the maze built. In 1838 Queen Victoria opened the former royal hunting grounds to the public.

Versailles.

A view from the upper terraces at Isola Bella.

Pitmedden. (Photographed by Martyn Rix)

Pitmedden in Grampian (Scotland) was laid out in the seventeenth century by Sir Alexander Seton, the 1st Baronet of Pitmedden, in the French Formal style of Le Nôtre. Sadly, the house and all its historical records, including the original garden designs, were destroyed by fire in the nineteenth century so the current restoration of the grounds is based on patterns of other contemporary gardens, principally those from the Palace of Holyrood.

Palácio de Seteais at Sintra.

Bussaco.

Vaux-le-Vicomte.

Drummond Castle.

Veitshöchheim.

Vaux-le-Vicomte.

Fronteira Palace.

Isola Bella.

Vaux-le-Vicomte.

The Huntington sculpture garden with giant camellias bursting into flower.

The Huntington estate in California (USA), comprising 600 acres of sprawling ranchland in the southern foothills, was bought by Henry Edwards Huntington in 1903. Shortly afterwards he retired to devote his attention to building the new home that was to house his superb art and manuscript collection. To help him create the kind of garden he wanted to match his mansion, he hired William Hertrich as curator of the grounds and for the next sixty years Hertrich worked at the Huntington, helping to create the world-famous Rose Garden with its 1200 different species of roses arranged in chronological order from the Middle Ages until the present day.

Vaux-le-Vicomte.

Hadrian's Villa.

Vaux-le-Vicomte.

The Château de Beloeil.

SCULPTURE

Belvedere.

Alton Towers.

Red valerian and fremontodendron at Bodnant.

Shugakuin Imperial Villa.

Veitshöchheim.

La Serre de la Madone.

Villa Garzoni.

Little Sparta.

The Donald M. Kendall Sculpture Garden.

The Donald M. Kendall Sculpture Garden.

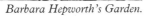

Barbara Hepworth's Garden.

Sissinghurst.

Vaux-le-Vicomte.

Versailles.

Versailles.

The Forbidden City.

Bragmansia at Herrenhausen.

Dumbarton Oaks.

Oranges trees at the Villa Gamberaia.

Hestercombe.

Weikersheim.

Parco di Mostri.

The urn-filled niches in the wall at Powis Castle, overgrown with ancient yews.

Falkland Place (Vitis cognetiae).

The Couple Garden.

Het Loo.

Vizcaya.

Knightshayes.

Bidens at Levens Hall.

Hanging lobelia at Powis Castle.

Vizcaya.

Alton Towers.

Rain daisies at Sissinghurst.

Villa Giulia.

Knightshayes.

Villa Gamberaia.

Hever Castle.

Levens Hall.

Hever Castle.

Somerleyton Hall.

1656–61 VAUX-LE-VICOMTE The finest example of Le Nôtre's work, this exceptional French formal garden is designed to be viewed from the Château, reminding its owner not only of his wealth and power but also of his control over all he surveys, including Nature itself.

View from the Château looking down the central, north–south allée to the distant statue of Hercules. Visited August 20.

Vaux-le-Vicomte's château and gardens were built between 1656 and 1661 for Nicolas Fouquet, Louis XIV's extremely wealthy and influential finance minister. Powerful men make numerous enemies and Fouquet was no exception to this rule, so when he was imprisoned for life in 1664, his wife, on the death of their eldest son in 1705, eventually sold Vaux to the Maréchal de Villars whose family lived there until 1764 when the estate was bought by the Duc de Choiseul-Praslin.

It was the Praslin home for over a hundred years until tragedy within the family – the 5th Duc murdered his wife and then committed suicide in prison – resulted in the sale of the estate in 1875. Already in a state of extreme disrepair, it seemed inevitable that the estate would be broken up and the château and outbuildings razed to the ground.

Fortunately, a local industrialist, Alfred Sommier, saw the potential behind the decaying buildings and derelict garden and decided that he would restore this relic of the Grand Siècle to its former glory. For the past 120 years the Sommier family and its descendants, who still own it, have worked assiduously and successfully to this end to such an extent that the layout of the garden today is almost exactly as it was on the fateful night, 17 August 1661, when Fouquet put on an extravagant fête and fireworks display to entertain the King and his court but

in so doing raised the question whether the King's finance minister was not, in fact, outshining the King himself in his lifestyle and power.

Fouquet was passionately interested in all kinds of beauty and a great patron of the arts in every field. When he decided to create a home from scratch, he gathered around him some of the most renowned and brilliant artists of his day: for the house, Louis Le Vau, for the interior decoration, Charles Le Brun, and for the garden, André Le Nôtre.

What makes Vaux-le-Vicomte exceptional and arguably the most perfect example of the French formal garden is that the whole project was conceived as a total entity right from the start. It was executed rapidly over five years and, most importantly, the château and garden were built on a new site, without existing buildings or structures having to be taken into consideration when conceiving the plans. It was a virgin drawing board and Fouquet, Le Vau and Le Nôtre were able to look at the entire design of both house and garden as an interlocking, unified whole. Never again was Le Nôtre to have such freedom.

Fouquet studied plans of renowned Italian, English and German gardens and he had, of course, visited the great gardens of France. Together with Le Nôtre, he read books on perspective and they embraced the Renaissance

The fountain ponds have been designed to show off reflections of the Château.

The intricate scrolls of the parterre de broderie are immaculately maintained.

The many sculptures of the grottoes include the reclining Anqueuil, a river god sculpted by Lespagnandel (centre) at Vaux-le-Vicomte.

Looking back through the allée of planes.

A pair of loving lions by Gardet.

ideas which emphasized the laying out of the gardens for beauty and pleasure rather than the medieval idea of the garden as an enclosed, private space for personal enjoyment or for growing plants for medicine and consumption. To Fouquet and Le Nôtre the huge, beautifully manicured garden laid out below and around and stretching beyond the château was a very public symbol of man's power and control over his environment. Each area of the garden, instead of being a separate compartment, was part of a single composition, a vast overall plan that could not be disassociated from the house; in fact the whole conception was of symmetry and balance both within itself and with the château.

Thus, the beautiful, intricate scrolls of the parterre de broderie are like an enormous carpet that extends out from the house. The view from the front steps down the huge, long, north–south axis, flanked by statues, fountains and clipped shrubs, looks across to a broad grassy slope between the limes in the distance which is topped by an imposing gold statue of Hercules.

What one doesn't see from the front of the moated château is the second major east–west axis formed by the great canal which is at right angles to the central *allée*. This canal, with its grand cascades on the one side and its grottoes on the other, comes as a great surprise to the visitor, for Le Nôtre's design and construction of the garden is such that the optical effect is one of foreshortening the view so that it seems that the grottoes

The great canal, La Poële (literally, 'the frying pan'), placed at right angles to the main north-south axis, cannot be seen from the Château and only comes into view as one proceeds down the central allée at Vaux-le-Vicomte.

rest on the far bank of the water-mirror, whereas in fact they are much further away behind the canal, La Poële.

As one proceeds down the garden past the parterres and fountain pools, one comes upon the water-mirror and at this point one sees the steep valley cut across by the canal and the visitor realizes that the statue of Hercules is considerably further away than it had first seemed. However, looking back at the château from beyond the mirror, Le Nôtre's second optical effect is achieved; the whole south front of the château is seen reflected in the water-mirror.

On either side of the main parterres and lawns, smaller east–west axis paths lead to other parts of the garden concealed, more or less, from the main view: the potager

(kitchen garden), the Grilles d'Eau (a stairway of fountains), the Water Garden and the woodland groves.

Vaux-le-Vicomte is incredibly impressive: the money, the organization, the dedication required both then in the seventeenth century and now in the twentieth century, to keep such a place in immaculate condition is mind-boggling but it is arguably the finest surviving example of Le Nôtre's work and represents more accurately than even Versailles the achievements of landscape architecture in France during the seventeenth century.

Address: Château de Vaux-le Vicomte, 77950 Maincy, France.

Looking across the water mirror to the east.

1661–1715 VERSAILLES Here, French formal gardening was at its most lavish, masterminded by Le Nôtre to reflect the power and overweening pride of his patron Louis XIV – The Sun King – with its main east/west axis emphasizing the King's identification with Apollo, the Sun God.

The fountain of Apollo with the Grand Canal stretching away behind it. Visited August 18, in a terrific thunderstorm.

Versailles – the palace, gardens, extensive grounds and other royal residences – is an enormous complex that had its origins in the reign of Louis XIII, but was predominantly expanded and developed under Louis XIV. Later changes and adaptations by Louis XVI and Louis XVIII did not significantly alter the overall conception of the garden as originally designed by Le Nôtre between 1661 and Louis XIV's death in 1715.

Versailles is the product of the imagination of a man who considered himself to be the most powerful man on earth and who wanted a palace and grounds that reflected his authority, influence and wealth in no uncertain terms. It is the most extraordinary example of man imposing himself on nature, changing, shaping, adapting, altering the environment to his will, at whatever cost.

The original hunting lodge built by Louis XIII was chosen as the place of Louis XIV's development of the ideal palace. After visiting Vaux-le-Vicomte (see pages 74–77) in 1661, Louis was so impressed by the work of Le Nôtre and Le Vau and so furious that the magnificence of Fouquet's château and grounds seemed to challenge his own power and wealth that he had Fouquet imprisoned for life and immediately commissioned the same group of talented artists to come and create a palace and gardens that would outstrip and

outshine that created by his minister.

Work on the grounds began before the extension of the palace was tackled. Louis XIV was passionately interested in gardens and worked in close partnership with Le Nôtre (of whom he was very fond) for almost forty years. The grounds surrounding Versailles were, according to one source, 'sad and barren . . . with no view, no water and no woods'. This did not deter Louis; it spurred him on. 'It is in difficult things that we show our quality,' he wrote. The lack of a view was rectified by gently sloping the ground in front of the house down to the canal and then letting it rise again slightly into the distance. The lack of water was a severe problem as, in some ways, the whole garden was conceived of as a water garden with the mile long canal and the numerous fountains that Louis loved to see playing.

However, a series of reservoirs were created at Saint-Cyr to supply the fountains and when that proved insufficient, fourteen giant water wheels and a huge pump were built to enable 5000 cubic metres of water to be pumped daily up the hill from the Seine so that Louis could enjoy the sight of over one thousand fountains spurting out water as he toured his garden. In fact the problem was never really solved satisfactorily and Claude Denis, the *fontainier*, had a complex system of runners and flagsmen on the alert to relay information about

View of the Palace of Versailles with the Green Carpet and Apollo's Chariot in the foreground.

In the summer months the oranges and palms are displayed outside in the Orangery Parterre.

The South Parterre at Versailles with intricate scrolls subtly planted with white impatiens.

The Colonnade by Mansart.

The Fountain of Winter by Girardon.

where Louis was in the garden, so that the fountains in his vicinity could be turned on and those no longer in view could be turned off.

As to the problem of no woods, Louis solved that too. A special machine for transplanting trees up to 1.5 metres in circumference was used to bring mature trees from nearby forests into the garden, to the *bosquets* (groves) on either side of the main axes.

The garden is built on two great axes: the east/west axis with the front of the palace facing due west, emphasizing Louis's identification with Apollo, the Sun God; and the north/south axis which, near the palace, links the Fountain of Neptune with the Lake of the Swiss Guards and the canal linking the Trianon in the north to the Menagerie (no longer extant) in the south.

The Petit Parc immediately below the palace with its parterres, statuary and fountains embraces the Fountain of Latona (mother of Apollo), the central grass sweep (the tapis vert) and the Fountain of Apollo before reaching the enormous cross-shaped Grand Canal. Parallel with the main east/west axis, and behind the long gravel paths adjacent to the grass slope on which stand twelve statues and twelve marble vases, are the *bosquets* which have seen changes over the centuries but still feature the Rockwork Grove, the Fountain of Winter, the Fountain of Spring, the Colonnade and the Grove of Apollo's Baths, which was created for the Grotto of Tethys but which was subsequently destroyed.

Looking out from The Grand Trianon in the pouring rain.

On the north/south axis, the main features at the north end are the Fountain of Neptune, the Dragon Fountain, Water Avenue and North Parterre, with its beautiful parterre de broderie and the Orangery and, beyond the road, the Lake of the Swiss Guards, with the equestrian statue of the King by Bernini at its south end.

The huge area covered by the Great Park of Versailles originally comprised almost 15,000 acres and was surrounded by 27 miles of wall (now it consists of little more than 2000 acres). It is hardly surprising, then, that even Louis XIV occasionally longed for a little respite from the grand and formal life of the Court of Versailles. So, as a kind of retreat, he bought the village of Trianon in 1668 (situated at the top of the northern arm of the cross-shaped canal) and commissioned Le Vau to erect a small pavilion decorated with blue and white tiles. However, when this deteriorated in 1687 it was demolished and a new château, by Mansart, was built in its place. This was known as the Marble Trianon, though it later became known as the Grand Trianon to distinguish it from the Petit Trianon which was built in the 1760s by Louis XV.

The crowning glory of the Grand Trianon gardens are the two large flower parterres. Louis XIV was passionate about flowers but Le Vau's plans for the Petit Parc in front of the King's state apartments in the main palace at Versailles did not enable him to indulge this passion. However, in the more enclosed, peristyle garden created between the two wings of the Trianon château, he could plant flowers to his heart's content. The *parterres de compartiment de fleurs* were filled with thousands of blooms overhung by orange trees. One account describes how flowers were bedded out even on freezing winter days so that Louis could proudly show his treasure to guests and any flowers that drooped in the icy conditions were changed during dinner so that the display remained immaculate. Louis's power and wealth defied the ordinary workings of nature.

The other features of these gardens are the various pools which act as mirrors for the parterres, the grove called the Hall of Classical Statues and the Jardin du Roi which contains parterres of floral embroidery.

Address: Versailles, Paris, France.

1762–74 THE HAMEAU in the **PETIT TRIANON** Marie Antoinette's rustic idyll was influenced by the English Romantic Landscape Movement, in marked contrast to the formal tradition that had dominated France in the first half of the eighteenth century.

The Mill, one of twelve houses built by Mique for Marie-Antoinette in 1783.

The whole estate of the Petit Trianon was originally landscaped to include a botanical garden, whose exotic trees now form part of the highly acclaimed collection of the Jardin des Plantes in Paris, and a menagerie which was later destroyed. The small château was built by Gabriel between 1762 and 1768. Originally intended for Madame de Pompadour, it was given to Marie-Antoinette by Louis XVI in 1774 and it was she who commissioned Hubert Robert and Richard Mique to turn the gardens into a kind of naturally irregular, miniature landscape extending into the countryside,

A planting of cottage garden vegetables.

reflecting the influences of English gardening ideals on the previously dominant French formal garden tradition. In the gardens an artificial river ran through hilly grounds and on a small island Mique erected a Temple of Love and on the river bank, the Rock Pavilion or Belvedere.

However, the garden is probably most famous for the Hameau, which was built in 1783 and based on a Normandy village. It attempted to create the rustic idyll that Marie-Antoinette saw as the perfect setting for the simple, carefree life that she and her entourage led.

In the centre of the hamlet is the lake, surrounded by half-timbered, thatched buildings: the mill, the farm, the dairy, the dovecote, the Marlborough Tower and the Queen's Cottage surrounded by the vegetables and fruit bushes of the kitchen garden.

Celebrated in its day for the festivities and expense involved in living 'the simple life', the Petit Trianon was stripped of its trappings after the revolution. Restoration work was started in 1867 by the Empress Eugénie and this continues today, with a brief that stresses the importance of historical authenticity.

For the student of garden history, seeing all these components of Versailles – the main Palace, the Grand Trianon, the Petit Trianon, the Hameau and the Potager du Roi – is a fascinating way of understanding the changes that took place in French gardening styles over a period of 125 years.

Address: Versailles, Paris, France.

The Queen's Cottage in the Hameau.

1677–83 THE POTAGER DU ROI The King's kitchen garden comprising a huge, walled, rectangular area, provided all the fruit and vegetables for the Palace of Versailles.

The Potager du Roi.

The Potager du Roi was created between 1677 and 1683 to provide fruit and vegetables for the greatly enlarged court of Louis XIV. The designer of the garden was La Quintinie, *jardinier en chef* to Louis XIV and author of the book which was translated by John Evelyn in 1693, *The Complete Gardener.* Although very near the Palace, adjacent to the Lake of the Swiss Guards on the east side, the actual plot was not eminently suitable for a kitchen garden as it was, in fact, a marshy pond. However, infilled with sand from the construction of the nearby lake, the level was raised above that of the surrounding land and fertile top-soil was imported from the hills of Sartory.

The Potager consists of a walled rectangular area of about 8 hectares divided into nine separate enclosures next to the walls, with four main areas in the centre surrounding a fountain. At the far end of the Potager access can be gained to the Parc Balbi. In Louis's day all kinds of fruit and vegetables were grown, including exotics, but nowadays the main concentration is on different varieties of apples and pears, supported by some soft fruits.

The Potager du Roi has been conserved in its original form and is designated the Ecole Nationale Supérieure d'Horticulture.

Address: Potager du Roi, 6 rue Hardy, 78000 Versailles, France.

1715–75 CHÂTEAU DE BELOEIL The most important French formal-style garden in Belgium with an enormous, central *bassin* bordered by *bosquets* and a series of *fabriques* – miniature buildings that explain the iconography of the garden.

The Temple of Pomone in the remains of the old Potager. Visited July 14.

Beloeil, the home of the Prince and Princess de Ligne, has been the family's ancestral seat since the fourteenth century and the existence of the estate dates back to the twelfth century. Originally consisting of a primitive fortress surrounded on three sides by a moat, the imposing château was first built in the seventeenth century by the 3rd Prince of Ligne, Claude-Lamoral I, and rebuilt in 1900 after being largely destroyed by fire.

The precise history of the gardens does not seem to be well documented but Beloeil's archives reveal that land was purchased in the sixteenth century for the purposes of building a park and the French formal-style gardens were laid out in the early part of the eighteenth century by Prince Claude-Lamoral II (1685–1766), the 3rd Prince's grandson and namesake. The *jardin-anglais* or deer-park to the south east of the gardens was landscaped in 1775 by his son the 7th Prince, Charles Joseph de Ligne (1735–1814), a well-known man of letters whose autobiography *Coup d'Oeil sur Beloeil et sur une grande partie des jardins d'Europe* (1781), contains a collection of witty and pithy ideas on the subject of gardens, his own among many others.

The garden as it exists today remains very much as it was designed by the father and son in the eighteenth century, assisted respectively by the two French architects Jean-Bâptiste Bergé and François-Joseph Bélanger, designer of the gardens at Bagatelle.

The principal feature and central axis of the formal garden is the huge rectangular expanse of water that stretches from the north front of the château towards the moat at the far end. Formerly the moat was crossed by a swing bridge that enabled visitors to enter the garden from the three-mile approach that extended through the forest beyond.

On either side of the lake on parallel axes are a series of *bosquets* and ornamental lakes with transverse and oblique views across the garden. On the left-hand side is the Boulingrin, a distortion of the English 'bowling green', which was frequently used as a theatre in the eighteenth century and then became a rose meadow which is now planted with the roses 'Madame A. Meilland' (Peace) and 'Dame de Coeur' but which originally contained the first Bengal roses to be introduced into Belgium in the eighteenth century. The Dean's Walk runs the length of the *allée* that borders the park. It is 600 metres long and the containing hedges are almost six metres high. A series of ponds, an oval lake and four, sky-reflecting pools succeed each other and bring one around the top end of the *bassin* which ends with an impressive statue of Neptune.

On the right-hand side of the lake, the series of *bosquets* are much more like garden rooms with the individual areas separated by huge clipped hedges. Here the quiet cloister is succeeded by the Bassin des Dames and the Bassin des Glaces. The Women's Pool is surrounded by a colonnaded walk of overarching hornbeams. Nature

The Bassin des Dames, the Women's Pool, surrounded by a colonnade of arching hornbeams.

La Ruine in the Jardin Anglais.

has been ruthlessly trained to create an enchanting architectural feature. Parallel to the *bosquets* on the right-hand side of the lake runs a canal beyond which the Orangerie at the far end can still be seen. Running up towards the house are the remnants of the potager in the middle of which stands Le Temple de Pomone. Sadly, that part of the garden is very overgrown and access is forbidden. Similarly, the overgrown maze and garden of miniature buildings in the children's play area near the Orangerie has also been closed to the public and the Orangerie itself, while retaining its grandeur from a distance, has sunk into a very shabby state inside – a small café stands at one end of it and a few pinball machines are dotted around the huge interior which could, with careful renovation, regain its original elegance.

The *jardin anglais* which represents probably the most important feature of the garden in terms of garden history, is also, unfortunately, closed to the public. From the fence can be glimpsed La Ruine, Le Temple de Morphée and the Obelisk which Prince Charles-Joseph built in keeping with his celebration of *fabriques*, 'a term I shall use to describe all the "show buildings" and all the constructions with which human industry supplements

the works of nature for the adornment of gardens.' Jean-Marie Morel (1776).

Fabriques are miniature monuments which explain the iconographic and symbolic design of a garden and Prince Charles-Joseph made a vast allegorical garden of his estate at Beloeil which traced life from the 'cradle of childhood' to the 'chamber of death' but he did not impose his allegories on visitors. 'I have sometimes been reproached for the names and walks in my allegory. Visitors who do not wish to be provoked to thought have only to accept the entire garden as groves and paths amid shrubs and flowers' he said in *Coup d'Oeil sur Beloeil*.

This garden is well worth visiting, although the enormous expense of maintaining such a labour-intensive garden is clearly taking its toll with the demise of the potager and the unclipped hedges, but herein also lies much of the charm – nature relentlessly struggling to reassert itself despite the centuries-long attempt by the Princes of Ligne to keep it under control and maintain its status as the most important French formal-style garden in Belgium.

Address: Château de Beloeil, B. 7970 Beloeil, Nr Leuze, Belgium.

Les Sources, the three springs.

A view from the Château down the lake.

1680–1700 POWIS CASTLE Early British example of an Italian Renaissance garden with the castle perched above the formal terraces from where extensive views of the rolling countryside and mountains beyond can be seen.

The view of the countryside from the garden at Powis Castle. Visited May 10.

Cistus and ceanothus on the terrace wall.

Powis Castle, built by the Prince of Powis around 1200, was given by William III to his favourite, the Earl of Rochford, while the Earl's family were in exile and they lived there from 1696 to 1722. Designs for the red limestone terraces, for which the castle and its gardens are so famous, were probably commissioned before the exile of the 1st Marquess of Powis, in 1688. It has been suggested that they were the work of the gentleman architect, William Winde, who was working on the Marquess's London home during the 1680s but the Frenchman, Adrian Duval, is also thought to have been involved at a later stage, possibly as an hydraulics' expert.

The importance of the formal terraces lies in the fact that they are an early extant British example of the Italian Renaissance Baroque Garden, with the castle poised above them and the views from there and the terraces looking spectacularly across the garden to the rolling countryside and mountains beyond. What is missing from the Italian comparison is the elaborate water fountains. They did apparently exist at the foot of the terraces but were replaced in the 1770s by the Great Lawn, in deference to the Landscape Movement. Now a small fountain garden is found on the far eastern side of the grounds built by Lady Powis at the beginning of the twentieth century, possibly to evoke memories of the larger fountain garden, long gone. It was she, too, who inaugurated the extensive diversification of planting on the terraces and the introduction of a formal garden in

Looking north towards the Castle terraces with golden- leaved maples in the foreground.

place of the kitchen garden which she felt had become too visible from the upper garden.

The original clear-cut lines and architectural formality of the terraces, with neatly clipped obelisks of yew and lead statues on the balustrade over the orangery, have been softened by the extraordinary growth of the yews which have expanded and rounded to such an extent that they seem to be falling over the balustrades. It is reminiscent of Isola Bella (see pages 40–41). Originally, too, there was an aviary and an orangery on the terraces. Some fruit trees remain but the terraces are planted mainly with a wide variety of herbaceous plants and shrubs, tender and hardy, which flourish well in the sun and alkaline soil to create a marvellous range of colours and foliage all year round.

Across the Great Lawn from the terraces, on the ridge opposite, is the Wilderness or Woodland Garden, which, from the early eighteenth century, provided a marked contrast to the formal garden and a fantastic place from which to view it. Stately oaks and yews are interspersed with numerous rhododendrons, magnolias and hydrangeas as well as firs, cedars and cypresses. The whole area is criss-crossed by woodland paths that pass the Ice-house, the Garden Pool and the Ladies' Bath.

Thacker in *The History of Gardens* says that Powis is, for him, 'The most beautiful garden in Britain' and there are not too many visitors who would disagree with this claim.

Address: Powis Castle, Welshpool, Powys, Wales.

Overgrown tunnel of ancient, clipped yews.

Diascia in a trough.

17TH CENTURY DRUMMOND CASTLE (Restored 1818–68) This important Scottish garden,
reflects a return of interest to the earlier French and Italian styles but also incorporates later ideas such as formal parterres and the introduction of exotic species.

Looking from the Castle terrace down over the formal gardens. Visited July 12.

Drummond Castle Gardens were almost certainly first begun in the late fifteenth century when the 1st Lord of Drummond built his fortalice on the land that had been granted to him by James IV. Records for 1508 mention that Lord Drummond sent cherries to the King when he was hunting in a nearby forest, and the survival of the obelisk sundial made in 1630 by John Mylne (Master Mason to Charles I) is further evidence of the importance of the garden at that date. Later historical evidence suggests continued work on the garden along with expansions of the castle, but the major development for which the garden is famous occurred in the nineteenth century with additional though complementary work continuing to the present day.

Drummond is a composite garden. It has all the hallmarks of a formal seventeenth-century Renaissance garden but, as it was totally remodelled in the early to mid-nineteenth century, the formal parterre layout also incorporated many other influences gleaned over the intervening centuries, as well as introducing exotic new plantings from the New World.

Which of two famous Victorian landscape gardeners had the greatest influence in the redesigning of the gardens is open to question but there is no doubt that both had input into what became probably the most famous garden in Scotland of its day.

Charles Barry, a leading Victorian architect and garden designer of two acclaimed Italian gardens, at Trentham in Staffordshire and Shrubland in Suffolk, exhibited a series of watercolours at the Royal Academy in 1828 showing plans to extend the castle and depicting the famous terracing and parterre garden as complete. Whether this reflected what had already been done in the gardens at Drummond or whether it gave Clementina Sarah Drummond and her husband the idea is not known. However, it was under the stewardship of Lewis Kennedy which lasted for about forty years from 1818 to 1868, that the remarkable formal garden was created. Kennedy came from a famous gardening family and was, in about 1812, working at Malmaison for Josephine Bonaparte to whom his father's nursery was supplying plants.

The Italian and French influences are found in the basic layout of the whole garden which can be seen from the vantage point of the castle. Immediately below the Italianate terracing is the parterre garden with a strong north-south axis centred on the famous sundial and leading to a classical archway flanked by a horizontal, thick, clipped yew hedge. Behind the hedge nestle extensive kitchen gardens (which cannot, of course, be seen from the top of the terrace) and a swathe of grassland beyond cuts through the woodland up to the

View of the Castle through an Acer japonicum 'Aureum' and a Prunus 'Pissardii'.

top of the opposing hillside. This is particularly reminiscent of French formal gardens such as Vaux-le-Vicomte (see pages 74–77), but the Italian influence is strongly felt in the numerous pieces of classical statuary strategically placed around the garden, and in the terracing, urns and quartz edging on paths and walls and fountains.

In its heyday, when Queen Victoria honoured the castle with a visit in 1842, she recorded her walk in the garden as follows: 'We walked in the garden, which is really very fine, with terraces, like an old French garden.'

A journalist covering the visit wrote: 'On the southside, and immediately fronting the principal face of the Castle, lie the matchless flower gardens of Drummond which, though situated in the north, are as well known by repute to every florist and man of cultivated taste in London.'

A picture by Jacob Thompson which depicts the event shows the planting as very lush and full, but during this century many of the trees and shrubs that had overmatured were cut back or replaced and many borders were replanted. The St Andrew's Cross shape, which is formed by the diagonal paths and the segmented beds of the parterre, is now either planted with roses, lavender or white-flowered, silver-leaved *Anaphalis triplinervis*, and the radically thinned shrubs and clipped topiary stand out against the smooth lawns and gravel areas. *The Oxford Companion to Gardens* prefers the more riotous planting exhibited in the

nineteenth-century pictures, feeling that it softened the very formal layout. Others prefer the more orderly, newer planting, feeling that it complements and emphasizes the fine structure.

Another wonderful feature is the incredibly long avenue of trees which line the drive from the outer castle gate at the road to the actual buildings and gardens, and which were planted by the 4th Earl of Perth in the mid-seventeenth century.

Address: Drummond Castle Gardens, Muthill, Nr Crieff, Perthshire, Tayside, Scotland.

The statues were brought from Italy by Charles Barry in 1830.

1690–1720 LEVENS HALL GARDENS Three-hundred-year-old topiary and the earliest known ha-ha still exist in this English garden designed by a Frenchman whose knowledge of French formal gardening can be detected in the geometry of the layout.

A view of the Topiary Garden looking out towards the park. Visited July 21.

The 300-year old topiary is clipped annually to keep it in shape.

Levens Hall Gardens were designed and laid out between 1690 and 1720 by a Frenchman, Guillaume Beaumont, who had been a gardener for James II until his abdication and was also reputed to have worked with one of the most famous of all French garden designers, Le Nôtre. Some garden historians claim they can detect Le Nôtre's influence on the formal layout of the garden into four quarters divided by an enormous beech avenue and a topiary parterre at the side of the house; others say that whether or not this overall design is attributable to Le Nôtre's influence, the scale and atmosphere of the garden is much more intimate and homely than are gardens of a similar period in France.

One reason for this could be the fact that in 300 years various branches of the same family have owned the house and garden, and there have been only ten head gardeners over this long period.

Colonel James Grahame who bought the house in 1688 was a friend of John Evelyn, the diarist and gardener, who encouraged him to realize the potential of the land around his new property. The Levens archives contain much correspondence between Grahame and Beaumont which describes the plans for and the development of the whole garden, particularly the topiary garden. The two men spent almost thirty years working together on implementing their ideas. Despite a period of decline during the eighteenth century when much of the topiary became so overgrown that, according to Brent Elliott in his book *Victorian Gardens*, visitors failed even to comment on it. Even though the topiary figures in golden yew, which were planted by

The Topiary Garden looking back towards the Hall with Heuchera 'Palace Purple' in the foreground.

Forbes (who was head gardener from 1810 to 1862), and the miles of box hedging had to be renewed after the Second World War, the fascination that the garden holds for the modern visitor (and particularly children) is that the overall garden plan and the majority of the topiary remains essentially the same as it was 300 years ago, as can be seen in a garden plan dating back to 1745.

Another interesting feature of the garden is the ha-ha which divides the house and main garden from the park. It is thought to be the earliest of its kind in Britain and the vistas, which can be seen from the garden looking out into the countryside beyond, presage the Landscape Movement, which was to become such an important element of eighteenth-century English gardening.

Another feature of the garden is the planting of the box parterres with colourful displays of spring and summer bedding. The latest innovation to celebrate the garden's tercentenary is the planting of the seventeenth-century garden on the right-hand side of the house which contains only plants that would have been used and available at that period.

Address: Levens Hall, Kendal, Cumbria, England.

Spirals, bells and chess pieces were popular topiary motifs.

Mixed lobelias in a trough.

Typical Japanese tree pruning.

Somerleyton Hall.

Crinkly-crankly hedge, Potager du Roi.

Longwood.

The Fushimi-Momoyama Castle and garden in southern Kyoto (Japan) was rebuilt in 1964 adjacent to the site of the original Fushimi Castle, which was constructed for the first time in 1594 by the great shogun Hideyoshi Toyotami and then reconstructed by him in 1596 after its collapse in the great earthquake of that year. This multi-storeyed castle-palace was a centre for Momoyama culture, nurturing the arts of the age such as Noh theatre, painting, poetry, gardening and the art of *o-karikomi* (tree shaping) and the tea ceremony. Nowadays, as well as promoting and displaying the history of the Momoyama era and having a spectacular display of cherry blossom in season, it boasts a funfair and pool.

The garden of William Waterfield.

Olive tree pruning in Palm Springs.

Doorways in the double hedge at Somerleyton Hall.

Somerleyton Hall in Suffolk (England) was originally an Elizabethan mansion that was extensively remodelled in an Italianate style when it was purchased in 1844 by Sir Morton Peto, the builder who won the contract to erect the Houses of Parliament and Nelson's Column. Bankruptcy forced him to sell the estate, which was purchased in 1863 by Sir Francis Crossley of Halifax, whose descendants own the house and grounds to this day. The twelve acres of formal gardens contain some lovely Italian statuary, a walled garden, a 300-foot long iron pergola covered with wisteria, a celebrated yew maze designed and planted by Nesfield in 1846 and unusual lean-to greenhouses by Paxton with ridge- and furrow-glazed roofs instead of the more usual flat ones.

Crowded topiary on the hillside gardens of the Palácio de Seteais at Sintra.

The Palácio de Seteais at Sintra (Portugal), now a beautiful hotel, was built in the 1790s by a Dutch consul. It was later owned by the Marquês de Marialva who, in 1802, doubled the size of the palace by adding a matching building linked to the original via a triumphal arch. At the back of the palace the typical Portuguese gardens of parterres of extraordinary clipped, box-edged beds overlook spectacular views of the Atlantic.

Fushimi-Momoyama Castle.

The Stilt Garden, Hidcote.

The fox, Knightshayes.

Looking across the valley to the laurel maze at Glendurgan Garden.

Glendurgan Garden in Cornwall (England) was one of several Cornish estates owned by the Fox Family in the nineteenth century. Keen gardeners and Quakers, Alfred and Sarah Fox started clearing the valley site which ran down to the sea in the 1820s and by 1833 they had laid out the complicated laurel maze in the middle of the garden and were planting the numerous trees and exotic and tender plants which were to flourish in the mild, sheltered climate. The garden was bequeathed to the National Trust in 1962.

Somerleyton Hall.

Turf Maze at Chenies Manor.

Blenheim Palace.

A Celtic maze design at Shanagarry Pottery.

Herrenhausen.

Shanagarry Pottery in Country Cork (Republic of Ireland) was built by the Irish potter Stephen Pearce in 1970. It is only two fields away from the remains of Penn Castle (the starting point for William Penn's historic voyage to America) where Pearce has recently built a new pottery and Emporium and work is underway on a restaurant and specially designed gardens. At Shanagarry Pottery a beech maze based on the pattern of a gold brooch has been planted. This maze and the garden at Penn Castle should start to flourish at about the same time and the plan is to have paths and walkways linking the two areas.

1670 THE FRONTEIRA PALACE Portuguese *azulejo* tilework at its best based on the Islamic tradition but with the geometric patterns abandoned by the Portuguese in favour of more representational subject matter, including famous kings and mythological characters.

View across the main parterre to the elaborately tiled Gallery of Kings. Visited April 18.

The Fronteira Palace was built in about 1670 by the Marquês de Fronteira and it was reputedly designed by an Italian architect though his name is unknown. Originally used as a hunting lodge, the Fronteira family made the palace their main home after their city residence was destroyed in the great earthquake of 1755 which devastated much of Lisbon. The Palace is still the family home of the Fronteira family and the twelfth Marquês de Fronteira, a direct descendent of the first Marquês, is the present incumbent.

The garden of the Fronteira Palace is an excellent example of a typical, seventeenth-century Portuguese garden in that it not only reveals the numerous influences that are the inevitable result of a nation that revelled in travel and conquest during the preceding centuries but also shows that the sum of its individual parts can create a whole that is quintessentially Portuguese.

The house, on a hill looking down over the garden below and out across the surrounding countryside (now very much developed but previously, of course, quite rural), is very much an Italian Renaissance development. The beautifully clipped box hedges of the geometrically patterned parterre, the shaped trees and the central fountain are reminiscent of the French formal garden movement and the numerous statues reflect the classical influence.

To the right, forming one side of the garden as one

looks down from the terrace along the house, lies the *pièce de résistance* whose antecedents are Moorish but whose characteristics have been developed into what is thought of as typically Portuguese – the *azulejo* work.

The importance of water and tiles in Arab gardens goes back many hundreds of years before its introduction into the Iberian peninsula by the Moors in the eighth century. *Azulejo* comes from the Arab word *zuleij* 'burnt stone' and although in Islamic tradition tiles could only have arabesque or geometrical patterns, by the time the Moors had left Spain in the fifteenth century the art of tile-making had traversed the mountains of the Sierra Morena and become firmly embedded in Spain and Portugal.

Azulejo manufacture was specifically associated with Portugal and by the sixteenth century it had broken out of its strict Islamic confines and under Christian influences was being used to depict a much wider range of subjects – human, mythological, animal – and rather than each tile being an individual entity, often one tile became part of a bigger overall picture or panel.

The importance of water and tiles to create coolness, tranquillity and relief within a garden, in contrast to the heat and dryness of the landscape outside, is an important concept in the Arab world and has been incorporated into many Portuguese gardens. But the water tank and *azulejo* work at the Fronteira Palace is the largest and most ornamental in Portugal. A wall, which runs the length of the water tank, is covered in beautiful *azulejo* paintings of twelve knights on prancing horses and reveals, through open arches, mysterious grottoes above which is a balustraded terrace. This has a little pavilion at each end and is reached on either side by flights of stone steps. The back wall of the balcony has fifteen niches containing busts of Portuguese kings and the entire surround is covered with blue tiles and decorated shellwork. The whole building is reflected in the still water of the tank and is quite stunning.

Behind the Gallery of Kings, concealed from the main vista, is another more private garden, the Garden of Venus and, more private still, the Chapel Walk. Between the two is the Casa de Fresco, the Cool House, its walls elaborately decorated with shell, glass and ceramics in complex designs. Apparently, this decorative work was done when the Palace was completed and King Peter II was invited to a banquet in the garden. The King enjoyed himself so much that he conferred the title of Marquês on his host and, in keeping with a time-honoured tradition that crockery and glass used by the royal party could not be used by anyone else, all the plates and glasses from the feast were broken up and used to decorate the Casa de Fresco outside which the banquet had taken place.

Unfortunately, at the time of our visit one could only see around the gardens in a guided tour which was a great shame. However, a great deal of restoration work was going on in the house so perhaps when it is completed things will be easier.

Address: Palacio de Fronteira, Largo de Sao Domingos de Benfica, off Estrada de Benfico, Lumiar, Lisbon, Portugal.

The Cool House.

The Gallery of the Kings showing the water tank.

Detail of the tilework in the Gallery of the Kings.

Circa 1720–60 QUINTA DOS AZULEJOS Enclosed Portuguese leisure garden developed in the Islamic tradition and designed as an *ambulatio*, a strolling walk, so that the visitor can appreciate the extensive and beautiful *azulejos* – painted tiles.

The Quinta dos Azulejos looking towards the house (now a school). Visited April 11.

Wisteria tunnel.

The Quinta dos Azulejos, built in the early eighteenth century by Antonio Çolaco Torres, is one of the finest examples of the Portuguese leisure garden which still reflects the Mediterranean Islamic tradition of the enclosed interior garden, rather than the ideas prevalent in many of the northern European gardens, which sought to incorporate the landscape beyond the immediate garden into the overall plan.

What makes the Quinta dos Azulejos extraordinary are the *azulejos* – the painted tiles. Every column, panel, bench and wall is covered in the most beautiful tile work. Although originally a Moorish tradition, to decorate gardens, water tanks and fountains with geometrically patterned tiles, the Portuguese did not confine themselves to Islamic precepts but painted and glazed tiles in a much wider variety of colours than had previously been used and ran riot with the subject matter. Stories from Greek and Roman mythology, from Christianity, from farming life, animals, fishes, birds and ornate patterns and borders are all to be seen as one walks round the sides of the garden. For, interestingly, although the garden is entered through an archway in the middle of the garden and the central path leads straight across the garden and out to a playground beyond, the purpose of the garden is to provide an *ambulatio* – a

Looking into the tiled garden from the direction of the house.

leisurely walk – so the visitor's natural instinct is to walk either to left or right in order to look at the *azulejos*.

The house was, according to a commemorative plaque, visited a number of times by the Royal Family between 1753 and 1760 but by the end of the nineteenth century it had been converted into a private school which it remains to this day. Sadly, the garden has now been built around at the far end with some extremely unattractive additions as dictated by the needs of the school with seemingly no consideration for the aesthetics of the garden and its historical importance.

While still very beautiful and well worth a visit, the Quinta dos Azulejos is suffering from the ravages of boisterous children using it as the main thoroughfare from the school to the playground and some of the newer classrooms. I saw one little boy vigorously push his friend into a box hedge and then receive payment in kind. It doesn't take much imagination to picture the condition of the hedge!

The tile paintings, particularly those that depict animals, are intriguing but it isn't a place for a long visit as it is rather small and confined. Also, it is a couple of miles out of the city in the suburbs of Lisbon so it is best to go by taxi rather than battle with the highly complex system of new roads that are springing up in and around Lisbon literally in front of one's eyes!

Address: Colègio Manuel Bernardes LDA, Quinta dos Azulejos, Paco do Lumiar, 1600 Lisboa, Portugal.

The tiled columns.

Detail of a tiled panel.

99

Advancing rain on the Grand Canal at Versailles.

Bowood, looking across the lake to the Doric Temple.

Denver Botanic Gardens.

Chicago Botanic Garden.

Denver Botanic Gardens in Colorado (USA) features an arboretum, a herb garden, collections of native plants and a huge conservatory filled with tropical plants and cacti. The botanic gardens also manage a large section of Mount Goliath (fifty miles away) and the alpine flowering plants to be seen blooming there between June and August are well worth the drive.

Chicago Botanic Garden in Illinois (USA) was constructed in 1965 on an area of marshland and landscaped as a series of lakes, waterways and islands. It features fine collections of native plants, demonstration gardens, an educational centre, greenhouses full of tropical and desert plants, and *Sansho-en*, a Japanese-style garden comprising three islands.

Virginia Water photographed in January.

Virginia Water Lake in Surrey (England) was originally a grand ornamental addition to Windsor Great Park built by the Duke of Cumberland in the eighteenth century. Dams, a grotto, cascade and rockwork adorned the lake; a fake Chinese yacht and pavilion and a gothic belvedere enhanced the atmosphere but these no longer exist. However, the graceful lake full of fish and fowl and the delightful surrounding woodland still survive.

A rustic bridge on Stow Lake, Golden Gate Park.

Golden Gate Park in San Francisco (USA), was created by the great landscape architect, Frederick Law Olmsted (1822–1903), in the late nineteenth century. 1000 acres of gardens, lakes, forest and waterfalls were constructed on an area that was originally wild sand dunes.

Stancombe Park.

Little Sparta.

The Obelisk Pool and Kent's Temple at Chiswick House.

Chiswick House Gardens in London (England) were designed by William Kent in the first half of the eighteenth century. Respecting the natural contours of the land, Kent, in collaboration with Charles Bridgeman, drew on many sources to create the semi-classical landscape of statues, monuments, vistas, terraces, water, domed temple, exedra and avenues that complement the Palladian villa built for Lord Burlington in 1729.

Arley Hall.

The semi-circular pool backed by the palisade of clipped cypress at the Villa Gamberaia.

The Plunge Pool at Painswick.

Veitshöchheim.

Stancombe Park.

Vizcaya.

Berggarten at Herrenhausen.

The central cascade looking towards the Upper Belvedere.

The Belvedere in Vienna (Austria) is a baroque masterpiece built between 1713 and 1732, comprising two gardens, the Upper and the Lower, cleverly linked by elaborate waterworks and cascades.

A detail of the stepped cascade at Belvedere.   *Villa d'Este.*

Blenheim Palace.   *Bowood House.*

The lake and waterfall at Longwood Gardens.

The cascade at Virginia Water in winter.

Looking down the water staircase at the Villa Garzoni.

Het Loo.

Het Loo.

Villa Aldobrandini.

Vizcaya.

The staircase at Bussaco with the water staircase running through the middle.

Castle Howard.

1666–1713 HERRENHAUSEN An original German baroque garden developed by Electress Sophie, mother of King George I, which escaped the ravages of the English Landscape Movement only to lose its central viewpoint – the house – during the Second World War.

Looking diagonally across the parterres towards the Bell Fountain. Visited August 1.

Herrenhausen, originally an estate outside the city of Hanover, was first developed as a summer residence by Duke Johann Friedrich. A site plan of 1666 shows the outlines of the first park which consisted of an almost square pleasure garden near the main house divided by a central avenue and flanked at the end by two fish ponds beyond which the avenue continued the line of the central axis as far as the River Leine.

The second major phase in the development of the garden took place around 1673 when both the house and garden were enlarged and the parterre in the pleasure garden was rearranged and richly ornamented and flanked on either side by *bosquets* and plantations of fruit trees. The Haute Cascade and the grotto were also built. The third, final and most important stage of the development of the '*Le jardin de Herrenhausen, qui est ma vie*' was overseen by the Electress Sophie, wife of Ernst August who spoke these words in 1713, a year before she died while walking in her beloved garden.

Sophie was the daughter of the Elector Palatine Frederick V and Elizabeth Stuart, a daughter of James I of England. She spent much of her childhood in the Netherlands and her favourite gardener was a Frenchman, Martin Charbonnier (who worked for her

The Orangery parterre.

The Great Cascade.

from 1682 onwards), so Dutch and French influences played a significant role in the design and layout of the garden.

In her first ten to fifteen years at Herrenhausen Sophie concentrated on developing the existing parterre garden by setting up new sculptures, building the Hedge Theatre (1689–93), Small Cascade and Gallery (1694–1700) for holding lavish banquets and musical entertainments.

In 1696 the final stage in the construction of the garden began. A square area, about the size of the parterre garden, was designed thus making the whole Grosser Garten (main garden) a rectangle of approximately 50 hectares surrounded by a wide ditch, known as The Graft (very much in keeping with the Dutch garden tradition of canals surrounding a garden). The Nouveau Jardin, to contrast with the parterre garden which was designed on a pattern of right-angled squares, was divided by crossed avenues, with the great fountain that spouts an 83-metre jet of water in the centre, to form four square areas occupied by star-shaped gardens. At the centre of each of these are round open spaces with octagonal fountain pools in the middle. The central axis continues down to an oval *bassin* and the avenue that runs along the east/west axis at the southern end of the garden has a round pavilion in either corner, designed by Louis Rémy de la Fosse in 1708.

In the centre of the Grand Parterre Garden stands the Bell Fountain which has 166 jets and the paths are lined with sandstone sculptures of gods, virtues, seasons and continents on plinths, painted white to simulate marble as was customary at the time. Between the Grand Parterre and the Nouveau Jardin, eight small gardens representing aspects of the history of gardening, such as a Renaissance Garden, a Baroque Garden, a Rococo Garden, a Rose Garden and a Water Garden, were substituted for the original designs when the Hanover City Council acquired Herrenhausen in 1936 and began a programme of much needed restoration work. Similarly, after the house and much of the garden were destroyed in the war, a programme of restoration was again embarked on and completed in 1966 in time for the 300th anniversary of the garden's foundation.

There has been some criticism of the historical authenticity of the planting in the triangular compartments in the Nouveau Jardin and the structure of the parterres beyond the Swan Lakes but, overall, the Grosser Garten at Herrenhausen is considered the best original surviving Baroque Garden in Germany. On Sophie's death, her son, King George I, and his descendants never had the time or inclination to oversee a massive transformation of the garden into the subsequently fashionable Landscape style and thus it avoided the fate that befell Het Loo (see pages 110–113).

Address: Grosser Garten, Herrenhausen, Hanover, Germany.

The Great Fountain reaches a height of 82 metres.

DUTCH BAROQUE

1684–99 HET LOO (Restored 1977–84) Seventeenth-century Dutch baroque garden on a grand scale with the emphasis on symmetry, water, statuary and planting reflecting the belief that creating order and harmony on earth mirrored the peace and unity to be found in Paradise.

The parterres are bordered by plates-bandes, where each plant is tied up and given its own space in the seventeenth century manner.
Visited July 19.

Het Loo, a moated medieval castle in the sparsely populated Veluwe region, was purchased by Prince William of Orange (1650–1702) in 1684 for use as a hunting lodge but with the idea of building something more palatial elsewhere on the estate. Plans were drawn up, probably by the Académie d'Architecture in Paris, and work commenced. By 1686 the main building of the new Het Loo and the wings were constructed, and the gardens laid out under the supervision of the Dutch architect, Jacob Roman (1640–1716), and the French designer, Daniel Marot (1661–1752).

The Narcissus Fountain.

Het Loo became the favourite hunting lodge and country palace of William III and Princess Mary and on their accession to the English throne in 1689 it underwent further extensions and embellishment in keeping with their increased wealth and status. However, pressing affairs of state meant that Princess Mary never had time to visit her beloved Het Loo again and only learned of the changes through the marvellously detailed description of it written by the King's physician, Walter Harris, published in London in 1699.

Kings William IV and V used Het Loo as a hunting lodge and summer palace during the eighteenth century but on William V's flight from Holland in 1795 the palace and grounds were abandoned and seriously plundered. In 1807 Louis Napoleon inherited the property as King of Holland and extensive alterations took place, the most drastic being the conversion of the garden into a landscaped park in the English style. The lower garden and canals were filled in, the fountains and statuary and parterres disappeared and a flat green sward ran directly behind the palace, ringed with clusters of different trees. Even the moat of the original medieval castle, now known as Het Oude Loo, was filled in.

Despite lamenting the loss of the old garden, the descendants of William V made no moves to undo the alterations to the Great Garden, although outside its walls other developments took place such as the conversion of six fish ponds into an artificial lake and the

Looking back towards the house from the Upper Garden through the King's Fountain.

addition of a tea pavilion, bath house and arboretum.

It was not until after the death of Queen Wilhelmina (1880–1962) that her daughter Princess Margriet decided to move, with her family, to another house on the estate and permit the palace to be turned into a national museum. The aim was to remove the nineteenth- and twentieth-century additions to the house and garden and restore the whole complex to its original seventeenth-century layout using as a blueprint the numerous contemporary accounts, records, paintings and drawings which still existed, principally Harris's account *A Description of the King's Royal Palace and Gardens at Loo*, the early eighteenth-century ground-plan of the garden by Christiaan Pieter van Staden, and the bird's eye view of the house and grounds in a drawing attributed to Jacob Roman (1640–1716). These documents, plus the archaeological evidence revealed during the reconstruction process that took place between 1977 and 1984, have enabled the house and garden to be returned as near as possible to the way they would have been at the time of William III's death: the quintessential example of a seventeenth-century Dutch baroque house and garden.

To the late-seventeenth-century mind, symmetry was

One of the eight main parterres de broideries, with the statue of Flora in the centre.

analogous to the order and harmony that existed in paradise and creating a garden in which this principle predominated was an attempt to reflect the order and harmony that King William III's skilful leadership would create for his people. Furthermore, the imposition of order and artifice on wild and unruly nature was an important way of asserting and proclaiming the power and authority of the King.

The first stage of the garden's development consisted of the section immediately behind the house known as the Lower Garden. It is walled and terraced on three sides (south, west and east) and bounded on the north side by the canal and an east/west avenue called Middendwarslaan that leads to the Het Oude Loo on the west side. The Lower Garden is divided into two main sections, by the Middenallée with the Venus Fountain in the centre of it and with four parterres on each side, and the east/west cross axis which has the fountains of the Celestial and Terrestrial Spheres on it and the Fountains of Narcissus and Arion at each end. The four inner parterres are parterres de broderies and the four outer ones are green parterres with ornamental grass edged with boxwood hedges. All the parterres are bordered by *plates-bandes*, which are beds of flowering plants with each plant carefully separated from the next by a controlling piece of string, and trimmed yews and junipers, and bordered by low, boxwood hedges.

The Upper Garden, begun in 1692, extends from the Middendwarslaan to the two curved colonnades at its far end and continues the north/south *allée* down its centre with the spectacular King's Fountain in the middle (with a jet spouting 13 metres into the air) and three parterres

on each side. Originally there were nine parterres on each side but as the decision was taken to retain some of the fine specimens of trees that had been planted in the Upper Garden when it was landscaped in the early nineteenth century, in particular two very fine copper beeches and a tulip tree, it was impossible to recreate the original number of parterres. Stairs at the back of the colonnades lead up to a flat terrace from which the whole garden and house can be viewed north to south just as the terrace at the back of the palace provides a south to north view of the garden.

The two other gardens which have been largely restored are the King's Garden on the west of the palace beneath the King's apartments and the Queen's Garden on the east below the Queen's apartments. Both were accessible from inside the palace as well as from the main garden itself. The King's Garden consists of two sections – a double parterre and espaliered fruit trees against the wall and a bowling green used for various ball games. The Queen's Garden only covers half its original area because work space for the museum necessitated retaining some of the early nineteenth-century building that had been erected at the southern end of the garden. However, about half of the original space covered by *berceaux* has been reconstructed. *Berceaux* are networks of arbours and pathways covered by clipped hornbeam that have grown to magnificent proportions. It must be the best and most extensive example of this work in existence and it is beautifully cool and shady. Between the *berceaux* and the terrace is an octagonal fountain bordered by parterres and numerous tubs of exotic plants and varieties of orange trees. In the corner

The Queen's Garden, at Het Loo, with tender plants put out for the summer.

DUTCH BAROQUE

The berceaux of clipped hornbeam at Het Loo.

between the palace and the terrace an aviary and a grotto can be seen, though not passed through, as was originally possible for Queen Mary, giving her access to both her own apartments and the main garden.

There is no doubt that the accurate reconstruction of this garden is a marvellous contribution to our understanding of seventeenth-century gardening on many levels. The overall design not only reflects contemporary philosophical thought but also shows the combination of French and Dutch influences on the layout of the garden and its ornamentation with the emphasis on symmetry, water, statuary and planting. There is no doubt that the influence of Le Nôtre can be detected but the Dutch assimilation and reinterpretation of his ideas to suit the dictates of the terrain and their own preferences is even stronger. The scale of the garden is much smaller, for instance, than Versailles (see pages 78–81) or Vaux-le-Vicomte (see pages 74–77); the emphasis on width rather than length and far perspective is seen in the shape of the square parterres; and the underscoring of the variety of the vegetation by clearly separating the plants is a very typical feature of the Dutch Baroque style.

In the ten years since it was first opened to the public everything has grown lush and it no longer has the rather bald, cold look captured in photographs of the mid-1980s. It looks much more like the magnificent coloured engraving published by Petrus Schenk *c*.1700.

Address: Rijksmuseum Paleis en Tuinen Het Loo, Apeldoorn, Holland.

The inner structure of the berceaux.

The Triton Fountain.

113

1708–23 WEIKERSHEIM CASTLE A German baroque garden combining French and Italian influences with a highly unusual Orangery in two separate sections, creating a spectacular view of the countryside beyond, and featuring numerous comic, satirical and grotesque statues.

Looking through the semi-circular opening of the double Orangery to the countryside beyond. Visited July 19.

Weikersheim Castle was extensively enlarged in the eighteenth century by Carl Ludwig (1674–1756), Count of Hohenlohe, whose family documentary evidence of the first moated castle dates back to 1156. Although the original Renaissance garden was laid out in 1600 to the south of the castle beyond the moat and terrace, it bore no axial relationship to the castle because French and Italian ideas about the links between house and garden had not yet filtered through to Germany. However, by

Looking back towards the house.

the time the baroque garden which we see today replaced the Renaissance garden, the central axis ran north from the Hall Wing in the Castle to the southern end of the garden overlooking the Tauber Valley.

As with many gardens in Germany, influences from their southern and western neighbours played an important role in the design of the seventeenth and eighteenth centuries (to the extent that there is no specifically German garden style) but the Italian Renaissance and French Baroque styles were assimilated and adapted to suit the individual predilections of various Princes, Counts and Electors of Germany.

Work on the garden at Weikersheim was carried out in two phases. The first phase, begun in 1708 after a plan by Daniel Matthieu, constitutes the main formal outline of a perfect rectangle with paths in the form of a cross, a central round pond and an oblong pond at the end. This was not completed before Count Ludwig's marriage to Elizabeth Friederike Sophie, Princess of Oettingen, in 1713, resulted in a new impetus and interest in the garden from her. She engaged the architect Johann Christian Luttich whose plan for a dramatic and unusual Orangery at the far end of the garden was executed between 1719 and 1723.

The design, position and purpose of this Orangery

The dwarf of the Court Garden Woman.

Statues along the moat with the Drummer in the foreground.

goes much further than orangeries built in France and elsewhere, although a precedent had been set at other German castles and palaces where Luttich worked. It extends on two wings across the entire width of the garden with an open semi-circular recess in the middle where an equestrian statue of Count Ludwig stood until 1865 (it now contains a regal figure of 'Europe'). This central break between the two halves of the Orangery provides a spectacular, panoramic vista over the fertile Tauber Valley that makes the whole countryside, as far as the eye can see, seem to be part of the garden.

The sculptures, fifty-two in all, are another important feature of the garden. Gods and goddesses, the elements, the winds and the continents are all represented. According to Thacker in *The History of Gardens*, what makes the garden fun and more akin to rococo than serious baroque classicism is the satire and humour evident in the sculpture; the gods sitting on the top of the

Orangery dangling their legs and the dwarves on the wall alongside the moat are grotesque caricatures of the court hangers-on: the cook, the court jester, the Master of the Hunt, etc. The overall effect is one of enjoyment and amusement.

Our visit, on a very hot summer's day, was made even more enjoyable by the fact that one of the two buildings (the Armoury and Gardener's House built *c.* 1710) that symmetrically flank the castle is now a music school and individual students can be found in quiet niches of the garden practising their instruments and delightful, orchestral strains accompanied us as we walked down the beech avenues alongside the rather derelict kitchen gardens that exist on the right-hand side of the main pleasure garden.

Address: Weikersheim, Nr Bad Mergentheim, Wurzburg, Germany.

The Hercules Fountain.

The statue of the Idler.

1675–1749 STOWE Superlative example of the eighteenth-century English Landscape Movement with sweeping lawns, water, classical buildings and a *fermé ornée*, created by Vanbrugh, Bridgeman, Brown and Kent who all worked on the grounds and buildings at various times.

Looking across the superbly maintained trees and parkland towards the Corinthian Arch. Visited May 25.

Stowe was owned by the Temple family from the end of the sixteenth century until the middle of the nineteenth century when bankruptcy forced the estates and collections to be sold. The house itself was sold in 1921 for conversion into a public school.

In terms of garden history the huge wealth and power of the Temple family during the eighteenth century, followed by its rapid decline in the nineteenth, is a major blessing because it resulted in one of the finest examples of English landscape gardening being preserved virtually intact. During the period of the garden's evolution (1593–1780) many of the most notable architects and landscape designers of the day worked on developing the grounds and buildings and these examples of their work are largely extant although a number still await restoration.

When Sir Richard Temple, later Viscount Cobham (1675–1749), inherited Stowe from his father in 1693 he acquired a house and garden that were less than twenty years old yet over the next fifty years he inaugurated an ambitious, ongoing programme of extensive changes and development which reflected his increasing wealth and political power.

The garden he inherited was formal with three terraces, an avenue of poplars along the central axis, and a walled kitchen garden. Between 1715 and 1725 Temple employed first Sir John Vanbrugh, then Charles Bridgeman to make changes that would be in keeping with his status. A grander entrance court was made on the north side of the house and the three terraces were redesigned to form one large grand parterre in the French style. This was shortly followed by the extension of the gardens down to the stream which was dammed to form the Octagon Pond. As the garden could not be extended eastwards because of the approach road on that side, Vanbrugh built a Rotunda out to the west, thus enclosing part of the area known as Home Park, and Bridgeman built a ha-ha to create a concealed boundary on the south and west which enabled views from the gardens to extend out into the countryside beyond, giving an impression of much greater space.

Between 1725 and 1740 the extensive works programme continued. On the west side the garden was completed with the entire Home Park pasture being incorporated into the garden and surrounded by terraced walks. In the south, the stream was dammed a second

The Gothic Temple folly in Hawkwell Field.

Looking up towards the south front of the house from the West Lake Pavilion.

The Palladian Bridge at Stowe.

The interior of the Palladian Bridge showing the plaster ceiling added by Borra.

The Corinthian Arch forms the focus of the Grand Avenue at Stowe.

time to create the Eleven-Acre Lake and a new approach road was built around the southern and western boundaries, freeing the eastern side for expansion and development.

After Vanbrugh's death in 1726 James Gibb and William Kent were largely involved with the development of the east garden which occurred in two phases. Firstly, the little valley running south-east of the main axis was laid out as the Elysian Fields with the buildings and whole conception of the area following William Kent's notion to create a landscape comprising a series of 'natural' pictures in the Claudian manner. Here are to be found the Temple of British Worthies, the Temple of Ancient Virtue, and the Shell Bridge, all by Kent. To the east of the Elysian Fields, the Hawkwell Field was, between 1739 and 1743, laid out in the manner of a *ferme ornée*, an ornamental farm, with the animals grazing right up to the buildings which were all designed by James Gibb.

In 1741 Capability Brown came to work at Stowe as Head Gardener so it is probable that he had a hand in the design of the Hawkwell Field. It was at about this time, too, that the formal parterre in front of the house was grassed over and all traces of the formal central axis disappeared under the expanse of lawn bordered by clumps of trees that led down to the Octagon Lake.

The last major innovation before Temple's death in 1749 was the enclosure of the area to the north-east of the house and the creation of the Grecian Valley and a new walled garden enabling the transfer of the old one from the south-west of the house to its new position and thus paving the way for the final opening up of the whole southern vista which was undertaken by Temple's nephew, Earle Temple. It was he too who remodelled the south front of the house so that it became one of the finest classical façades in England and aptly reflected the grandeur and beauty of the garden.

To list every building in the gardens at Stowe would be to rewrite the National Trust handbook but enough has been said to indicate the importance of this garden as possibly the finest representative example of the eighteenth-century English Landscape Movement.

Address: Stowe Landscape Garden, Buckingham, Buckinghamshire, England.

The Temple of British Worthies.

The Hermitage.

1700–26 CASTLE HOWARD A garden of epic proportions in the heroic Landscape manner in which Vanbrugh used the natural contours of the land and the rolling vistas of the surrounding countryside to create a panoramic environment.

The Atlas Fountain designed by Nesfield with the Castle in the background. Visited July 12.

Castle Howard and its grounds, built between 1700 and 1726, was commissioned by Charles Howard, the 3rd Earl of Carlisle (1699–1738), at a time when country houses were the ultimate status symbols and he wanted one that outshone those of his contemporaries.

The original castle and village of Henderskelfe had existed for several hundred years on the site but in 1693 the castle was seriously damaged by fire which is when Charles Howard conceived the idea of a grand new house. After discarding the first plans drawn up by

The Rose Garden.

Talman (who had worked at Chatsworth), he asked Sir John Vanbrugh, the successful stage designer and dramatist of such plays as *The Provok'd Wife* and *The Relapse*, to submit designs for a new castle and the grounds.

Vanbrugh (1664–1726) was not an architect or a landscape gardener by training but he had an intuitive feel for the setting of a building within a total landscape and, as such, he has been claimed, according to Geoffrey Jellicoe in *The Oxford Companion to Gardens*, as one of the pioneers of the English Landscape Movement. He was, said Sir Joshua Reynolds, 'an architect who composed like a painter' and the commission to design Castle Howard was his first attempt at putting his ideas into practice. Unlike at Stowe, Blenheim and Claremont, Vanbrugh was able to conceive the project at Castle Howard as an entity, a unified plan to create an environment of epic proportions in the heroic manner. Thus, by using the natural contours of the land to determine the landscape and by putting the house parallel to the main approach, rather than at right angles to it, he was able to take advantage of the rolling vistas on all sides of the house.

The south front of the castle looks out on a formal garden with immaculate lawns, framed by yew hedges, in the centre of which stands the Atlas Fountain. To the south-west is the original kitchen garden now given over to beautiful rose gardens in memory of the present owner's mother, Lady Cecilia Howard, who died in 1974. To the east the lake, pond and river extend into the distance with Vanbrugh's bridge crossing the river and the Mausoleum (by Hawksmoor) in the distance. From the south front of the house the Broad Walk leads, to the east, into the diagonal Terrace Walk that runs along the old Henderskelfe Village main street up to the beautiful Temple of the Four Winds (designed by Vanbrugh but not completed until two years after his death).

The north side of the house looks down over a rolling grass slope to the Great Lake (built in the 1790s but obviously part of the original plan, as in 1724 Hawksmoor refers to it in a letter to the Earl). To the east of this lake, and stretching across to the Temple of the Four Winds, stands Ray Wood. It was already full of mature trees when Vanbrugh started work on the Castle, and the decision to let it remain in its natural state with the addition of a maze of twisting paths and walkways and strategically placed statuary and fountains (lost or eroded over the centuries) was an important one in terms of garden history. This early example of the 'natural' in the landscape movement has now made an easy transition into the currently fashionable natural woodland garden with an enormous collection of rhododendrons, hybrids, shrubs, trees and special spring, summer and autumn walks through the wood.

On the edge of Ray Wood, next to the Great Lake, is a terrific adventure playground very near the Lakeside café and boat rides (open only in the summer months).

Address: Castle Howard, York, North Yorkshire, England.

The New River Bridge from the Temple of the Four Winds.

The gateway to Ray Wood.

A view across the lakes to the Mausoleum in the distance.

1705–64 BLENHEIM PALACE The Romantic Landscape Movement's search for Naturalism exemplified here with Capability Brown's sweeping grass lawn, curving lake and rushing cascades, together with Vanbrugh's bridge.

Looking west towards the Palace across the Italian Garden. Visited June 25.

Blenheim Palace and its grounds, designed by Sir John Vanbrugh (1664–1726) in conjunction with Charles Bridgeman and Henry Wise, had its foundation stone laid in 1705. However, despite Vanbrugh's initial optimism that the main body of building and planting would be completed within a year, the work took much longer and its owners, the Duke and Duchess of Marlborough, did not move in until 1719. After the Duke's death in 1722, the Duchess continued to oversee the garden plans he had initiated and subsequent Dukes have made major changes and additions to the grounds over the centuries.

Blenheim today is very different from its original conception although it retains the air of enormous grandeur and impressiveness which it has undoubtedly always had.

Bridgeman's signed plans of 1709 show the bastioned military state garden which Henry Wise and his gardeners built on the south front of the house facing towards Bladon Church. This garden had a four-sided, 250-yard parterre of dwarf box in patterns which led into a hexagonal-shaped, formal wilderness. This was surrounded by stone-built curtain walls with eight, rounded bastions 150 feet high at each corner. These were not only majestic in their aesthetic effect but highly practical, providing protection for the garden and vantage points from which to view the paths and parterres within and to look outwards at the vistas beyond.

The military state garden contained no flowers. These were provided in profusion for the first Duchess in the formal garden planted on the east front of the palace – lavender, pinks, rosemary, lilies, roses, jasmine and honeysuckle – all of which she could see from her window overlooking the garden.

To the south-east of the military garden lay the 8-acre vegetable garden, which was enclosed by brick walls, 14 feet high, with stone dressings to mirror the martial theme of the state garden. Here, Wise planted and nurtured a huge variety of fruit trees – figs, mulberries, quinces, apples, cherries, plums and nectarines. He recommended 28 varieties of peach and 72 of pear. Marlborough took an enormous interest in the proceedings and wrote to the Duchess from his camp at Meldert in 1709: 'If possible I should wish that you might taste the fruit of every tree so that what is not good might be changed. On this matter you must advise with Mr Wise.'

Today, this part of the garden is very different from the original design and execution. The military state garden only lasted fifty years before Capability Brown (1716–83) replaced it in 1764 with the rolling green lawn that sweeps down to the lake and cascade he created by damming the River Glyme and allowing it to flood on either side of Vanbrugh's Bridge.

Vanbrugh's monumental bridge facing the north front of the house was built between 1708 and 1710 and in the original layout appears only to span a ravine on either side of which are separate lakes. After her husband's death, the first Duchess, with his chief engineer Colonel Armstrong, created a canal that linked the two flat pools of water. But it was Capability Brown's scheme to change the landscape by allowing the River Glyme to run beneath the bridge, creating natural shaped lakes on either side, that gave Vanbrugh's bridge a purpose and created a park that exemplifies the main tenets of the English Landscape movement. In the south-western corner of the lake, Brown, in the 1760s, designed the Grand Cascade where the River Glyme falls from the lake and resumes its slow, winding course to eventually join the Evenlode, a tributary of the River Thames. The

The water terraces on the west front.

picturesque, romantic and deafening rush of water was intended to remind spectators of the savage scenes painted by Salvator Rosa (1615–73).

As well as creating the lakes, the lawns and the cascades, Brown initiated the planting of thousands of trees. The transition from formality to naturalism was virtually complete. Fortunately, however, Brown did leave the formal approach avenues of elms to the north and east of the house untouched (though, sadly, Dutch Elm disease did not and they have been replanted with limes and planes) and the walled kitchen garden, both of which remain today to indicate the military overtones that originally imbued the whole garden.

Innovations that have taken place this century include the replacement of the first Duchess's flower garden in the east wing with the Italian garden. Despite its name, the intricate parterre de broderie and the central pool with the Mermaid Fountain, recreated by the 9th Duke and Achille Duchêne, the French landscape architect, are much more reminiscent of the great French châteaux such as Vaux-le-Vicomte (see pages 74–77).

On the north front, the Duke repaved the Great Court which Brown had grassed over and in 1925 he and Duchêne began work on the water terraces on the west front of the palace. This was a costly business but resulted in a formal garden of delightful water parterres reminiscent of those at Versailles, ornamented with Bernini's Fountain of the River Gods, together with the lead sphinxes and carved caryatids. In 1932, Sir Sacheverell Sitwell urged the Duke to recreate the military state garden that had existed on the south front 200 years before in order to complete the formal gardens but the Duke, it is said, shrugged, knowing such a task would be impossibly expensive.

The importance of Blenheim Palace and its grounds lies firstly in the perfect synthesis between the rolling grassland, sunken ha-ha, water vistas and Vanbrugh's bridge, exemplifying the Romantic Landscape Movement at its most magnificent and dramatic and, secondly, in its eclecticism. It is as important for what is no longer there and for what has been changed and added to the original conception, as for what it is today.

The Pleasure Gardens include the Marlborough Maze, a narrow gauge railway, the Butterfly House, Adventure Play Area, Garden Café and Garden Centre.

Address: Blenheim Palace, Woodstock, Oxfordshire, England.

Bernini's River-Gods Fountain on the lower water terrace.

The Vanbrugh Bridge.

1754–71 BOWOOD One of Capability Brown's best-preserved Landscape gardens with a man-made lake that looks like a natural river disappearing behind the trees and vistas of great simplicity and beauty.

Looking down over the ha-ha to the lake. Visited July 4.

Bowood estate, bought in 1754 by John Petty, Earl of Shelburne, comprised, at that time, a half-built house and a park which had originally been a royal hunting ground dating back to 1614. Lord Shelburne employed the architect Henry Keene (1726–76) to suggest how the house should be completed and although Lord Shelburne died in 1761 and Keene returned to Ireland in the same year before the work was completed, Keene's designs for two service courts to the north-west of the house have largely determined its character as it exists today.

The 2nd Earl of Shelburne, William, was created Marquess of Lansdowne in 1784, and it is he who was predominantly responsible for developing the house and park in a manner that reflected the wealth and power of his family. He employed Robert Adam (1728–92), the most fashionable architect in England, not only to design his London home in Berkeley Square but also to work at Bowood on linking Keene's courts to the Big House. However, the two men fell out and in 1771 Adam was paid off.

In the meantime, work was progressing on the garden. In 1757, the 1st Earl of Shelburne had asked Lancelot

'Capability' Brown (1716–83) to look over the grounds and suggest some ideas for landscaping it. Brown was paid a fee of 30 guineas for three days' work but no plan seems to have been produced before Lord Shelburne's death in 1761. However, by 1763 a plan had been agreed and records show Brown receiving payments until 1771 when his final account was settled.

Bowood's interest to the garden historian rests on it being, according to Christopher Thacker in *The History of Gardens*: 'The best preserved of Brown's major landscapes'. Here, Brown's hallmark, the man-made lake which looks totally natural, can be seen to great effect. As was his usual method, Brown created the lake by damming the pond and the stream at the foot of the valley and allowing the water to accumulate behind it and spread out on either side of the valley behind the dam, thus creating a lake with totally natural lines. He then concealed the dam – in the case of Bowood, behind a line of beeches – so that from a distance it looked as though the lake were a large river disappearing into the distance.

Brown has been accused of creating landscapes that are plain, verging on stark, but one man's meat is

Looking back towrds the house with the ha-ha in the foreground.

another man's poison. The starkness for which he has been criticized might equally be described as landscapes of simplicity and subtlety which can be lost in striving for too picturesque an effect. Stowe (see pages 116–119) and Stourhead (see pages 132–133), for instance, have numerous symbolic buildings in the landscape, but at Bowood there are few.

Brown himself was probably responsible for the Doric Temple at the north-eastern end of the lake, although there seems to be some uncertainty about this. It provides a focal point in the constantly changing, evolving landscape while, at the same time, says Thacker, unifying the garden into a multi-dimensional composition in which trees, grass, water and land create 'not many different and separated pictorial compositions but innumerable variations on a single theme'.

Although Brown had made several suggestions for cascades at the dam at the northern end of the valley, it wasn't until after he'd left Bowood that the proposal by Charles Hamilton (1704–86), creator of Painshill, Surrey (see pages 134–137) was executed in 1785, apparently in imitation of a painting by Gaspard Dughet (Poussin) (1615–75). The Hermit's Cave, close to the head of the Cascade, with its gothic overtones, is especially interesting because it is lined with fossils and mineralogical specimens collected by the geologist, the Reverend Joseph Townsend of Pewsey.

The formal gardens, of which Brown would probably not have approved, were laid out at the front of the house – the upper terrace in 1818 and the lower one in 1851. Together they comprise the Italian Garden. The Mausoleum built by Robert Adam in 1761 is set some distance from the house at the northern end of the rhododendron woods which are only open for six weeks a year when the flowers are at their peak.

A beautifully constructed wooden Adventure Playground is a strong inducement to children who moan when told they will be spending a weekend afternoon 'visiting gardens'.

Address: Bowood House, Derry Hill, Calne, Wiltshire, England.

The Cascades.

Looking out from the far end of the lake into the parkland at Stourhead.

View over Bucklers Hard in autumn from Exbury Gardens.

Exbury Gardens in Hampshire (England) were created by Lionel de Rothschild in the 1920s from an area of land that had formerly been part of the New Forest. Comprising some 200 acres in all, these beautiful woodland gardens have been planted over the last seventy years with thousands of trees, shrubs and bulbs. Over a thousand hybrids of rhododendrons and azaleas have been bred and raised here by the Rothschild family. Ponds, bridges, rock gardens and walks provide the backdrop against which to appreciate the huge variety of plants.

The landscape beyond Lochan Eck at the garden of Little Sparta.

Bi Shu Zhan Zhuang.

Powis Castle.

The Villa Gamberaia seen from outside the garden.

The Living Desert Reserve.

127

Looking from the meadow back towards the garden at Arley Hall.

Castle Howard.

Rousham House.

Arley Hall, looking from the garden out over the meadow.

Rousham, showing the detail of the ha-ha from the parkland.

1720–50 ROUSHAM HOUSE William Kent's picturesque landscaped garden, designed as a series of pictorial compositions, illustrates Alexander Pope's dictum that: 'All gardening is landscape painting'.

Scheemaker's Lion Attacking the Horse. Note the 'Eye Catcher' on the horizon. Visited June 11.

Rousham House is considered one of the finest examples of the work of the renowned eighteenth-century garden designer, William Kent (1685–1748). Garden historians, both contemporaneous with Kent and in the present century, have felt that at Rousham Kent was able successfully to translate into garden design all the ideas and theories he had accumulated during his period in Italy as a painter and student of paintings by Claude Lorrain, Gaspard Dughet and Salvator Rosa; from his work for Lord Burlington as an architect; and from his experience editing two volumes of designs by Inigo Jones and to hone these into a cohesive landscape philosophy.

Horace Walpole said of Kent: 'He leaped the fence and saw that all nature was a garden'. His great friend, the poet Alexander Pope, who believed that 'All gardening is landscape painting' expressed an idea that was to become central to Kent's work at Rousham.

Owned by the Dormer family, two sets of plans for Rousham were drawn up during the 1720s. One, which had a number of formal elements, was probably the work of Charles Bridgeman. The other, which was drawn up by Kent, eliminated most of the formal elements suggested by Bridgeman but retained the large lawn in front of the house and the straight elm walk terminating in the Statue of Apollo. Apart from these two 'controlled' features, the designs follow the natural contours of the land. The River Cherwell running to the south and east of the house is incorporated into the design without any artificial damming or diverting of the water as occurred in so many other landscaped gardens such as Stourhead or Blenheim (see pages 132–3 and 122–3).

The rest of Kent's designs for the garden were conceived and executed in such a way that the visitor experiences the walk as a series of pictures or compositions that strike him not only visually and aesthetically but also reverberate with allusions to

The serpentine rill.

The Vale of Venus.

Praeneste Terrace, inspired by the Roman town of Praeneste (modern Palestrina).

antiquity. That is why, according to a letter written by the gardener John Macclary in 1750, one should walk around the garden in a particular way to ensure that every view, every vista, every 'picture' is seen in the way that Kent intended.

One of the most acclaimed features of the garden is the Cascades and the Vale of Venus, a chain of ponds in a long valley, which Kent designed to be approached from below yet which visitors are sometimes encouraged to view from above. Kent's planting was done so as to enhance the perspective, breaking up the levels of the land and framing views. Other features that came in for critical acclaim were the ruined, gothic, tripartite arch built over the river and a mile beyond the house to provide a focus on the horizon that helped bring the distant landscape into the garden; the complex underplanting of roses, lilacs and syringas beneath the evergreen screens to create a surprising effect of intertwined flowers and trees; and the planting of open groves for a dramatic, rather stage-like perspective.

Although this remark by Sir Thomas Robinson was describing Kent's work on the Prince's garden at Carlton House, it could equally well sum up what Kent achieved at Rousham. 'It has the appearance of beautiful nature, and without being told, one would imagine art had no part in the finishing.'

Address: Rousham House, Steeple Aston, Oxfordshire, England.

The upper level in the Vale of Venus.

The walled gardens.

1724–85 STOURHEAD A Romantic, picturesque landscape in which water, buildings and plants were designed to create vistas that sought to imitate the paintings of Gaspard, Rosa and Lorrain with numerous allusions to the glories of the classical past.

The Pantheon built to honour Hercules. Visited October 2.

Stourhead was bought by the famous Hoare banking family in 1717. The old house, originally called Stourton House, was demolished and a new Palladian villa was built in 1718 and named Stourhead. When Henry Hoare II (1705–85) inherited the estate in 1724 the new house overlooked walled gardens to the south, a railed forecourt with an oval lawn to the east and a large pasture to the west. Over the next sixty years the grounds were utterly transformed to create, in Horace Walpole's often quoted words, 'one of the most picturesque scenes in the world'.

What Henry Hoare succeeded in doing at his beloved home was designing a landscape that, by being at a slight distance from the house, provided both literally and metaphorically an escape into another world. Everything in the landscape – water, buildings, plants – was designed to create pictures and views that were not only beautiful vistas in themselves but reminiscent of the glories of the classical past. Henry Hoare owned many paintings of Italian scenes including a Gaspard and a copy of Claude Lorrain's *View of Delphi with a Procession* which undoubtedly influenced the way he envisaged and created the landscape at Stourhead. Hoare travelled widely in Europe and Italy between 1738 and 1741 and almost certainly knew and was influenced by the ideas expounded by Leone Battista Alberti (1401–72), who had this to say on the siting and building of a country house: 'Nor should there be wanting in the prospect remains of Antiquity, on which we cannot turn our eyes without considering the various revolutions of men and things and being filled with wonder and admiration . . . there should be Columns, Pyramids, Obelisks and other memorials to remind us of great men . . . and where these are a good number of them strewn up and down the country they afford a most beautiful prospect.'

After the death of his second wife in 1743 Henry Hoare started working on Stourhead in earnest. By that time he had already made the great Fir Walk that terminated in the Obelisk although that itself was not built until 1746.

The architect Henry Flitcroft (1679–1769) advised Henry Hoare on all his buildings until his death in 1769. He was a close associate of William Kent. Their first venture was the damming of the water basin to form, eventually, a three-cornered lake and the Temple of Flora which, sited on the water springs, honoured the sources of the river in the pagan fashion (according to Kenneth Woodbridge in his excellent booklet *The Stourhead Landscape*). Then, the Pantheon on the opposite side of the lake was built to honour Hercules, considered a great moral hero in the Renaissance, and to house the statue of him by Michael Rysbrack which Hoare commissioned in 1747.

By the time the Pantheon was completed in 1757 the

The Temple of Apollo.

lake had more or less achieved the shape we see today and other building works followed: the rock bridge across Zeals Road, the Temple of Apollo, the Bristol High Cross (a medieval monument that Hoare had found lying about in pieces in the Cathedral and got permission from the Dean to erect on his land), the Grotto and River God's Cave; the Gothic Cottage and further afield, two miles north-west of Stourhead House, Alfred's Tower, and below it the gothic style Convent.

Everything that was built by Hoare had classical or historical themes and associations which reflected the considerable learning and wide reading of this cultured man but, apart from his belief that he was creating at Stourhead 'the enchanting paths of paradise' overlaid always 'by the hand of prudence and supported by perseverance in well-doing and constant watchfulness over the main chance', in his later years his letters reveal that it was the delight of his daughter and grandchildren in the gardens that meant most to him.

In 1776 he wrote to his friend Lord Bruce: 'I mounted the Tower Thursday with the dear children. The Temple of the Nymph (i.e. the Grotto) is all enchantment to them, and the Cross new painted fills them with rapture.'

On Henry Hoare II's death his grandson Sir Richard Colt Hoare (1758–1838) inherited the estate. His contribution to Stourhead was in the extensive planting programme he initiated. The overall structure of the grounds was retained, in accordance with his grandfather's vision, with a few projects such as the Rockwork Boathouse and the Gothic Cottage either inaugurated or completed by him but the numerous species of rhododendrons, azaleas, cypresses, tulip trees, copper beeches, pines, spruces and many other trees which give such huge pleasure to twentieth-century visitors were planted by Richard Colt Hoare and his descendants.

Address: Stourhead, Stourton, Wiltshire, England.

Rockwork outside the grottoes.

The pebble floor of the Grotto.

1738–73 PAINSHILL PARK A picturesque landscape in which numerous vistas, moods and contrasts are evoked by the mixture of formal, wild and parkland areas dotted with ruins and follies, created by the imaginative eighteenth-century landscape architect, Charles Hamilton.

Looking across the lake to the Gothic Temple. Visited July 20.

Painshill Park was created on an inauspicious tract of barren heathland bought by Charles Hamilton (1704–86), youngest son (and fourteenth child!) of the 6th Earl of Abercorn in 1738. Always hard pressed for money despite his background and a number of sinecures, Charles Hamilton was a gifted artist, plantsman and landscape designer who advised and worked on projects at Stourhead, Bowood and Holland Park. For thirty-five years Hamilton worked, ceaselessly developing his garden, acquiring more land and building the estate up to over 200 acres but, in the end, his inability to live within his meagre means overwhelmed him and in 1773 he was forced to sell Painshill to repay his debts.

Fortunately, the succession of owners who acquired the house over the next 175 years left the garden basically intact, maintaining it in the manner in which Hamilton had created it. Sadly, however, in 1948 the estate was sold, divided into several ownerships and the gardens abandoned. Miraculously, no significant building work was done so that when, in 1975 and again in 1981, Elmbridge Borough Council bought 153 acres of the original estate (principally the area around the lake and to the west), they were able to grant a lease to the newly established Painshill Park Trust under the Patronage of HRH The Prince of Wales and a long-term programme of restoring the garden to its former glory commenced.

Painshill Park was renowned in its heyday, as numerous references in letters, diaries, notebooks, paintings and drawings testify, and its importance in the history of gardening is obvious. Not only was it the creation of one of the most imaginative garden designers

of its day but, because it grew and evolved and changed over the thirty-five years in which Hamilton lived there, it is a superb example of changing ideas and fashions in a very productive and creative period of garden history.

The garden is basically divided into two parts: the intensively ornamented pleasure grounds around the lake and the wilder, freer areas to the west of the lake; and the stretch of open parkland north of the lake running from east to west across the estate. This parkland area is not owned by the Trust although it contains the remnants of the Turkish Tent which originally stood where the present boundary line now bisects the property. The site of the newly constructed tent has therefore had to be moved 50 yards south of its former position. The parkland's open aspect dotted with clumps of trees here and there (in the manner so favoured by Capability Brown) was undoubtedly part of the overall atmosphere and contrast that Hamilton envisaged and which the restoration project has been unable to recreate.

First and foremost, as Giles Worsley in his excellent articles on the garden for *Country Life* magazine has stressed: 'The planting of Hamilton's park is all about vistas, of scenes to be viewed from a specific spot, and at the end of most of the vistas lies a garden building, each one intended to evoke a different mood.'

One of the earliest parts of the garden to be reconstructed was the Amphitheatre, its regular grass area backed by tiered evergreens and its formal planting arrangement reflecting the style of the 1740s. The Elysian Plain on the other side of the lake, however, was planted twenty years later with thickets of trees, colourful shrubs and broad grass walks, reflecting the much more

The Chinese Bridge.

Rockwork outside the Grotto.

View from inside the Grotto.

Looking down from the Gothic Temple.

The ancient Cork Oak.

The Ruined Abbey at Painshill Park.

The interior of the Ruined Abbey.

informal style that became fashionable in the 1760s. Originally, in the middle of this 'shrubbery' area stood a classical Temple of Bacchus which was considered one of Hamilton's finest buildings but it has now completely disappeared except for a portico that has been moved to the back of the present Painshill House. Apart from the calm, idyllic, peaceful Claudian mood that this classical temple would have evoked, more wild and savage moods of the type induced by Salvator Rosa's paintings are invoked by the approach to the Hermitage perched on the side of a steep slope. Long gone, it will eventually be reconstructed.

The Gothic Tower and the Ruined Abbey have a stark, haunting appearance but both look out over wonderful vistas – from the top of the Tower three counties can be seen and from a sheltered spot inside a concealed roof in the Abbey tranquil views of the lake can be enjoyed. Like the Abbey, the Mausoleum was built as a ruin and its purpose was to suggest a classical era long past and arouse melancholy thoughts of the transitory nature of life. The Gothic Temple, built in the 1750s, was the first building to be restored in 1985 and it provides delightful views down to the lake and creates a beautiful vista when looked at from the carefully restored lake. This has been thoroughly dredged and once again has water from the nearby River Mole constantly pumped into it by the restored Bramah Water Wheel which dates back to the 1830s. This replaces the original one installed by Hamilton almost a century earlier.

Two other features of note are the Chinese Bridge and

The Turkish Tent.

A view through the Mausoleum at Painshill Park.

the Grotto Island which it links to the lake's edge. The original influence here is interesting. Despite its name, the bridge bears only a slight resemblance to bridges in Chinese gardens but the tufa limestone rocks with their pitted water-worn appearance on the Grotto Island, are reminiscent of the Chinese penchant for Taihu rocks (see page 262). The grotto was built by Joseph Lane in the 1780s and consisted of a huge, central chamber and various side passages. Lined with plaster and embedded with fluorspar and various coloured crystals, the vaulted ceiling was hung with plaster wood stalactites. The whole cavern is currently in the process of being restored and, contrary to the expectations conjured up by the word grotto, it is already far enough advanced to show that it is a surprisingly light, glistening and water-reflecting space.

Hamilton has been called a master of illusion. Mood-making areas like the lake and the alpine wood seemed larger than they were because he designed a circuit that undulated around the garden so that it could constantly be seen from different angles and heights. Recreating Hamilton's original concept is the Trust's aim: 'The whole park will be restored not to what we *think* it may have been, but as we *know* it was.' The visitors of the future will be able to judge for themselves how successful and important Hamilton was in creating and shaping garden history.

Address: Painshill Park, Portsmouth Road, Cobham, Surrey, England.

The Gothic Tower.

1766–78 ERMENONVILLE A French picturesque landscape garden influenced by the ideals of the English poet and gardener William Shenstone and the French poet and philosopher Jean Jacques Rousseau, who was originally buried there.

Looking across the lake to the Temple of Philosophy. Visited July 22.

Ermenonville, or Parc Jean Jacques Rousseau, has a long history dating back to the eighth century but it is for the landscaping of its grounds in the eighteenth century by René-Louis de Girardin, who inherited the estate in 1766, that it became famous and important in the history of gardening.

Girardin was a cultured man who had travelled widely in Italy, Germany and England. There he had visited the poet and gardener William Shenstone (1714–63) at his home in Leasowes who had landscaped his garden into a *ferme ornée*. Only traces of the garden still exist but it was much celebrated in its day for the amazing variety of vistas it presented as one walked around the prescribed route. Numerous benches, urns, waterfalls, bridges, small buildings and inscriptions gave the visitor views and scenes to delight the eye and concentrate the mind.

Enormously impressed by Shenstone and the English Landscape Movement's emphasis on the picturesque aspect of nature, Girardin was also a great admirer of the French philosopher Jean Jacques Rousseau (1712–78) whose love of nature untouched by man's controlling and shaping hand made a strong impression on his acolyte. Rousseau's view of gardening, expressed in his

novel *La Nouvelle Héloïse* (1761), was one of the major influences on Girardin when he drew up plans for the development of his estate around the house at Ermenonville.

Originally the land around the château comprised 1000 hectares: to the north of the house was the Grand Parc, the Potager, the Desert, the big Lake and the Farm; to the south was the smaller lake, with the Ile des Peupliers at the far end, surrounded by a path that takes one through woodland overlooking the lake and passes a number of symbolic buildings placed strategically to make one pause, think, and take in the view from a variety of angles.

The château is not open to the public nor are the grounds to the north of it but the southern gardens, now known as the Parc Jean Jacques Rousseau, are owned by the Touring Club of France and are open to the public several days a week in the summer months.

Befriended by Girardin in the last weeks of his life, Rousseau obviously found great comfort and enjoyment in the wild and natural environment that Girardin had created. Visiting it now, with its rather overgrown and unmanicured air, one feels that the spirit of Rousseau

The Tomb of Jean Jaques Rousseau on the Isle of Poplars (cut to the ground 1994).

still haunts the place although his bones were removed in 1794 from their resting place in the tomb on the Ile des Peupliers, where he had been buried by Girardin, and reburied in the Pantheon in Paris by a decree issued by the Revolutionary Convention.

However, his original burial place remained a place of pilgrimage and imbued the garden with an air of melancholy and a sense of the mortality of life in keeping with the other buildings in the garden with their historical and philosophical undertones: The Cascade and Grotto of the Naiads, the Shrine of Reverie, the Arcadian Prairie (now inhabited by some lovely horses) the Ruined Temple of Philosophy, the Sepulchre of Meier, the Sepulchre of the Unknown Man and the Prehistoric Grotto.

Despite its name, there is little evidence of poplars on the island but this is apparently because they became so large that they were affecting the stability of the man-made island and had to be cut down. However, new young poplars are now starting to grow and in future years the island will presumably once again look as it does in most of the old pictures one sees of it.

Ermenonville is an important place for the garden historian because it provides such a marked contrast to the dominant tradition of French formal gardens which were so influential throughout Europe. Here one sees the influence of the English landscape tradition at work in France although the effect of the hotter climate resulting in very little grass makes the overall effect very different from that of Ermenonville's role models such as Stourhead or Stowe (see pages 132–3 and 116–9).

Address: Parc Jean Jacques Rousseau, Ermenonville 60950, Nr Senlis, Oise, France.

The Dolman.

The Sepulchre to Friedrich Meier.

The Shrine of Reverie.

The vine arbour at Villandry.

Painswick.

The Huntington.

Dumbarton Oaks.

Dumbarton Oaks.

The semi-circular vine arbour at Powis Castle.

Masses of Cleome spinosa at the Parco della Villa Pallavicino.

Parco della Villa Pallavicino, on Lake Maggiore near Stresa (Italy), is a nature park with an interesting garden within it that is cunningly planted almost entirely with annuals.

Lobertia at Bodnant.

Het Loo.

1738–70 PAINSWICK ROCOCO GARDEN The best example of an English rococo garden, in which formal and informal elements combine to capture the light-hearted, frivolous mood of that pleasure-loving era.

A view across the Kitchen Garden towards the Eagle House. Visited August 25.

Painswick Rococo Garden was principally built by Benjamin Hyett, the son of Charles Hyett. Charles built the main house at Painswick, 'Buenos Aires', to benefit from the hill air, for he suffered from asthma. He died in 1738 only three years after completing the building and it was then that his son Benjamin undertook the development of the garden. The house and garden remained in the family for the next 200 years but saw a number of changes over the centuries with the disappearance of the Exedra Garden and the geometric kitchen garden. In 1965, problems with finance and maintenance resulted in the current owner, Lord Dickinson, planting a new wood in the sheltered combe where previously the kitchen garden had been. By 1983 the area had become impenetrable.

Who designed the original garden at Painswick is not known. One theory is that Thomas Robins (1716–70), a painter of numerous houses and gardens in the middle of the eighteenth century, including a very detailed one of Painswick, may in fact have designed it himself. His highly acclaimed picture of the house and garden at Painswick might have been a proposal for the layout of the grounds around the house rather than a record of what it looked like when someone else had finished work on it. However, whichever came first is not as important as the fact that Robins' painting exists and is a wonderfully detailed record of what this eighteenth-century rococo garden looked like.

An exhibition of Robins' work held in 1976 coincided with a major resurgence of interest in Britain's historical gardens and the importance of Painswick as one of the very few surviving rococo gardens of its era was recognized and resulted in a courageous decision by the Dickinson family. In 1983 they agreed to a programme of restoration to return the garden to its original form.

The first stage necessitated clearing away the new wood, regrading and levelling the area above the Bowling Green, regravelling the paths, draining and repuddling the fish pond and starting work on the derelict garden buildings. In all this Robins' painting provided invaluable clues and, as work progressed, archaeological evidence from the restoration itself provided further information about how the original buildings were constructed and how the layout was designed.

By 1988 it was evident that the cost of the reconstruction work had been seriously underestimated (as is so often the case in this kind of work) and the Painswick Rococo Garden Trust was set up as a registered charity. Money from other trusts and charities could then be applied for to ensure the completion of the work and to enable the garden to remain open to the public.

Each year one of the major features of the garden has been restored and so far a great deal has been achieved. The kitchen garden has been recreated re-establishing the centre pool revealed by archaeological surveys and

The Eagle House.

The Exedra.

with plantings of varieties of fruits and vegetables that would have been available in the eighteenth century. The Exedra has been rebuilt, the Red House renovated and the Eagle House restored using only materials available at the time of its original construction. Throughout the garden numerous trees, shrubs and bulbs have been planted and will continue to be as the works programme proceeds. One spectacular feature of the garden is the snowdrops. Huge drifts of them carpet the woodland below the Fish Pond and along the banks of the stream. How they got there is not recorded but a photograph of 1895 shows children in the Snowdrop Grove sitting among masses of them. One of the varieties to be found in the garden is *Galanthus nivalis atkinsii* which may have been acquired from James Atkins (1804–84), a snowdrop grower who lived for a time at Rose Cottage in Painswick.

Painswick's importance in the history of gardening lies in the fact that it is the best and most complete example of an English rococo garden that exists. More frequently

a term applied to the arts and architecture, the word rococo is derived from two words *rocaille* meaning 'rock work' and *coquille* 'a shell' and referred to scroll and pattern shapes made from rocks, shells and other natural forms. However, in gardening terms it represented the transition period between the French formal influence and the Landscape Movement when experiments were taking place to mix the two styles so that formal and informal elements were juxtaposed. Straight vistas and winding serpentine paths compete with each other in a relatively small space and a mixture of architectural influences are captured in the buildings – Classical, Gothic, Doric and Rustic. The overall mood is light-hearted and flamboyant, capturing the pleasure-lowing spirit of the age.

Address: Painswick Rococo Garden, The Stables, Painswick House, Painswick, Stroud, Gloucestershire, England.

From inside the Red House.

The outside of the Red House.

1763–76 VEITSHÖCHHEIM One of the best preserved German rococo gardens with numerous *salons* and *cabinets*, intimate spaces and partitions, light-hearted treatment of classical iconography and dramatic *rocaille* work in the grotto.

Looking over the Kleiner See to the statue of Pegasus in the Grosser See. Visited July 17.

Vietschöchheim, renowned as the best surviving example of an eighteenth-century rococo garden in Germany was developed on land first purchased by the Prince-Bishops of Würzburg in 1680 with the intention of developing a summer residence and garden there. By 1686 all the land which now comprises the schloss and hofgarten had been purchased and covered an area 475m by 270m. Right from the start the house and its immediate garden at the north end of the site were separated from the hunting park, as it initially was, in the south. This was not the norm at that period as the French influence dictated a central axis from the house leading down through the parterre garden and on to the *bosquet* and park beyond. However, the site and the positioning of the house made this impossible. Between 1699 and 1721 the Prince-Bishop Johann Philipp von Greiffenclau initiated a programme of enlargement and development of the property.

The entire site was enclosed within a high perimeter wall. The house and its pleasure garden were separated from its surroundings by retaining terrace-like walls, and the wooded park was divided into three main, longitudinal sections of varying widths: the section running north/south on the western side containing two artificial lakes: the Grosser See and the Kleiner See (the large and small lakes); and the main north/south and

east/west axis paths were also established.

However, it was not until 1763, at the end of the Seven Years War, that the final shape of the garden as we know it today was formed. During the reign of the Prince-Bishop Adam Friedrich von Seinsheim, from 1755 to 1779, a number of architects, sculptors and gardeners, namely Johann Philip Geigel, Ferdinand Tietz, Johann Pieter Wagner and Johann Prokop Mayer worked closely with him to remodel the pheasantry into its present composition.

In the Grosser See a huge sculpture of the Parnassus Rock surmounted by Pegasus was commissioned and a hedge border with niches for sculptures was planted all round the lake. The *bosquet* area was redesigned with a large circular space at its centre where the cross axes met. Numerous allegorical statues were placed here and along the avenues and paths and in the *salons* and *cabinets* (little garden rooms and partitions).

In 1767–8 work began on the third section, the densely wooded area, which was replanted with spruce and divided in three to bring control and order into what had become a very overgrown part of the garden. The Hedge Theatre was created in the section nearest the house, thus facilitating access via a flight of steps from the schloss. Fountains and Chinese pavilions adorn the central section and a Linden Grove was planted in the

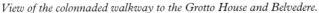

View of the colonnaded walkway to the Grotto House and Belvedere.   *A spyhole cut through a series of hedges.*

southernmost part.

A triangular piece of land between the eastern perimeter wall and the wooded area was the last section of the garden to be developed in 1773. Here, the east/west cross axis that runs from the sculpture of the Parnassus Rock through the garden to the perimeter wall terminated in a cascade, which was unfortunately destroyed by a bomb in 1945. Numerous statues line this area and the path leads to the Belvedere and Grotto in the south-east corner. Unfortunately not open to the public, this garden building has the most stunning and well preserved *rocaille* work all over the walls – animals, fish and mythological beasts glare out at any trespasser and through the locked basement doors of the Belvedere one can see the most tantalizingly well-preserved grotto.

The garden was opened to the public in 1776 but almost immediately decline set in. Reports of losses and thefts of the garden artefacts were commonplace but owing to the intervention of King Maximilian I, Joseph of Brava in 1823, who was an incurable romantic, the then unfashionable rococo garden was spared the fate of so many of its contemporaries – being turned into a fashionable landscape garden.

If entered through its west or north gate, the garden looks rather drab, unkempt and uninspiring. The tall hedges lining the west avenue conceal what lies beyond – the parterres around the schloss and the house itself are undergoing restoration work which creates a dowdy impression. But once you enter the main garden and walk along its numerous criss-crossing paths of seemingly labyrinthine complexity but in fact, designed along highly ordered and symmetrical lines, you soon become captivated.

Although Veitshöchheim has numerous views through the sculptured hedges and paths and pavilions, it is not intended to extend the visitors' vision to the countryside beyond. It is totally enclosed and in that way so different from the French Baroque or Italian influences that one can see, for instance, at Weikersheim (see pages 114–15). Here, what is important and what is quintessentially rococo is the creation of intimate spaces and the playful, light-hearted treatment of classical themes and forms that can be seen in the iconography of the classical statuary which has been interpreted as representing the resurgence of man's creative and intellectual energy after the Seven Years War.

A very pleasant restaurant in the square, in the centre of the outbuildings which adjoin the north entrance, provides fuel or reward (whichever way round you do it) for tackling the whole garden circuit.

Address: Schloss Veitshöchheim, Würzburg, Germany.

The Belvedere stands on the Grotto decorated with a series of fantastic rocaille work figures.

Sissinghurst.

La Serre de la Madone.

Villa Torrigiani.

Fronteira Palace.

La Serre de la Madone in Menton (France) was created by Lawrence Johnston in the 1920s and 1930s and he spent much of his time there for health reasons. Although now sadly fallen into decay and seriously overgrown, the wonderful terraces that form the backbone of the garden still retain much of their former grandeur. The whole garden has now been designated a heritage site and is being cleared and renovated for future public opening.

Barnsley House.

Isola Bella.

Tresco Abbey.

Hestercombe.

Gravetye Manor.

Dumbarton Oaks.

Rose Constance Spry, Eccleston Square.

The Generalife.

Hever Castle.

La Mortola.

La Quinta dos Azulejos.

Chenies Manor.

Isola Bella.

Rousham House.

Alton Towers.

Gravetye Manor.

Tintinhull House.

Arley Hall.

1795–1800 SEZINCOTE A Persian-style, chahar-bagh garden in which the extraordinary combination of Muslim, Hindu and Classical architectural features and planting influenced by Humphrey Repton and Graham Thomas make this place unique.

The Snake Pool and Indian Bridge. Note the cobra on the dead tree. Visited July 27.

The Orangery behind the Indian Garden.

A Brahmin Bull.

Sezincote is derived from the French word *Cheisnecote* which means, literally, the hillside of the oaks, and the history of the small parish in which the present house stands goes back as far, if not further, than the Domesday Book in which it is recorded.

In 1795 Colonel John Cockerell returned to England from Bengal, where he had worked for the East India Company, and bought the estate from the Earl of Guildford. On his death in 1798 his brother Charles Cockerell inherited the property and commissioned his brother Samuel Pepys Cockerell (named after the great diarist from whom the family was descended), who had been a surveyor for the East India Company, to build him a house in the Indian manner. Working closely on the plans with Thomas Daniell, an artist who had recently returned from ten years in northern India, S. P. Cockerell's original designs for the house had no fewer than five large domes and a complex design for the south facing elevation of the house. In execution the plans were watered down to a large central dome and four smaller ones at each corner of the main building. Charles Cockerell's bedroom was a separate, octagonal building to the north of the house reached by a curved passageway and decorated to resemble a tent with wooden spears to support a canopy. Despite the strong Mughal influence in the Tent (as Charles's bedroom was known) and the various garden buildings, as well as the roof of the main building, the interior was almost exclusively classical in style with no attempt at Indianization.

Moghul roof work.

Temple to Surya.

The layout of the Thornery, the Water Garden to the north of the house, including the Bridge, the Temple and the Rock Pool are generally attributed to Daniell. Much of the planting and layout of the Park, however, and the original south garden are thought to be heavily influenced by Humphrey Repton (1752–1818) who, while not producing one of his famous 'before' and 'after' Red Books for Sezincote, did produce a sketch of his ideas for the south garden which still exists and he mentions his work at Sezincote in several writings.

However, much of the credit for the garden must go to those who have rejuvenated it since the Second World War when it became very run down. In 1944 the estate was purchased by Sir Cyril Kleinwort and it is to Lady Kleinwort, helped by Graham Thomas, that we owe the present planting and layout of the south garden. It was on her return from India in 1965 that the 'paradise garden' design much favoured by the first great Mughal emperor Babur (1483–1530) was introduced. The chahar-bagh, 'the fourfold garden' which is divided into four equal parts by intersecting water channels, is the basis of all Persian gardens going back 4000 years and it was this design that lay at the heart of many of the gardens Babur built.

The crossing canal is accentuated by the planting of Irish yews (hardier than the Italian cypresses favoured in hotter climates) and the garden is backed by the wonderful curving conservatory and overlooked by a grotto (part of the early nineteenth-century design) and a tennis pavilion, built in 1961, copying decorative architectural features from the house.

Similarly, Graham Thomas's 'wild garden'-style planting around the Thornery and down the stream has added great interest for the garden lover but here it is the original architectural features that create the Mughal feel rather than the planting *per se*.

Sezincote's extraordinary mixture of Hindu, Muslim and classical influences in the architecture are unique and the garden buildings with the Temple of Surya (a Hindu God), the Brahmin bulls and the Snake Pool are unlike anything else to be found in Britain. This, together with the present owners' continuing development of the garden and house in the same eastern Mughal tradition, make it the best example of its kind in the West.

Address: Sezincote, Bourton-on-the Hill, Nr Moreton-in-Marsh, Gloucestershire, England.

The Tennis Pavilion.

Planting along the Water Garden.

1811–18 SHERRINGHAM PARK Probably the best surviving example of Humphrey Repton's work based on plans drawn up in one of his famous Red Books in which he showed 'before' and 'after' views and sought to balance propriety, convenience and a picturesque effect.

The view of the rhododendrons from the top of the tower in the woodland. Visited May 20.

Sherringham Park, or Sherringham 'Bowes' as it was originally called, was bought in 1811 by Abbot Upcher, who asked the elderly but still famous Humphrey Repton (1752–1818) to produce designs for a new house and landscaped grounds. In 1812 Repton produced one of his famous Red Books in which with skilful 'before' and 'after' drawings he was able to show his client what the effect of his suggested improvements would look like. Upcher was delighted with the plans that Repton drew up for 'a gentlemanlike residence' in a sheltered position in the park, protected from the cold sea winds by the wooded hill behind it and enabling the inhabitants to enjoy the rolling landscape of hills and woods in front of it, from where at several designated vantage points spectacular views towards the sea could be enjoyed.

Work commenced at a rapid pace but in 1818 Repton's patron died before he could move into his recently completed property and Humphrey Repton himself only outlived him by a few months. However, Upcher's son Henry, realizing the uniqueness of the house and park and its location, moved in in 1839 and the house remained in the family until 1988 when it was taken over by the National Trust.

Sherringham Park is the best surviving example of

Humphrey Repton's work and one that he considered his favourite. Repton was probably the most famous landscape gardener after his predecessor Lancelot 'Capability' Brown and he became embroiled in a very public argument with two of his contemporaries, Uvedale Price and Richard Payne Knight, about the nature of gardening. In fact, like many arguments, it can be seen in retrospect that the two sides were not as far apart in their views as they supposed but the bare bones of the controversy lay in what each side considered the function of landscaping to be.

Knight and Price favoured striving to achieve a 'picturesque landscape' above all else. Price wrote at great length on what he meant by this and it seemed that he believed that the principles of painting such as composition, harmony of tints, unity of character and the effects of light and shade 'are in reality the general principles on which the effect of of all visible objects must depend . . . I am therefore persuaded that the two opposite qualities of roughness and of sudden variation, are the most efficient causes of the pictures.'

Price damned the work of Capability Brown as being too smooth, predictable and insipid and was critical of Repton who stood up for Brown's work. Repton argued

Across the parkland to Thomas Upcher's Temple.

that the picturesque, while important, could not be the landscape gardener's sole or overriding consideration. 'Propriety and convenience are not less objects of good taste than picturesque effect.' Repton claimed that English gardening had to be 'the happy medium betwixt the wildness of nature and the stiffness of art'. The truth was that Repton was a pragmatist and Price a philosophical theorist and while in essence Repton sympathized with much of what Price and Knight said, the practical considerations that pertained to each garden or park he was asked to 'improve' had to be taken into consideration.

Perhaps the reason why Repton felt so happy about his work at Sherringham was because the site had so much natural potential that it wasn't hard to achieve the picturesque, the propriety and the convenience required, simultaneously.

In 1975 Thomas Upcher built the Temple which Repton had planned to overlook the sea from a vantage point in the woods in front of the house. It is not on quite such a high and dramatic spot as originally planned but nevertheless presents beautiful views of the park and house. On the hillside behind the house a gazebo overlooking the sea on an ancient lookout post was built by Mrs Mildred Cordeaux, Thomas Upcher's cousin, and formally opened by the Prince of Wales in 1988. The steep climb is well rewarded by the dramatic coastal vista that it affords.

The grounds are particularly well worth a visit in May or June when the numerous rhododendrons are in flower, many of which were grown from seeds gathered in the Himalayas on botanical trips undertaken by Ernest Wilson (1876–1930) sponsored, in part, by the Upcher family.

Address: Sherringham Park, Upper Sherringham, Norfolk, England.

The woodland paths.

Detail of Thomas Upcher's Temple.

1820s STANCOMBE PARK A Victorian folly garden at some distance from the main house with winding paths, dripping ferns, temple and lake; and bone-encrusted grottoes which are all reminiscent of a gothic horror film.

The house seen from the central axis of the Upper Garden. Visited June 20.

Stancombe Park, dating back to Roman times (as the recent discovery of a Roman mosaic reveals), was built in the late eighteenth century though it was partially destroyed by fire in the latter part of the nineteenth century which explains its mixture of architectural styles.

Standing at the head of the valley below Stancombe Hill, the house has, effectively, two separate gardens. The one around the house has been created out of the elegant sweeping parkland that formerly came right up to the house. This garden consists of herbaceous borders (redesigned in 1988 and approached by York stone steps flanked by Irish yews), a gazebo that overlooks the valley and an avenue of pleached limes that leads to a seat surrounded by cherubs.

The other, the famous historic folly garden, is separated from the main house by a long sweeping drive and is reached by a narrow path along the valley. Legend has it that this garden was built in the 1820s by the Reverend David Edwards who, having married a wealthy girl whose dowry could help with the upkeep of the estate, found that his very fat wife did not appeal to him sexually and so took up with a local gypsy girl. He built the romantic folly garden for their trysting place, making all entrances to it so narrow that his wife, Mrs Purnell-Edwards, was unable to enter the garden and discover them.

The less romantic but possibly more historically correct reason for the building of the folly garden was that it provided much needed work for the jobless soldiers who had returned from the Napoleonic Wars. It might also explain the Egyptian influence in the area near the ice-house, a common feature in constructions of the period, to celebrate Nelson's victories on the Nile.

The narrow path and tunnel guarded by a dog through which the visitor goes to reach the lake has a marvellous dark and mysterious feel about it – dripping ferns, enormous roots, fossils, whale bones and grottoes all combine to create the perfect setting for a gothic horror film. Sadly, the Doric Temple overlooking the lake has lost its furnishings and the two small houses surrounding the Swan Fountain which were originally used for the propagation and preservation of exotic plants via an elaborate water system that has fallen into disrepair, have been targeted by vandals. But, like the Swiss Garden (see pages 156–7), this part of the garden is a superb example of the Victorian folly garden and extremely popular with visitors at its annual Open Day for the National Garden Scheme.

Address: Stancombe Park, Stinchcombe, Gloucestershire, England.

A copy of the great boar sculpture.

Two small houses by the Swan Fountain, forerunners of the modern greenhouse.

The Font.

The Egyptian style entrance to the Grotto.

Stained glass window in the Doric Temple.

Bones from a whale stranded in the nearby Severn.

155

1830–80 THE SWISS GARDEN A Victorian gothic folly garden, strongly influenced by the mid-Victorian fashion for the Swiss Picturesque, which seems much bigger than it really is because of the numerous small hills and paths that wind around it.

The Swiss Cottage in the centre of the garden. Visited May 20.

The Thatched Tree Shelter.

The Indian Kiosk.

The Swiss Garden was originally part of a Bedfordshire estate called Old Warden Park which was bought at the end of the seventeenth century by the Ongley family who had made a fortune in trade. The earliest development of the Swiss Garden is associated with the 3rd Earl of Ongley (1803–77) of the East India Company, who succeeded to the estate in 1830, and it was developed by him until, heirless, he sold the property to Joseph Shuttleworth in 1872. Shuttleworth demolished the old manor house and built the gothic-style Victorian mansion that still exists today. He also developed the Swiss Garden, gothicizing here and there but remaining very much in tune with the original designs.

Financial difficulties dating from the Second World War resulted in the closure of the Swiss Garden from 1939 until 1976 when The Shuttleworth Trust asked the Bedfordshire County Council to take over the restoration and future management of the garden. They agreed and after extensive restoration work the garden was once again opened to visitors in 1981.

The Swiss Garden is wonderfully charming and romantic. Its four-acre site seems much bigger than it is because the naturally flat terrain has been remodelled by extensive digging to create pools and mounds that impose an up-hill, down-dale landscape with numerous intricately winding paths and hump-backed bridges that create new vistas for the eye at every turn. You never see the whole garden at any time, there is no overview from

A view over the ponds.

the house or any other point and it is this secretive, clandestine quality that gives it its charm. Could this also be because there is truth in the legend that the 3rd Earl of Ongley built the garden as a trysting place for himself and his Swiss mistress and made it impossibly difficult for them to be followed or tracked down by his wife or her spies? Rumour also has it that this young mistress died very young and still haunts the garden.

Whether it was truly to celebrate his mistress's nationality or whether the Earl was influenced by the contemporary fashion for the Swiss Picturesque, the Swiss Chalet that stands on a small knoll virtually in the middle of the garden is a delightful summer house and, since its restoration, one of the most charming of its period. Although there appears to be only one level with an intricate fretted and panelled interior and split hazel work and pine cone decorations on the veranda, there is in fact a semi-concealed basement at the back of the cottage, formerly linked by a bell-pull and a flight of exterior wooden steps which have, unfortunately, long gone.

Also built in the 1830s, though altered and adapted by the Shuttleworths, as evidenced by the year 1876 carved above both entrances, are the grotto and fernery. The grotto, a cool cavernous, gloomy area made of tufa-stone, has a wonderfully dark, mysterious atmosphere about it which contrasts markedly with the dazzling lightness of the fernery which is an important and early example of English cast-iron glasshouse construction.

The Terrace, the Dogs' Cemetery, the elaborate flower beds and the planting of variegated species and specimen trees are other features that are specifically attributable to the Shuttleworths' tenure and, bit by bit, the old cast-

iron arches are being used again for trailing roses. Urns, stone books with inscriptions, a thatch-roofed seat around a tree and stone dolphins are just some of the Victorian features of this romantic garden.

Bedfordshire Council have undertaken the restoration programme just in time; if it had been left much longer Shuttleworth would soon have reached the point of no return and this prime example of a romantic Victorian garden would have been lost for ever.

Address: The Swiss Garden, Old Warden, Biggleswade, Bedfordshire, England.

The Grotto and Fernery.

The Temple of Universal Peace at Bi Shu Shan Zhuang.

The Exedra at Painswick.

The Gothic Temple at Stowe.

The Ruined Abbey at Painshill.

The Temple of Philosophy at Ermenonville.

Laugier's Hut at Little Sparta.

The Hypothetical Gateway at Little Sparta.

William Waterfield's stuffed fox.

A view cut through the mature woodland at Stourhead.

The Grottoes at Painshill positioned to give wonderful reflections.

Stowe.

The Swiss Garden.

Stourhead.

Bowood.

Bussaco.

Blenheim.

Barnsley House.

Biddulph Grange.

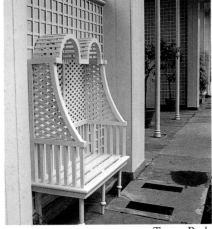

Tatton Park.

Rousham House.

Tatton Park.

Tatton Park.

Hatfield House.

Rousham House.

Tatton Park.

Dumbarton Oaks.

Tatton Park.

Knightshayes Garden.

Little Sparta.

Ermenonville.

Veitshöchheim.

Stancombe Park.

Hidcote Manor.

Dumbarton Oaks.

Het Loo.

Shisen-Do Temple.

Stourhead.

Villa Garzoni.

Villa Garzoni.

Villa Garzoni.

Veitshöchheim.

Ji Chang Yuan.

Levens Hall.

Quinta dos Azulejos.

The Camomile seat at Sissinghurst.

Painshill.

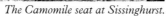

Bi Shu Shan Zhuang.

Somerleyton Hall.

The Swiss Garden.

Villa Gamberaia.

Somerleyton Hall.

Bodnant.

Dumbarton Oaks.

Knightshayes.

1840–60 ARLEY HALL GARDENS A long herbaceous border and a number of 'garden rooms' were created here half a century before Gertrude Jekyll popularized these features in her writings and garden designs.

Looking in towards the herbaceous borders. Visited August 10.

Arley Hall Gardens were laid out in their present manner by Rowland and Mary Egerton-Warburton between 1840 and 1860, although in the previous century there had been walled gardens and a pleasure ground built on the site in 1746 by the present owners' ancestors, Sir Peter and Lady Elizabeth Warburton.

The gardens are, perhaps, most famous for one particular feature, the herbaceous border. Originally called the Alcove Walk because of the classical style pavilion at the far end, it is one of the first of its kind to

The avenue of pleached limes.

have been planted, as an extant garden plan of 1846 shows. Many years before Gertrude Jekyll and William Robinson popularized the planting of herbaceous borders, a visitor to Arley Hall in 1886 records in the Visitors' Book: 'The herbaceous border much improved and altogether quite lovely'.

The improvement mentioned probably refers to the addition in the 1870s of the clipped yew tree buttresses which divide the border at regular intervals adding a majestic form to the long walk, particularly in the winter period when the border is not in flower.

Gertrude Jekyll visited Arley Hall Gardens and reproduced Elgood's water-colour of the herbaceous border in her book *Some English Gardens*, 1904. Did her ideas about garden rooms also spring from these gardens or did the family get their ideas from her? Certainly the gardens have many separate 'rooms', some part of the original design, others developed over the century by successive generations of the family. The little half-timbered tea cottage and garden was originally planted with topiary (uprooted in 1961 owing to severe neglect during the Second World War which made them too expensive to maintain) and is now full of wonderful scented species and shrub roses. The walled garden, part of Rowland's original design, was formerly a large kitchen garden but has become a pleasure garden, while the second of the original enclosures is a kitchen garden

The ilex avenue.

The Tea Cottage.

and still used as such. The pretty flagstone garden was built by Antoinette Egerton-Warburton as a private sanctuary, while the adjoining herb and scented gardens and later innovations, and the ilex avenue, with its strange cylindrical clipped trees (originally shaped as pyramids but grown so huge after the First World War that they could only be shaped into cylinders), were part of the original plan, as was the sunken bowling green which was later converted into a tennis court and is now a fish pool garden.

Two other early features are the perfect avenue of pleached limes from the car park to the entrance and the Rootree, originally a romantic alpine rock garden though now much more of a shrub garden. At the far end there is the Rough, a bit of waste land that in recent years has been turned into an animals' drinking pool and a sort of semi-wild site for shrubs and naturalized bulbs.

Last, but not least, the present owners are developing a Grove and Woodland Walk to the north east of the house. In the nineteenth century local children walked through the Grove to the Chapel but later the area became very overgrown until it was little more than a wilderness. However, since the 1970s the area has been cleared to create a woodland grove of 'planned informality' where visitors can wander freely, enjoying a wide variety of woodland shrubs and plants as well as many rhododendrons, azaleas and exotic trees.

Address: Arley Hall Gardens, Nr Great Budworth, Northwich, Cheshire, England.

The flag garden.

1840–71 BIDDULPH GRANGE A picturesque series of 'garden rooms' provided the backdrop and conditions for growing the huge variety of plants that were becoming increasingly available in the mid-nineteenth century.

Looking from the Grange towards the lake and the Rhododendron Ground. Visited May 18.

Biddulph Grange was purchased in 1840 by James Bateman (1811–97) and his wife Maria Egerton-Warburton who moved there from the neighbouring house, Knypersley Hall, owned by James's father. James Bateman was a horticulturist well known for his work on orchids, *Orchidaceae of Mexico and Guatemala*, published in 1857. His wife, Maria, was interested in herbaceous plants, particularly fuchsias and lilies, and was the sister of Rowland Egerton-Warburton who, with his wife, created the gardens at Arley Hall in Cheshire (pages 166–7).

The Grange from the lake.

The Batemans lived at Biddulph Grange until the late 1860s when, because of financial difficulties, they made it over to their son who sold it in 1871 to Robert Health, a leading local industrialist. In 1923 Biddulph was converted into a hospital. By the 1960s the garden had fallen foul of vandalism and neglect and in 1988 the National Trust acquired it and embarked on an extensive project to restore it to its former glory as one of the most famous gardens of its day.

Biddulph Grange became famous in the mid-1850s by which time the Batemans, in collaboration with their friend, the marine painter Edward Cooke (1811–80), had virtually finished working on the garden they started in 1849.

According to Brent Elliot in his book *Victorian Gardens*, in the 1840s the garden landscape fraternity was locked in a debate as to the purpose of landscape design. Writers such as John Lindley in *Gardeners' Chronicle* and Edward Kemp in *How to Lay out a Small Garden* stressed the need for congruity of design. The artificial yoking together of art and nature such as had occurred in places like Chatsworth, where fine lawns were edged with wild undergrowth or formal staircases were made of 'rude natural-like' rockwork, were, according to Joshua Major in *The Theory and Practice of Landscape Gardening*, inappropriate; the associations created by these juxtapositions were disharmonious and congruity or

China (The Chinese Garden).

The Gateway to China.

The tunnel from the Rhododendron Ground into the Pinetum at Biddulph Grange.

The Lake.

The stone vase at the top of the Wellingtonia Avenue.

harmony and appropriateness of vision should be the ideals sought after in garden design. The importance of the plants and the *genius loci* were also re-emphasized in contrast to the importance of the gardener and the architect of garden buildings. Arbitrariness was out; unity of expression and propriety of associations was in. However, universal agreement on what precisely constituted propriety and unity was hard to find so the discussion veered back and forth.

Kemp felt that Biddulph Grange Garden succeeded in creating a garden of congruity despite its numerous elements. To the novice garden historian it might appear that Biddulph is anything but unified – on paper it reads like a catalogue of totally different 'pictures' that bear little relation to one another with its Italian Garden, Pinetum, Arboretum, Rhododendron Ground, Stumpery, China, Egypt, Lime Avenue, Cherry Orchard, Cheshire Cottage. But, in fact, each area was designed to create an appropriate space for the specific plants within it. For example, the Rhododendron Walk was planted by Bateman with all the species of rhododendrons and azaleas and their early hybrids then available. The section known as China was created to display the numerous exotic plants being brought back from the Far East at that time, especially those discovered by the plant hunter, Robert Fortune.

As well as each area being designed as an appropriate setting for plants, the buildings or landscaping within the areas were designed to enhance the overall effect. Thus

The entrance to Egypt at Biddulph Grange.

the part known as Egypt with its stone sphinxes and pyramidical topiary; the lake and temple after the Chinese fashion introduced by W. Chambers at Kew (see pages 54–5) and the ornate wooden bridge over the lake and the stretches of the Great Wall of China, all attempt to create an appropriate backdrop for the plants. I say 'attempt' because some critics think it bears no relationship to the original it purports to imitate while others, such as Thacker in *The History of Gardens*, think it bears more resemblance to the Chinese garden depicted in T'ang I-fen's painting of 1862 than any other 'Chinese' garden in the West.

The overriding reason why Kemp and others admired Biddulph, despite 'the excessive multiplication of parts . . . . which interferes with unity and connection', was because of Bateman and Cooke's creation of harmony through architecture, together with a whole variety of screening devices used throughout the garden, such as rockworks and tunnels to divide and link different sections and the use of extensive planting to partition areas near the house. These factors gave unity and congruity to the whole.

Excavations made by the National Trust in 1988 revealed the original structure of the more formal garden areas around the house including the Dahlia Walk which was one of the first parts of the garden built by the Batemans. A walk along the herbaceous border at Arley Hall (see pages 166–7) will give you some idea of how it must have looked 140 years ago.

Address: Biddulph Grange Garden, Biddulph Grange, Biddulph, Stoke-on-Trent, Staffordshire, England.

The Cheshire Cottage.

The Stumpery.

171

1814–60 ALTON TOWERS Probably the best example of Victorian 'gardenesque' in which the design of the garden is characterized by a great mixture of styles and, some feel, a noticeable loss of artistic unity.

Looking down into the garden in the valley with the Towers in the distance. Visited June 15.

Alton Towers is built on a site whose history dates back to the eighth century yet it was not until the early nineteenth century that the huge building and development programme began which made the house and grounds so famous in the Victorian era.

When Charles Talbot, 15th Earl of Shrewsbury, inherited the enormous Staffordshire estate from his uncle in 1787, he found that it appealed to him much more than his other home at Heythrop. So, having extended the original farmhouse known as Alverton Lodge into a large, gothic-style mansion renamed Alton Abbey and having obtained an Enclosure Act that enabled him to enclose the land and turn it into a private park and woodland, he spent the years from 1814 to 1827 developing the gardens.

J. C. Loudon (1783–1843), author of the famous *Encyclopaedia of Gardening* (1822), originally coined the term 'Gardenesque' to describe a style of planting in which each individual plant was allowed to develop its own character as fully as possible. Although he was one of a number of architectural designers who were asked to draw up plans for the garden his ideas were rejected. Possibly because he was miffed about this, he wrote scathingly about the eventual outcome: 'We consider the greater part of it in excessively bad taste, or rather, perhaps, as the work of a morbid imagination joined to the command of unlimited resources.' However, the eclectic mixture of styles that is evident in the design of Alton Towers is typical of the Victorian period and came

to be known as 'Gardenesque' after Edward Kemp popularized the term in his highly successful book *How to Lay Out a Small Garden* (1850), even though his definition was very different from the one Loudon had expounded twenty years earlier, it now referring to an eclectic mixture of styles.

In fact, the garden architects employed by Charles Talbot to execute what were essentially his own ideas and design for the gardens were Thomas Allason (1790–1852) and Robert Abraham (1774–1850). With their help the dramatic sloping terrain overlooked by Alton Abbey and sweeping down to the River Churnet was transformed from dry, treeless desolate scenery into a dramatic, romantic vista of woodlands, lakes, pools, fountains, terraces, walls, paths, staircases and architectural features.

The most important garden buildings were the Chinese Pagoda Fountain, with its 70-foot-high water jet, reputedly modelled by Abraham on the ToHo Pagoda in Canton and reflecting the fashion for *Chinoiserie* that was sweeping through western Europe; and the Grand Conservatories, also by Abraham, which housed the palm trees and other exotic plants which were flooding into Europe from all over the world. A stone structure called Stonehenge, though bearing little resemblance to its namesake, was erected as was a Swiss Cottage in which lived a blind Welsh harpist employed to enchant the Duke's family and guests with his music.

When the 15th Earl died in 1827, the estate was

inherited by his nephew John Talbot (1791–1852), the 16th Earl of Shrewsbury, who completed the laying out of the formal gardens near the house, put the finishing touches to the Valley Gardens, perfected the Rose Garden and the Rock Garden, laid out the Star Garden, Terraced Gardens and Dutch Gardens and erected the Choragic Monument at the head of the Valley Gardens as a monument to his uncle, bearing the inscription: 'He Made the Desert smile'.

He also employed the gothic architect Pugin (1812–1852), among several others, to gothicize and extend the Abbey with halls, galleries and fortifications, a chapel and a Banqueting Hall before renaming it Alton Towers.

On his death in 1852 and that of his cousin Bertram in 1856, the senior male line of the Earls of Shrewsbury died out and after a protracted legal battle the estate reverted to Henry Talbot (who claimed direct descent from Gilbert, third son of the 2nd Earl of Shrewsbury). He became the 18th Earl of Shrewsbury, taking up possession of Alton Towers in 1860.

It was Henry Talbot's idea to open the gardens to the public and the first tickets were sold in 1860, netting a total income for the year of £116 17s. 5d. but it was during the era of his grandson Charles Talbot (1860–1921), 20th Earl of Shrewsbury, who inherited the estate in 1877, that the gardens had their heyday.

Throughout the 1880s and 1890s the gardens were kept in immaculate condition and opened daily in the summer for visitors. During August each year grand fêtes were held lasting several days to which crowds of up to 30,000 people came from all over the Midlands. An advertisement for one such fête in 1893 outlines some of the thrilling events to take place at The Fête of the Year at Alton Towers 'Horse leaping, water jumps, lady riders, bands, constant dancing, high wire, the man with the iron head, celebrated clowns, renowned bird impersonator, fireworks, gorgeous flowers, grand conservatories, quiet woodland walks. Fête ticket passes everywhere.' It almost replicates the words of the modern brochure for Alton Towers, right down to the all-in-one price!

Separation and legal wrangles with his estranged wife resulted in the Earl moving out of Alton Towers around the turn of the century and the house and grounds started what was to be a headlong decline. The Earl's death in 1921, preceded by that of his son in 1915 and followed by that of his wife in 1923, meant that after 700 years of ownership the Alton estates passed out of the hands of the Earls of Shrewsbury and were broken up.

However, in 1924 Alton Towers and its grounds were bought by a group of local businessmen who restored the gardens to their former glory for the benefit of the public. During the war years, the house was requisitioned for use by the Army and by the time it was returned to the owners in 1951 it was in such a bad state of repair that the interior had to be gutted. This was the start of an ongoing, long-term programme of renovation and change that has seen the restoration of many of the finest garden features and the added attraction (to some) of a Theme Park.

But while my blood chills at the thought of all those terrifying rides and my intellect rebels at the thought of the nastier aspects of the twentieth century dominating the rich history of a famous nineteenth-century garden, I have to admit that it really isn't so different from the garden it was a hundred years ago. The only real difference is that in 1894 the spectacular events only lasted for half a dozen days a year, while now they happen every day for over six months of the year.

If you have older children who can be left to their own devices in the Theme Park while you go round the gardens, it makes the perfect family outing. They can scare the wits out of themselves while you can escape to the gardens which, to our great surprise, were not only beautifully kept up but surprisingly peaceful and remote from the monster rides. If you don't have children and want to visit the garden, the best time to go is at 9.00 a.m. because the rides don't start until 10.00 a.m. but you will still have to pay the full rate if you go in the high season between March and November. However, if you visit the garden in the winter period, November to March, the Theme Park is closed and you can enjoy the garden with very little competition from crowds.

Address: Alton Towers, Nr Cheadle, Staffordshire, England.

The bridge across the canal.

The Pagoda Fountain.

1680–1958 TATTON PARK An authentic Japanese garden and an example of Loudon's gardenesque style are just two reasons why this superimposed layering of numerous garden styles is important historically.

The Italian Garden, planted in very simple style with clumps of thrift. Visited June 10.

Tatton Park was the family home of the Egerton family for nearly four hundred years until, on the death of Maurice Egerton in 1958, it was bequeathed to the National Trust who rank it in their 'Top Ten' English Gardens. Archaeological remains indicate that the area on which Tatton now stands was inhabited in 8000 BC and every age since then has left evidence of settlement. Extensive documentation dating from the Middle Ages provides a detailed account of the history of the house and gardens.

The first house of 1680 was surrounded by small formal gardens in accordance with the fashion of that time but during the eighteenth and nineteenth centuries

The African Hut.

the grounds were extensively developed in keeping with the gardens of the present mansion, completed in the early 1800s. The straight beech avenue planted in 1737 which was originally the main drive to the house still exists (although it is no longer the main drive) despite Humphrey Repton's proposal in his Red Book to break it up into clumps as part of his vision of landscaping the parkland. The old beech maze of 1795 still exists too and is a prime example of an early maze.

The formal Italian gardens in front of the house, with their imposing flights of steps, central fountain and colourful beds best seen from the upper floors, were laid out by Paxton (1801–65) in 1847 and completed by 1890. From the terraces the view extended across the formal garden to the deer-filled parkland. Although the gardens were neglected and altered in the middle of the twentieth century, they have now been restored following the original layout as closely as possible.

Similarly, the tiered fountain and trellised shelter, which were the only remains of the early nineteenth-century flower garden known as Lady Charlotte's Arbour, (after Lady Charlotte Egerton, wife of William, the first Baron Egerton [1806–83]) designed by Lewis Wyatt in 1814, have undergone extensive renovation to restore the Arbour to its original design.

Wyatt also designed the orangery in 1818 (though its roof was raised later in the nineteenth century to accommodate the ever-increasing height of the palms). For the same reason, the roof of the fernery, built by Paxton, the celebrated creator of Crystal Palace, in the

1850s, was raised at the end of the century because of the rapid growth of the tree ferns.

In 1910 the 3rd Baron Egerton, Alan de Tatton (1845–1920), brought Japanese workmen over to the estate to landscape the Japanese Garden, which resembles, in miniature, the landscape of that country with streams, stands of tall trees, a thatched teahouse, paths, stone lanterns and shrubs. The Shinto Temple on the island in the middle of The Golden Brook was transported from its native home to complete the authentic Japanese atmosphere of the garden.

This Japanese Garden is the most important example of its kind in England and is one of the reasons why Tatton Park is so important historically. Another reason is that, having remained in the hands of one family for so long, it is an important record of the changing fashions and styles of gardening over the centuries – it is an amalgam or palimpsest (superimposed layering) of numerous different garden ideas. Thirdly, it is important as an example of the Victorian 'Gardenesque' style. Gardenesque, that is, in the sense of eclectic Victorian gardens which combined a great mixture of styles often with a noticeable lack of artistic unity. Tatton Park, Biddulph Grange (see pages 168–71) and Alton Towers (see pages 172–3) are other gardens in this category.

Tatton Park has many other interesting features such as the African Hut, the Leech Pool, the L-Borders, the Tower Garden, the Rose Garden, the Arboretum, the Pinetum and the Topiary, as well as a Home Farm, adventure playground and restaurant.

Address: Tatton Park, Knutsford, Cheshire, England.

Paxton's Fernery.

The Golden Brook.

The Japanese Garden.

Circa 1500 HEVER CASTLE (Reconstructed 1903–8) Edwardian folly combining Renaissance features with a classical Italian garden built by William Waldorf-Astor around the medieval castle where Henry VIII courted Anne Boleyn.

The Loggia and the Piazza viewed from across the Lake. Visited June 20.

Hever Castle was built in the fifteenth century around an ancient thirteenth-century gatehouse by the grandfather of Anne Boleyn, who built the Tudor house, moat and drawbridge. Historically, the house's fame rests on the fact that it was here that Henry VIII courted his second wife but after her death the property reverted to the crown and was given to Henry's fourth wife, Anne of Cleves, as part of their divorce settlement. The castle

The Italian Garden.

was, over the centuries, associated with a number of illustrious families but in 1903 it was bought by William Waldorf-Astor who instigated a series of developments that brought it back into prominence.

The transformation of Hever Castle and its grounds took place remarkably rapidly. Early plans drawn up by Cheal and Son for the former owners, the Sebrights, were discarded in favour of the much grander scheme envisaged by Astor. However, he still employed Joseph Cheal and between 1904 and 1908 over a thousand men worked on totally reconstructing the land. A 35-acre lake was created out of a marshy bog, vast quantities of soil and rock were moved around or brought into the grounds by steam engines and railways, and mature trees were transported from Ashdown Forest, all done to create natural and interesting contours and shapes to make the rather flat site more topographically interesting. Furthermore, a vast planting programme was initiated which today, ninety years on, is reaching its full maturity and beauty.

The historical importance of Hever's gardens lies in its presentation of the Edwardian vision and dilemma of gardening – which roots would gardening revert to after the excesses of the romantic landscape movement? It is interesting to note at Hever that the two areas of the garden are kept quite separate as though to indicate, both literally and metaphorically, the two quite different paths

The Topiary Garden.

The astrolabe in Anne Boleyn's Garden.

that can be followed. On the one hand, it attempts to capture the English medieval and Renaissance tradition in keeping with the history of the house and, on the other, it imitates the classical tradition in the huge and elaborate Italian Garden influenced, no doubt, by Edith Wharton's *Italian Villas and their Gardens*, which was published in the same year that work on the garden began.

Near the castle, between the inner and outer moats, the late medieval/Renaissance influences abound. Anne Boleyn's garden, for instance, is laid out as it might have been in her day. It is a series of small, simple, sheltered gardens with neatly clipped yew hedges. One is a herb garden, in the Tudor style, planted with a variety of English herbs, another is a chess garden with clipped golden yew chess pieces modelled after designs from the Tudor period to be found in the British Museum. In its centre the astrolabe, used for telling time and latitude from astronomical data, dates from the reign of Queen Anne (1665–1714).

Within the outer moat are three other features that reflect the early Renaissance character of the house: Anne Boleyn's orchard; the maze, with its two, elegant clipped yellow yews and its pretty broderie of box hedging encompassing the initials H and A for the fated lovers; and the section of topiary in fanciful and abstract shapes such as a corkscrew, a dovecote, a table and chairs, a peacock, a crown and several others. The formal art of topiary had been rejected by the Landscape Movement but found favour again with the Victorians as manifest here.

Outside the outer moat and extending to the lake lies the formal Italian Garden.

Astor had been American Minister in Rome and while there had amassed an enormous collection of antique statuary which he promptly shipped to Hever. Statues, urns, sarcophagi, columns, vases, busts and well-heads decorate the Pompeian wall which runs for an eighth of a mile down one side of the garden while down the other side runs the Pergola Walk and its grottoes inspired by the Pathway of One Hundred Fountains at the Villa D'Este (see page 33). In the middle of the enormous lawn lies the peaceful sunken garden surrounded by a tall clipped hedge. At the far end, alongside the lake, the loggia, fountain and piazza provide a beautiful summer setting for concerts and plays. Other features of the garden include the Rose Garden, the Blue Garden, the Sisters' Pool Lawn, the Anne Boleyn Walk, the Half-Moon Pond and the Cascade Rockery.

The overwhelming impression that one comes away with is that it is a glorious folly – an Italian junk shop stuffed to overflowing where collecting and planting have run riot and been indulged in for their own sake rather than to fulfil an aesthetic vision. Great fun, but what exactly is the point?

Address: Hever Castle, Hever, Edenbridge, Kent, England.

Statuary in the Italian Garden.

1870s KNIGHTSHAYES (Renovated 1937–72) A Victorian garden re-shaped by its twentieth-century owners' philosophy of creating new vistas, never repeating plantings and giving unexpected pleasure at the turn of every corner.

The Pool Garden with the weeping silver pear tree. Visited September 1.

The Paved Garden.

Japanese anemones by the curved stone bench.

Knightshayes Court Garden was originally laid out by the celebrated parks' superintendent Edward Kemp in the late 1870s as the large, late Victorian gothic mansion, begun in 1869 and designed by William Burges, was nearing completion. This 'typical Victorian garden' as Lady Heathcoat Amory subsequently called it was typical of its day with several clearly defined areas such as the formal terraces, clipped yew topiary, paved rose beds, a kitchen garden, an avenue of Douglas Fir, bowling green and large expanse of lawn.

Here was enormous potential for change thought Sir John and Lady Joyce Heathcoat Amory when they inherited Knightshayes in 1937 and for the next forty-five years they devoted themselves to creating a wonderful twentieth-century garden on their 50-acre site that bore little resemblance to the garden they inherited before the Second World War which was typical of the previous century. In 1972, on Sir John Heathcoat Amory's death, the garden was bequeathed to the National Trust, which has carried on the consecutive planting of trees established by Lady Heathcoat Amory as an essential part of a programme for replacing trees that have died from old age, disease or drought.

In *The Englishwoman's Garden* edited by Alvide Lees-Milne and Rosemary Verey, Lady Heathcoat Amory describes how and why her garden developed in the way that it has. Neither she nor her husband had any specialist knowledge or training in gardens and plants but their amateur enthusiasm and desire to beautify their home soon became an obsession. Consulting friends like Graham Thomas and Lanning Roper, they developed their ideas about the changes they wanted to make. Their first move was to tackle the terraces in front of the house which had been elaborately bedded out in Victorian days. All ill-thought-out and hurried conversion of part

Looking away from the house across the terraces to the parkland.

of the terraces into a rose garden was soon recognized as a mistake when Lady Heathcoat Amory realized that the height and garishness of the roses she had planted was ruining the vista of the rolling countryside beyond the terraces. She eventually grassed the beds over and converted the two rose beds at either end of the terrace into patchwork circles of scented thyme around a stone ornament. Ever since that first abortive attempt, subtle colours have become a trademark of the planting at Knightshayes.

'The main object of all our efforts was to introduce new vistas, never if possible to repeat former plantings, and to give unexpected pleasure at the turning of corners.' This philosophy, allied with their acceptance that 'a garden never stands still', explains why the Heathcoat Amorys' garden expanded from one project to another in the decades after the war. The three formal gardens to the east of the house date back to the last century. The Paved Garden, hedged in by large yews, and the adjoining battlement-hedged enclosure surrounding the Pool Garden (which Lanning Roper helped to redesign), originally surrounded Kemp's bowling green. South of the Pool Garden, topiary hounds chase a topiary fox cut by Sir Ian Heathcoat Amory in the 1920s to commemorate his passion for hunting.

But, it is in the newly developed areas of the garden that Sir John and Lady Joyce sought to incorporate their philosophy of gardening and their passion for plants.

One of their most exciting projects was the creation of the 'Garden in the Wood' which necessitated the removal of hundreds of trees but enabled about 30 acres of woodland to be filled with a great variety of shrubs and plants such as magnolias, rhododendrons, cornus, hypericum, camellias, Japanese maples, peonies, hellebores and geraniums, to name but a few.

Unable to resist the urge to extend their garden ever further into the surrounding woodland, the Heathcoat Amorys planted other areas such as The Glade, The Willow Garden, Holly's Wood, Michael's Wood and Sir John's Wood, at every move aiming 'to create a continuous and unexpected combination of flowers and foliage throughout the spring, summer and autumn'.

An inspiration to visitors, Knightshayes is a marvellous example of twentieth-century gardening at its best; when space, time, inclination and money are all in plentiful supply.

Address: Knightshayes, Tiverton, Devon, England.

View from the back of the Paved Garden.

Aralia elata 'Variegata'.

Long borders planted with delphiniums at Falkland Palace.

The Royal Palace of Falkland in Fife (Scotland) has a long history as the hunting palace of successive Scottish monarchs until Charles II left Falkland in 1651 to face defeat and exile. Although technically a property of the Crown, Falkland Palace is now looked after by the National Trust for Scotland. Since the Second World War, when it was used as a forest nursery, the garden has been redesigned by Percy Cane who has skilfully developed the herbaceous borders and rose garden against the dignified backdrop of the Palace.

Pitmedden Garden.

Arley Hall.

Powis Castle.

Chenies Manor.

Dumbarton Oaks.

Knightshayes.

Great Dixter.

Bodnant.

Carpet bedding demonstration at The Royal Horticultural Society's Garden at Wisley.

Wisley.

Wisley.

Colegrave Seeds demonstration garden.

The Moon Garden at Colegrave Seeds.

Belvedere.   Massed lobelias at Colegrave Seeds.

French marigolds at the Hameau.   A typical Cornish cottage wall in Rinsey.

The Inner Circle Gardens at Regent's Park.   Distinctive white snapdragons at Pitmedden.

1835–38 TRESCO ABBEY One of the most extensive and exotic collections of sub-tropical plants and shrubs in northern Europe, many collected and grown from seed by the Dorien Smith family over the last century and a half.

Exotic plantings among the remains of the ruined Abbey at Tresco. Visited August 25.

The Neptune Steps. (Photographed by Martyn Rix)

Tresco Abbey on the Isles of Scilly was built between 1835 and 1838 by the new Lord Proprietor of the Islands, Augustus Smith, on a site just above the ruins of the old priory which had been established there in 938 by the Benedictines. The new house looked down over a south facing slope to the sea and other islands beyond, and here Smith envisaged a terraced garden of about 14 acres while the back part (50 acres) could remain in its wild state providing a sheltered backdrop to the more formal laid out gardens.

Over one hundred and fifty years of collecting by the Dorien Smith family, descendants of Augustus Smith and still owners of Tresco Abbey, has resulted in one of the most extensive and exotic collections of sub-tropical plants and shrubs in northern Europe. Situated within the waters of the Gulf Stream and protected from the Atlantic gales by a wind-break of elm, sycamore, oak and poplar that Augustus Smith had the good sense to plant as one of his top priorities when he took on the proprietorship of the islands, Tresco enjoys a mild climate.

It must have required great vision to see the possibilities of the site he had chosen but he spent the next thirty-four years developing the home farm and the garden terraces and collecting seeds from all over the world to nurture on his new estate. Smith also had an enduring and occasionally stormy relationship with the Royal Botanic Gardens at Kew but overall the mutual exchange and supply of seeds and plants was highly beneficial to them both. Many of the plants that grew so successfully at Tresco are recorded in the paintings of Augustus Smith's great friend, Lady Sophia Tower, who visited the island many times in the mid-nineteenth century.

The steep terraces of the garden are reached by steps and a network of main paths and criss-crossing minor paths. In 1920, Sir Arthur Hill, the Director at Kew, wrote an article comparing the gardens at Tresco Abbey with Sir Thomas Hanbury's garden at La Mortola (see pages 186–7). Both were situated on a sloping hill that leads down to the sea and both contained magnificent collections of exotic plants from the southern hemisphere that were invaluable to the botanist and horticulturist.

Proteus, geranium maderense, cinerarias, acacias, palms, arum lilies, pelargoniums, eucalyptus, ferns, melaleuca, agapanthas and echiums are just some of the myriad species that flourish and often self-seed in this extraordinarily rich and diverse garden, creating a riot of colour and texture that is nevertheless given a strong sense of order by the formal divisions of the terraced slopes into specific areas – the Top Terrace, the Middle Terrace, the Cyprus Rockery, the West Rockery, Mexico, Father Neptune, etc.

A plants person's heaven, Tresco Abbey can easily be visited by helicopter or boat from Penzance.

Address: Tresco Abbey, Tresco, Isles of Scilly, England.

An unnamed bust. (Photographed by Martyn Rix)

The Ruined Arch. (Photographed by Martyn Rix)

Watsonias in full bloom across the fountain pool. (Photographed by Martyn Rix)

1867–1939 HANBURY BOTANIC GARDEN A world-wide collection of tropical, sub-tropical and exotic plants and shrubs flourish in this warm, mild and sheltered spot poised on an Italian hillside site that drops down to the Mediterranean coast.

The classical terrace at the north of the villa. Visited September 15.

Steps and terraces lead down the steep slopes of the garden.

A view of the south side of the villa.

Hanbury Botanic Garden, or La Mortola as it was originally called, was purchased by Sir Thomas Hanbury (1832–1907) in 1867. Recognizing the potential of the site, which was bounded by mountains on three sides providing shelter from the wind, Hanbury, with his brother Daniel and later his son Cecil and the German botanist Ludovico Winter, set about designing a garden that would be home to an eclectic collection of fascinating botanic specimens from all over the world. Trees and exotics from the Far East, Australasia, Central and South America and South Africa flourished in the mild climate.

The garden was planted as a series of special areas descending in terraces from the house, which is at the top of the garden, down to the coast 100 metres below. A wood of Aleppo Pines, an orchard of several kinds of citrus fruit, numerous specimens of Mediterranean maquis, tropical and sub-tropical plants all made the garden world famous at the turn of the century.

Sir Cecil's wife, Lady Dorothy, devoted the years between the two world wars to landscaping the garden so that its panoramic views and walks could be enjoyed by visitors. Paved pathways, fountains, statues and arbours were added to the garden and an Italian Formal garden planted with aromatic herbs, lavender and box was designed for the south-facing front of the villa.

The Hanburys had to leave the house during the Second World War as numerous bombings and shellings made occupancy unsafe. Much of the infrastructure of the garden was destroyed in this period and by 1960 Lady Dorothy was forced to sell the property to the

Italian Government. Despite good intentions, the amount of money needed for extensive renovations was not available and the garden fell into an even greater state of disrepair.

However, in 1983 the Italian Government assigned the property to the University of Genoa who, since 1987, have carried out a massive regeneration programme involving clearing vast areas of all-pervasive weeds and huge numbers of dead trees and shrubs, restoring paths and pergolas, buildings and statuary, and replanting extensively.

As is so often the case when rejuvenation of a once famous garden takes place, there is the thorny question of how far one tries to create an exact image of the past versus how far one tries to create a new type of garden for the future. Here a balance is being sought between capturing the flavour of the garden in its heyday and creating an exciting, new botanic garden which allows exotic plants to live freely in a natural environment.

The villa has been renovated along with other virtually derelict buildings on the property – one of which is lived in by the Hanburys' descendants – and many of the special areas of the garden have been restored, such as the Garden of Perfumes, the Australasian Forest and the arbours. The work continues apace on all parts of the property to return it to its former status with rarities from all over the world flourishing on its terrain.

Address: Giardini Botanico Hanbury, La Mortola, Ventimiglia, Italy.

A bottle palm in the Cactus Garden.

The view from the villa at sunset.

1884–1935 GRAVETYE MANOR Home of William Robinson, influential garden designer and author of *The English Flower Garden* and *The Wild Garden* which emphasized the importance of naturalness in planting as opposed to artificiality in garden design.

Free and natural planting maintains the spirit of William Robinson. Visited July 10.

Gravetye Manor, first built in 1598 by Richard Infield for his bride Katherine Compton, was bought in 1884 by one of the most influential gardeners of his time, William Robinson. He continuously developed the gardens and grounds in accordance with his own ideas and theories until his death in 1935, when the fortunes of the house declined. Occupied by the Canadian Army during the war, there was neither the money nor the manpower to devote to the gardens. However, in 1957 Gravetye was purchased by Peter Herbert (the present owner) to convert into a country house hotel and restaurant and a long-term programme of restoration commenced, based on Robinson's numerous detailed plans and accounts of his work, with the result that it once more looks very much as it did in Robinson's day.

An Irishman, William Robinson (1838–1935) began his gardening career in his native country, working first at Curraghmore for the Marquess of Waterford, then at the Irish National Botanic Garden at Glasnevin. He then emigrated to England and took a job at the Royal Botanic Garden in Regent's Park under the Curator, Robert Mainock (1800–80) with a brief to research and plant the English Garden. This enabled Robinson to

study plants in their natural settings and necessitated travelling all over the country in order to do so. This provided material for his journalistic work which in turn was a springboard for his independent career as a writer. Two early books on French gardens were followed in 1870 by *Alpine Flowers for Gardens* and *The Wild Garden*. The following year he established his own weekly journal *The Garden* (now part of *Homes and Gardens*), which he edited until 1899. In 1883, his most famous book *The English Flower Garden* was published which, together with his earlier book *The Wild Garden*, propagated his views on plants and planting and greatly influenced several generations of gardeners.

The most significant of Robinson's ideas was his emphasis on the *naturalness* of gardening as opposed to the *artificiality* of garden design with its stress on architectural structure and formality and the, to him, abhorrent passion for bedding plants. He loathed, for instance, Versailles, which he found indescribably empty and ugly. Robinson's idea of garden design was that it should be dictated by the colour, form and foliage of the plants, not by architectural features.

Like many good and influential ideas, his were better

when interpreted with intelligence rather than strict adherence to 'rule'. One sees this in Robinson's own garden at Gravetye. Over the decades he modified, changed and enlarged his garden in ways that do not always seem to be in keeping with his strongly declared principles. For example, Christopher Thacker, in *The Genius of Gardening*, relates an amusing story in which Robinson, in an article for *Country Life* in 1912, explains that his flower garden is divided into stone-edged beds in order 'to contain the greatest number of favourite plants in the simplest way'. However, when a visitor exclaims in surprise that he, too, has 'a formal garden', Robinson dismisses him as a 'silly person to make such a remark instead of looking at the flowers'. Robinson was obviously sensitive to the implied paradox – the south and west gardens at Gravetye are formal in the sense of a fairly strict geometrical layout of rectangular beds bordered by flagstone paths but what isn't at all 'formalized' or 'controlled' is the planting within the beds or the natural growth of the plants spilling out and over the paths. What Robinson said in *The Wild Garden* was that naturalized planting should be practised in areas outside the formal flower garden such as woodland paths, sides of streams, edges of shrubberies, copses and woods. Wild gardening was a part, possibly the most important part, of a garden but not the whole part.

In Gravetye this philosophy can be seen at work. Running from east to west on the south side of the house, a terraced wall separates the levelled flower garden from the sloping wild flower meadow that runs down to a small lake. The garden and the meadow are planted with numerous bulbs that create great drifts and banks of flowers in the spring.

To the north of the house the land slopes upward and is planted with shrubs and trees divided by the Long Lawn into two separate areas: the Azalea Bank and the Heath Garden, by the Long Lawn. Sadly this latter area was devastated in the Great Storm of 1989 and over 200 Corsican Pines were lost, just a year short of their centenary, as well as several hundred other trees both around the house and in the 1000 acres of Gravetye Forest. A further thirty trees and much of Robinson's original planting were lost in the 1990 storms but an extensive replanting programme has already taken place.

In view of Robinson's aversion to architectural features in a garden, it is interesting that he initiated such an unusual one for his kitchen garden. Built in 1898–1900 the huge, oval-shaped garden to the north of the house is situated dramatically on a slope with a stepped surrounding wall. It is extremely striking. The kitchen garden supplies all the summer fruit and vegetables for the restaurant and much of the winter requirements too, although rabbits and deer create problems.

A delightful touch on the rectangles of lawn in the main flower garden is the way the blue and mauve canvas of the deck chairs tone in with the predominantly blue and mauve planting in the herbaceous beds.

The gardens are only open to patrons of the hotel and restaurant.

Address: Gravetye Manor, Nr East Grinstead, West Sussex, England.

Looking from the paved garden to the Wildflower Meadow.

The Gazebo with a crowded path of lavender and nepeta.

Steps up towards the Long Lawn.

1908 HESTERCOMBE A superb example of Lutyens' and Jekyll's partnership where symmetry of form, artistic planting and attention to detail in colour and texture created a masterpiece of Edwardian gardening.

The Great Plat seen from the Original Terrace. Visited June 18.

The Grey Walk.

The Pergola.

Hestercombe House Gardens had little to recommend them except a broad upper terrace at the front of the house and spectacular views over Taunton Deane across to the Blackdown Hills beyond when, in 1908, its owner E. W. Portman commissioned Edwin Lutyens to design a garden for the house while retaining the two aforementioned features. Working in collaboration with his favourite partner, Gertrude Jekyll, plans were drawn up and executed in the same year.

Its heyday was the period between the two world wars but between 1939 and 1945 the house was occupied by American troops and the gardens were badly neglected. Mrs Portman still retained accommodation on the estate until her death in 1951 when the house and grounds reverted to the Crown and were leased to Somerset County Council, which designated it as the headquarters of the Somerset Fire Brigade. Under their guardianship, the historical importance of the garden was recognized and with the discovery of the original planting plans, systematic restoration of the gardens began in 1973 and continues to the present day, under the aegis of a 'Garden Panel' as the managing body. The County Council have won several awards for their restoration and conservation work in the garden.

Many consider Hestercombe to be the finest example of the dynamic and prolific partnership of Lutyens and Jekyll. Here the combination of Lutyens's formal symmetrical layout with Jekyll's artistic, 'painterly'

The semi-circular East Rill Pool.

The West Rill.

planting and their mutual attention to detail in the choice of materials, the design of steps, pools, paving and the combination of colour and texture have created a masterpiece of Edwardian gardening whose creators' influence has percolated down the century to the present.

Although the house front and terrace were rather uninspiring, Lutyens took advantage of the sloping ground below the house to form a series of terraces and vistas around a formal sunken parterre with diagonal axes, flanked east and west by water rills and bounded on the south by a long pergola whose circular windows (*clairvoyées*) give views out over the surrounding countryside.

The other section of the garden, which contains the Dutch Garden and the Orangery (the only building Lutyens actually built at Hestercombe), is linked to the main symmetrical *plat* at the front by the clever device of the Rotunda. This lies at the house end of the East Rill, opposite the Rose Garden, and has exits and entrances that lead out towards the terraced *plat* garden, on one side, and out towards the Orangery and the Dutch

Garden on another; so skilfully is it done that one is barely aware of the change in angle.

Links between the various sections of the garden are made by the repetition of small details such as the contrast in the bands of different stonework.

Influenced by Jekyll's interest in and knowledge of the Arts and Crafts Movement and its support of rural traditions and craftsmanship, Lutyens used to full advantage the special characteristics of two local materials that were near to hand: the rough split stone that was quarried from behind the house and the smooth, easily worked Ham Hill stone that came from nearby Yeovil. Tiles, flints and cobbles were also used to great effect, all of them in close conjunction with the colours and textures of the plants that Miss Jekyll chose for the long herbaceous borders in the Grey Walk and elsewhere. Throughout the garden the interlocking relationship between architecture and planting leaves one wondering where the one begins and the other ends.

Address: Hestercombe House Gardens, Cheddon Fitzpaine, Taunton, Somerset, England.

The Dutch Garden.

A Gertrude Jekyll thumb-print: a series of sunken terracotta pots

Cornus contraversa 'Variegata' at La Vasterival.

Le Vasterival (France) has been created by Princess Sturdza since 1958. Covering 7 hectares of acid soil near the sea, the huge range of plants nevertheless thrives in the carefully composted earth. The design is informal with paths, woodlands, glades and immaculate grass walks enabling one to enjoy the richness of the flora in a variety of settings all year round.

The woodland garden of Martyn and Alison Rix.

Geoffrey Dutton's Marginal Garden.

Miriam Rothschild's wild garden.

Miriam Rothschild's wild garden.

Rhododendrons in the woodland at the Bois des Moutiers.

Le Bois des Moutiers in Normandy (France), situated in woodland above the coast, has a house that was designed by Edwin Lutyens in 1898 and a garden which reflects the influence of his great friend and collaborator, Gertrude Jekyll, with its White Garden surrounded by clipped box hedges and its pair of profuse, mixed, herbaceous borders. Below the formal areas of the garden, woodlands full of rhododendrons tumble down the valley to the sea.

Looking out over the moors from Geoffrey Dutton's Marginal Garden.

Geoffrey Dutton's Marginal Garden, situated on five acres of hillside in the Scottish Highlands, is the product of over thirty years' part-time work. Dutton calls the garden 'marginal' because its basic design has been imposed by nature in terms of the site and the kind of vegetation that grows on it. Furthermore, his interference as a gardener, in terms of both time and philosophy, has, of necessity, been marginal too so the dramatic landscape has not been ruined. What Dutton has achieved by 'marginally' shaping and perfecting the trees, plants and shrubs that flourish in this bleak, wind-swept environment is the creation and maintenance of a garden that looks totally natural yet is, in fact, subtly fashioned as a series of enclosures linked by paths that lead one ever upwards to the dramatic views at the top of the garden.

The natural planting of watsonias at Kirstenbosch. (Photographed by Martyn Rix)

The Huntington Cactus Garden.

Gwen and Roger Elliot's Australian Native Plant Garden.

Leucospermum at Kirstenbosch. (Photographed by Martyn Rix)

Gwen and Rodger Elliot's Garden of Australian Native Plants in Montrose (Australia) was started by them in the early 1980s after they purchased the land from an estate agent who had 'improved' it by bulldozing nearly all the understorey plants! However, the Elliots' intention 'to foster the development of the native vegetation and total ecology of the area' with little help from man, has resulted in the regeneration of the natural vegetation to such an extent that the garden, which was designed with the aim of blending the ornamental garden with the native plants in the bushland beyond, has been so successful that the two areas are almost indistinguishable from one another.

Kirstenbosch Nature Reserve in Cape Province (South Africa) is founded on land that dates back to the seventeenth century when the southern boundary of the Dutch Settlement ran through the area. It was purchased in 1895 by Cecil Rhodes, who bequeathed it on his death to the South African government which, in 1913, chose it as the site for the foundation of the National Botanic Gardens of South Africa. The Botanic Gardens are informally planted with the huge range of native plants for which the South African Cape is famed and, extending up into the Reserve where the native flora grows wild, they cover, in all, more than 1000 acres around Table Mountain and extending to its highest point.

Santa Barbara Botanic Garden with a field of Californian Poppies which are not open as it was a very dark day.

The Santa Barbara Botanic Garden in California (USA), situated between the Santa Ynez Mountains and the Pacific Ocean, was founded in 1926 with the purpose of preserving and displaying the native flora of California. It has splendid specimens of Californian live oak and Douglas fir as well as special collections of wild, meadow and desert flowers, including many rare and endangered species. Panoramic views of the surrounding mountains and ocean can be enjoyed from the network of trails that run through the gardens.

Joe Pye weed in the wild-flower meadow at Longwood Gardens.

1906–21 LONGWOOD GARDENS Created by the industrial tycoon Pierre S. du Pont, the formal gardens imitate all the major European gardening styles but in an historical sense it is the vast native wild-flower meadow that is the original contribution to gardening.

The Fountain Garden, a tribute to the work of Le Nôre at Versailles. Visited July 26.

Longwood Gardens were bought in 1906 by the industrial tycoon Pierre S. du Pont (1870–1954), principally to save its century-old arboretum which was threatened by lumbering interests in the area.

The original, 200-acre lot of land had been purchased from William Penn by a Quaker farmer named Peirce, in 1700, and it was his great-grandsons Samuel and Joshua Peirce who planted the 15-acre arboretum on the farm in 1798. The wooded park set in the midst of the rolling hills has now grown to over 1000 acres, of which the gardens occupy about one third.

Between 1906 and 1921 when Longwood was first opened to the public, du Pont worked on developing numerous aspects of the garden, drawing on a wide range of gardening traditions for the development of his ideas.

The raw material on which he was working was very much that of the New World – rolling hills, native trees and space – while the influences on which he drew were largely those of the Old World. Features of Italian Renaissance gardens, French Formal gardens and the English Landscape Movement can all be recognized (indeed for the sake of authenticity were supposed to be recognized) in the various gardens and features he created.

Having originally trained as an engineer, du Pont was fascinated by the complex hydraulic feats required to install the numerous water features he wanted for the garden: in excess of 5 acres of pools and canals feed the water systems. There is an open air theatre based on the Villa Gori close to Siena which has hundreds of hidden fountains. The Italian Garden composed of water parterres was inspired by the garden at the Villa Gamberaia (see page 38) outside Florence. The water wall is modelled on a similar feature at the Villa D'Este (see page 30) in Tivoli and du Pont's favourite, the Fountain Garden, was a tribute to Le Nôtre's work at Versailles (see page 78). However, the summer displays of coloured floodlights which illuminate the 229 jets of the main fountain garden might be considered rather 'glitzy' by more sedate-minded gardening buffs and visitors.

In marked contrast to the extensive formal gardens

The Topiary Garden.

A detail of the fountains in the Fountain Garden.

The Water Wall inspired by the Villa d'Este.

Victoria water-lilies.

and display collections are the wild-flower meadows and woodlands which du Pont left in a natural state. Influenced, no doubt, by the English gardening tradition and possibly by the work of Jens Jensen, a planner for Chicago's West Park System, who was one of the early exponents of the movement for more flowing forms and indigenous planting, du Pont allowed fields to be developed naturally. Native flowers and grasses bloom side by side, with the only sign of man's controlling hand being the rough mown paths that allow visitors to wander from clumps of bergamot to clumps of Queen Anne's lace and on to clumps of goldenrod without trampling the delicate flowers underfoot.

Whether he intended it as such, the wild-flower meadows will surely be seen by modern garden designers and historians as one of the earliest and finest examples of the wild-flower movement initially expounded by William Robinson (see page 188) and Gertrude Jekyll (see page 190).

Other features of the garden include: a herb garden, a vegetable garden, a rock garden, a topiary garden, a heather garden, a maze, a dwarf conifer collection, one of the world's greatest conservatories, a lily pond, an arboretum, a special collection of orchids, ferns, roses, palms, desert plants, vast displays of annuals and perennials in season and our favourites, the two silver gardens.

Address: Longwood Gardens, Route 1, P.O. Box 501, Kennett Square, PA 19348, USA.

Liatris spicata in the wild-flower meadow.

197

1914–21 VIZCAYA An 'Old World' Italian garden, combining Renaissance, baroque and rococo influences, recreated in the tropical 'New World' of Florida by the Europhile industrialist James Deering.

The Stone Barge in the shallow waters of Biscayne Bay. Visited April 12.

Vizcaya was built between 1914 and 1916 by the industrialist James Deering (1859–1925) on a huge tract of land (some 180 acres in all) bought from Mrs William Bricknell (whose family was one of the original pioneers of Miami) at a time when the total population of the young city was little more than 10,000. Ten per cent of them were employed in the construction of the house, garden and estate. The house was finished by 1916 but the gardens were not fully completed until 1921. James Deering enjoyed eight winters at his Florida mansion before his early death in 1925 when, childless, his estate passed to his brother Charles's daughters.

They used the house infrequently and in about 1945 they sold two sections of the estate for development: the cultivated land south of the farm estate (of which more in a moment) for housing and the south garden area behind the casino, adjacent to the Bay, for a school and hospital complex, retaining only the house and about 30 of the original 180 acres bought by James Deering. In 1952 Dade County purchased the land and buildings from the family who donated all its contents and art works for the establishment of a Museum of European Decorative Arts. This self-sustaining venture now receives over a quarter of a million visitors a year.

Vizcaya is the product of four men's imaginations and its success lies in the fact that they each brilliantly fulfilled their particular roles yet worked together to create a spectacularly lavish and unified whole. James Deering had the money, taste and inclination to commission and sustain the snowballing costs of his dream. Paul Chalfin (1874–1959) was the interior designer who advised on styles and purchases. Francis Burrall Hoffman Jr (1884–1980), a friend of Chalfin's, was commissioned to draw up the architectural plans.

Diego Suarez (1888–1974), a young landscape architect who had worked with Arthur Acton on the historic restoration of the Villa La Pietra in Florence, was asked to design the gardens.

Although originally a Spanish style of architecture in keeping with Florida's Spanish heritage had been muted, it soon became apparent that the passion for Italy, and, in particular, the houses and gardens of Renaissance Italy, which was shared by the four men, would dictate the architecture, conception and style of Vizcaya. The structure of the house has the appearance of a huge Italian Renaissance villa with its seventy rooms arranged around a central courtyard. Deering and Chalfin had bought a huge variety of decorative artefacts to furnish the house spanning three major stylistic periods, Renaissance, Baroque and Rococo. It is indicative of Hoffman's architectural skill that by designing a house that appeared to have been lived in for over 300 years with each successive generation adding and adapting to what had gone before, he was able to create a harmonious entity that combined both grandeur and homeliness, luxury and intimacy.

The gardens, too, emphasized these contrasting but not mutually exclusive elements. The large formal gardens extending from the south front of the house are reminiscent of a number of famous Italian gardens such as the Villa Lante (see page 34) and the Villa d'Este (see page 30). Fan-shaped, with a central axis that continues the north–south axis of the house up to the mount at the far end of the garden, it is essentially one vast room walled in with terraces and backed by formal vegetation and forests. The floor of the 'garden room' is like a richly patterned carpet with the low, clipped hedges of the parterre de broderie revealing a distinctly French influence, as do the *allées* that flank the section of the garden that leads to the water stairway which rises to the casino on the mount. From the casino, the imposing south face of the villa can be seen. Walls, balustrades, urns, sculptures, shell-lined grottoes, pools and fountains combine to create the atmosphere found in the great, classically inspired Renaissance gardens of Italy. Between the south garden and the east front of the house which faces Biscayne Bay lies the *giardino segreto* (the walled secret garden), which was an important feature of many Italian gardens, providing a more private, intimate space in which to read or dream or tryst.

The long promenade and flight of steps on the east front of the house terminates at the water's edge in a sort of wide horseshoe shape and ahead lies, not as you would expect, a vast expanse of ocean, but a large stone barge 'parked' in the harbour, achieving not only a breakwater there but also an extraordinary visual impact. Forever stationary, defying the law of the sea by its stone weight, and breaking up the expanse of the horizon by making a focal point in the middle distance, this baroque fantasy is reminiscent of Isola Bella on Lake Maggiore (see page 40).

What is different and unusual about the whole concept of Vizcaya – villa and garden together – is that it is the creation of the totally foreign 'Old World' Renaissance culture in the tropical surroundings of the 'New World', synthesizing the two by using the plants and materials of the New World to recreate the cultural ideas and images of the Old World in a tropical setting.

Visiting Vizcaya in the late twentieth century is an extraordinary experience, especially for those who have been to many of the Italian villas and gardens from which its inspiration was drawn. On the one hand, its slightly overgrown, lush, decaying grandeur is very appealing in a city where modernity is rampant but to look out from the casino and see the ghastly hospital development (albeit worthy and necessary) where once stood the south garden – an area of tropically planted islands connected by decorative bridges as well as a boathouse, tennis courts and a domed garden house linked by groves and palms – is rather depressing as it is so antithetical to Deering's original conception. Across the main road from which Vizcaya is approached many of the buildings of the original farm estate still exist and it was intended that they be restored to their original condition and incorporated into the Museum complex but I was unable to find out if this had, in fact, been done.

The heat in Miami when we visited in April was overwhelming for us northern Europeans but the numerous fountains in the garden and the delightful grottoes dripping with icy water helped to cool our overheated bodies as did the fresh lemon slush drinks in the little café adjoining the delightful gift shop full of the most charming and tempting artefacts, knick-knacks and *objets d'art*.

Address: Vizcaya Museum and Gardens, 3251 South Miami Avenue, Miami, Florida 33129, USA.

The Water Stairway.

The giardino segreto.

Decorative term at the entrance.

The Lizard Fountain.

1921–41 DUMBARTON OAKS Beatrix Farrand's creation of an 'illusion of country life' in a city garden was influenced by her admiration of French, Italian and English landscape traditions yet it remained a uniquely American adaptation of the transatlantic prototypes.

In the Pebble Garden the wheatsheaf in the shallow water symbolizes the motto: As you sow, so shall you reap. Visited April 1.

Lovers' Lane Pool.

An aerial hornbeam hedge encloses the Ellipse.

Dumbarton Oaks has a rich and varied history that goes back almost 200 years. Known as the Rock of Dumbarton when the original house was built by William Hammond Dorsey in 1800, it was renamed Acrolophus in 1805 when purchased by Robert Beverley of Virginia but by 1825, its then owner John Caldwell Calhoun (1782–1850), Vice President of the United States, was referring to his house as Oakly. In 1846 this was changed briefly to Monterey when Edward Magruder Linthicum (1797–1869) bought the house and undertook an extensive programme of additions and alterations, principally to the house front, but by 1860 he had settled on The Oaks as a tribute to the huge white oaks surrounding the house and dominating the landscape.

It retained this name for sixty years until the property was purchased by Mildred and Robert Woods Bliss in 1920 when they settled for the name Dumbarton Oaks. by which it was known during their twenty years of occupancy and by which it continues to be known since their generous endowment of 16 acres of property and gardens to Harvard University in 1941 for the purpose of establishing the Dumbarton Oaks Research Library and Collection.

The heyday of the garden was during the twenty years between 1921 and 1941 when Mildred Bliss and her husband worked in close conjunction with the highly acclaimed landscape gardener Beatrix Farrand to create a garden that would give an 'illusion of country life' to its city-bound owners. The task was a challenging one: the

The Fountain Terrace.

The herbaceous borders.

house was large and imposing, the land had numerous levels and grades, and the owners were specific about certain requirements such as a swimming pool and a tennis court, plenty of green foliage in winter and flowers for enjoyment in spring and autumn as the Blisses spent most summers elsewhere. Nevertheless, despite these strictures or perhaps because of them, Farrand created a garden that has been admired and praised over the decades for its variety, complexity and resonance. It represents 'a uniquely American adaptation of the classical Mediterranean garden form which travelling Americans came to admire in the late 19th century and which was so eloquently described by Edith Wharton in *Italian Villas and Their Gardens*, as Diane Kostial McGuire puts it in her foreword to Beatrix Farrand's *Plant Book for Dumbarton Oaks*.

The Italian, French and English influences (particularly those of Gertrude Jekyll whose planting designs Farrand greatly admired and whose notes and papers she bought when they were auctioned by Jekyll's nephew after her death) are very strong throughout the garden but always as inspiration, not as prototypes to be copied slavishly.

Thus the more formal areas near the house are arranged on the eastern side as a series of 'garden rooms' each with its particular characteristics or themes, each separate but linked so that the visitor is enticed from one to the next: the Star Garden, the Green Garden, the Beech Terrace, the Urn Terrace, the Rose Garden, the Fountain Terrace, to the Lover's Lane Pool. On the north side of the house a series of graded, descending terraces creates an interesting false perspective that makes the vista seem larger than it actually is and looks down over the less formal areas of the garden which, in spring, are ablaze with masses of flowering bulbs. The lower garden also includes the dramatic area known as the Ellipse where a double row of American hornbeams, clipped into an aerial hedge 16 feet high and 15 feet wide, surrounds an antique fountain. Coming back up the slope towards the house from the Ellipse, there is an English style herbaceous border on the left and, on the right, the Pebble Garden whose wheatsheaf symbolizes the motto: 'As you sow, so shall you reap'.

When Mildred Bliss bequeathed her beloved garden to Harvard University, the first Director of Dumbarton Oaks, John S. Thacher, realized that the transition from private to public garden would inevitably result in changes and a diminished standard of maintenance. He conceived the brilliant idea of asking Farrand to write a plant book that would become a guide for the future upkeep and development of the garden. Although it was an arduous and time-consuming task for a woman reaching seventy, her meticulous documentation, not only of the plant lists for each part of the garden but her explanations of how and why each area was designed and planted in the way it was, has left the Trustees with a valuable record of the development of the garden at Dumbarton Oaks and a blueprint for how to proceed in the future, despite the garden's changing role.

Although Dumbarton Oaks was a complex and intricate garden with formality, freedom and naturalness combined in equal measure in the planting, we felt that the overwhelming factor that gave unity to the numerous styles was the *genius loci* which permeates the whole place.

Address: Dumbarton Oaks, Georgetown, Washington D.C. 20007, USA.

The Star Garden.

1907–47 HIDCOTE MANOR The quintessential 'garden rooms' garden, described by its creator, Lawrence Johnston, as 'a wild garden in a formal setting' which summarizes its dual characteristics perfectly, was the first garden to be taken on by the British National Trust.

Looking across the Old Garden to the Manor. Visited June 3.

Hidcote Manor Garden was created by Colonel Lawrence Johnston on the Hidcote Bartrim estate purchased at auction by his mother Mrs Gertrude Winthrop in 1907. The estate comprised an early nineteenth-century manor house, a village of about half a dozen cottages and nearly 300 acres of farmland. The house had virtually no garden to speak of except a small walled area to the south-west of the house which was planted with roses and cabbages and dominated by a

Mrs Winthrop's Garden.

huge cedar of Lebanon. Beyond the old garden walls lay fields of mediocre soil and the whole site, set high on the hillside and assailed by wind, seemed inauspicious for the creation of what was to become one of the most admired and influential gardens of the later twentieth century.

Its importance in the history of gardening is emphasized by the fact that it was the first garden to be taken on by the National Trust in 1948 when Lawrence Johnston offered it to the nation. Although Johnston was unable to bequeath an endowment to support it, it was considered so important by the National Trust's Board of Trustees that they accepted the bequest and have since worked assiduously to maintain it in the inspirational manner it was conceived and maintained by Johnston in his lifetime.

Hidcote Manor Garden covers about 10 acres and is roughly T-shaped. The top of the T is the axis that runs from the back of the house, through the Old Garden, the Circle, the Red Borders and the Stilt Garden to the gate that leads out to the fields that overlook the Vale of Evesham. The leg of the T is the axis that runs down from the two gazebos (between the Red Borders and Stilt Garden) to the ornamental gates at the edge of the fields beyond and known as the Long Walk. Around these two axes Johnston designed his garden as basically a series of

The White Garden planted with the rose Grüss an Aachen.

clearly defined compartments or 'garden rooms' as they have been popularly named. Each compartment is divided from the next by walls of high hedges that enable each section to have a complete life or atmosphere of its own. Entry from one 'room' to another is through doorways in the hedges that not only provide a passageway but create a frame through which the visitor gets an enticing view of the room which is about to be entered and through to other 'rooms' beyond.

The original Old Garden was the part Johnston worked on first and its division into small rectangular beds with low box hedges, clipped topiary and potted plants has a distinctly Tudor feel about it. Outside the Old Garden, the Circle, the Bathing Pool Garden and the circular grass garden beyond it create a charming long vista viewed from either end but at the same time present three totally separate and intimate garden rooms. Running between these three gardens on the eastern side of the Long Walk are Mrs Winthrop's Garden, a paved area with exotic plants such as agaves, yuccas, palms and day lilies, many in pots; the Green Dell, Back Border and Upper Stream Garden; and the large wooded area called Westonbirt named in honour of the famous arboretum. On the western side of the Long Walk, below the Stilt Garden, are the Terrace and the Pillar Garden with a formal framework of smooth yew topiary and below and beyond that the Lower Stream Garden, the Rock Bank and the Spring Slope. The top of the T-shape, the formal Stilt Garden flanked to the north by the immaculately cut grass and trimmed hedges of the Theatre Lawn and

Clipped laurel by the Lily Pool.

Bridge in the Stream Garden.

203

Looking through to the Bathing Pool Garden at Hidcote Manor.

The Stilt Garden.

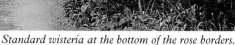

Standard wisteria at the bottom of the rose borders.

A clipped beech doorway.

to the south by the carefully structured and designed garden rooms, gives way to the west, east and south of the Long Walk to the wilder, more 'natural' areas of the garden which stand in marked contrast to the areas above. Thus, when Johnston, in later years, described Hidcote as 'a wild garden in a formal setting', he seems to have summed up perfectly the philosophy his garden espouses, a philosophy which manages to synthesize harmoniously the two opposing schools of thought that existed at the turn of the century.

There was, on the one hand, a group of architects and designers who supported the view expressed by Sedding in *Garden Craft New and Old* (1891) and Blomfield in *The Formal Garden in England* (1892) who, influenced by English medieval and Roman Renaissance garden traditions, recommended that the garden be treated as an extension of the house by creating a series of rooms.

On the other hand, William Robinson in *Garden Design and Architect's Gardens* (1892) berated the formalization favoured by Sedding and Blomfield, saying that only a thorough knowledge of plants was essential for planning a garden and he condemned the artificiality of formal plans, terracing and clipped hedges.

According to Ethne Clarke in her excellent book

Hidcote: The Making of a Garden, the argument might have continued unchecked if Gertrude Jekyll hadn't stepped in as arbiter and declared that both sides had a point. Plants were important as Robinson said and the new varieties made available in the nineteenth century could be used to great effect but, she pointed out, the effect might be seen to greater advantage in the more formal setting advocated by Sedding and Blomfield.

Hidcote proves her point. It is a highly successful marriage of the two views. Therein lies its importance in modern garden history. Johnston has drawn on numerous garden traditions in the creation of Hidcote and, by his particular vision, succeeded in synthesizing all the disparate elements into a new and original whole that has come to be seen (ironically since he is American by birth and European by upbringing) as quintessentially English.

Hugely popular, this garden is the most visited National Trust Garden after Sissinghurst and deservedly so.

Address: Hidcote Manor Garden, Hidcote Bartrim, Chipping Campden, Gloucestershire, England.

View down the Long Walk.

Potting sheds as you enter the garden.

(1578) 1926–73 CRATHES A Jekyll-inspired colour garden which is a fine example of a plantsman's garden, in which colour, texture and type of plant dominate the design, set within the formal structure of an ancient Scottish castle.

In the Lower Garden the subtle blues and greys of the border augment the stronger pinks, whites and reds of the roses. Visited July 18.

Crathes Castle and gardens date back to the mid-sixteenth century although the Burnett family who built it and lived in it until the mid-twentieth century had lived in the area for the previous 250 years on a small island fort in the middle of the Loch of Leys, now a partially drained marsh near Banchory. The political and religious struggles of the Reformation benefited the Burnett family in terms of land acquisition so this, combined with the needs of a rapidly expanding family, prompted Alexander Burnett (1529–74) to start building the castle at Crathes in 1749. Unfortunately, he became embroiled in fighting for Mary Queen of Scots and it was not until his great grandson Alexander inherited the property in 1578 that the last stage of the building was completed.

Very little seems to be known about the early layout of the, gardens at Crathes but there is no doubt that the huge, clipped yew hedges and the enormous, clipped yew topiary which dominate and frame sections of the gardens on the upper level are very ancient. They were planted in 1702 by the 3rd Baronet, Sir Thomas, who also planted the avenues of limes and extended the castle by an extra wing. All this in between fathering twenty-one children with his wife Margaret in the space of twenty-two years!

The walled garden has eight sections: four on the upper level and four below and each area is planted in a particular way reflecting the interests of the family members during this century.

The importance of the garden and its current splendour is due, in great part, to the passion, flair and energy of Sir James and his wife Sybil Burnett of Leys who inherited the property in 1926. Their design and planting reflect the influence of William Robinson (see page 188) and Gertrude Jekyll (see page 190) whose belief that the plants themselves (their colour and type) were the most important aspect of garden design had obviously been incorporated into the consciousness of Sir James and Lady Sybil.

Gertrude Jekyll did, in fact, visit Crathes in about 1895 and a painting, done by George Ellwood at that time and used to illustrate her account of it, shows a garden much tidier and more controlled than that which exists today. Jekyll praised the 'brilliancy of the colour masses' and it is this which Lady Burnett successfully captured in her plantings of the herbaceous borders and the Colour Garden which was completed in 1932 and is considered a unique achievement in the style of modern gardening. In 1973, with the aid of her head gardener, the Golden Garden was constructed, fulfilling a plan conceived by Lady Burnett from Gertrude Jekyll's book *Colour Schemes for Flower Gardens*. Beyond the wall by the north walled borders at the end of the garden farthest from the house, a gate leads into the Wild Garden, an area where autumn colours are particularly striking and would have undoubtedly met with William Robinson's approval.

The glasshouses, originally built at the turn of the century, had become very dilapidated over the decades but in 1978 they were completely rebuilt. They now house some very rare plants and collections such as the Malmaison carnations and it is hoped eventually to display the kinds of fruit, flowers and ornamental plants that would have been originally grown there.

Crathes is considered a plantsman's paradise and though it is one of Scotland's finest gardens many consider that it has a peculiarly English feel to it.

Address: Crathes Castle Garden, Banchory, Grampian, Scotland.

The June Borders.   A centrepiece to one of the tiny lawns.

Topiary in the Upper Garden.   The White Borders.

Gate leading to the Wild Garden.   Climbing roses on an impressive wooden trellis.

1910–80 GREAT DIXTER A Lloyd and Lutyens design of 'garden rooms' enclosed with topiary to create a feeling of intimacy and to provide protection for tender plants, together with the later addition of a Robinson-inspired, wild-flower meadow.

The Topiary Garden. Visited May 30.

Great Dixter is a fifteenth-century Manor house which was purchased by Nathaniel Lloyd in 1910. A well-known garden writer himself, he employed Edwin Lutyens to make alterations to the house and redesign the gardens which, having remained in the family (it is now the home of his son, the author and plantsman Christopher Lloyd) have been beautifully maintained and developed over the past eighty years as a series of gardens including a topiary garden, a rose garden, a mixed flower and vegetable garden, a wild-flower meadow and a long mixed border.

In 1915 Nathanial Lloyd published his book *Garden Craftsmanship in Box and Yew* which was an authoritative

Tree Lupins.

guide to making garden enclosures and topiary, and many of his ideas were put into practice in the design of his own garden. With the house at the centre of the plot and the garden all around it, the various hedged 'rooms' give a feeling of intimacy and accessibility to the whole garden. Creating small, intimate, enclosed areas was a clever way of providing shelter and protection for the numerous new and other tender plants that were becoming available from all over the world in the early decades of the twentieth century.

Christopher Lloyd doesn't share his father's passion for creating topiary but he feels that the formality it creates in the garden's design counterbalances and offsets the informality of the planting in the English cottage garden tradition which he favours.

Although William Robinson poured scorn on Nathanial Lloyd's book, in fact Lloyd had a great deal of sympathy for the ideas Robinson expressed in *The Wild Garden* and *The English Flower Garden*, as can be seen in the planting at Great Dixter, and this has been developed even further by Christopher Lloyd in the wild-flower meadow that he has planted on the property. In this century, there is no other garden of this kind that has allowed nature to take its own course so close to a garden which has been largely and, of necessity, continuously shaped by man. The field contains masses of orchids in spring and is a delight to walk through.

Address: Great Dixter, Dixter Road, Northiam, East Sussex, England.

Welsh Poppies create an informal atmosphere in the garden.

The wild-flower meadow.

Daisies and valerian maintain the informal feel.

Libertia formosa through a brick archway.

1930–67 SISSINGHURST CASTLE A series of separate gardens or 'garden rooms', each with its own individual planting schemes and arrangements, is the inspired creation of the combined talents of Vita Sackville-West and her husband Harold Nicholson.

The exuberant planting in the White Garden. Visited June 7.

White Wisteria floribunda 'Alba'.

Brick paths lead from one 'garden room' to another.

Sissinghurst Castle Garden was developed in the second quarter of the twentieth century by Vita Sackville-West and her husband Harold Nicholson on a virtually derelict site that they purchased in 1930 which had a fascinating history going back many centuries.

In medieval times a moated manor house stood on the site which was subsequently replaced in the sixteenth century by an elaborate mansion, built by the Baker family, who were related by marriage to the Sackvilles of Knole – Vita's family home during her childhood. Queen Elizabeth I spent three nights at Sissinghurst in 1570 but the family fortunes declined during the seventeenth century when Sir John Baker backed the wrong side in the Civil War. By 1756 the house was let to the Government as a prison camp for French prisoners of war. The damage they did during their seven-year tenancy was so great that two-thirds of the house was demolished at the end of the war. What was left was used as a Poor House until 1855 when the estate reverted to the Cornwallis family who built the imposing farmhouse and left the original, almost uninhabitable remains of the house to decay still further.

Vita Sackville-West fell in love with it when she viewed the estate in 1930 and within three weeks of her first visit she had paid £12,375 for the castle ruin, the castle farm and 350 acres of surrounding land, knowing instinctively that here lay the potential for the new garden she wanted to create, as her old one at Long Barn near Knole had become inexorably threatened by encroaching

The Rose Garden.

The Cottage Garden.

development. The Nicholsons spent the next thirty-two years creating the garden which was then given to the National Trust in 1967 by their sons, a year before Harold's death and six years after Vita's, because the escalating costs of maintenance could only hope to be covered if the garden was made over to that guardian of so many wonderful gardens.

An early aerial photograph of 1932 shows the coach house/stable/cottage block, the lone tower, the Priest's House and the south cottage surrounded by lawn and endless beds of cabbages yet, from this inauspicious, overgrown mess, Vita and Harold created a garden that was to become regarded as the epitome of Englishness and recognized as one of the most influential gardens of the twentieth century.

Influenced by Gertrude Jekyll (Vita was taken as a child to visit her at Munstead Wood), William Robinson and Lawrence Johnston, Sissinghurst nevertheless has its own unique character, created by blending the talents and vision of two very different personalities to produce a perfect harmony: Harold's love of architectural classicism and strong sense of symmetry and form together with Vita's romanticism, strong sense of colour and texture and intimate knowledge of plants, combined to create a garden that is, in their son's words, very much 'their joint achievement'.

The garden covers about 4 hectares and is arranged as a series of separate gardens or 'garden rooms,' linked by vistas between them. Despite its relatively small size, this layout makes the visitor feel that it is considerably bigger than it actually is. 'A combination of expectation and surprise' was the Nicholsons' aim and each garden is designed with that philosophy in mind.

The Rose Garden with its *rondel* in the centre, a disc of mown grass surrounded by a circle of yew hedges, designed by Harold, and the White Garden, which is composed almost entirely of white flowers and pale grey foliage, are the two most famous of the separate gardens at Sissinghurst but the Herb Garden, the Lime Walk, the Orchard, Nuttery, Moat Walk, Yew Walk and Tower Lawn each have their own individual planting schemes and arrangements that are much admired by the numerous visitors from all over the world that visit the garden daily.

The sheer volume of people that pass through the garden each year (more than the number that visit any other National Trust Garden in England) has created problems in maintaining the garden's structure according to the Nicholsons' vision, so the National Trust actively pursues policies (such as high entry charges) to try and discourage too many visitors at Sissinghurst. For this reason, we originally intended to leave the garden out of this book but it has been so important and influential in the history of twentieth-century gardening that we felt we couldn't ignore it.

Address: Sissinghurst Castle Garden, Sissinghurst, Nr Cranbrook, Kent, England.

Harold's rondel at the centre of the Rose Garden.

The Nuttery.

1933–61 TINTINHULL HOUSE Home of Phyllis Reiss and now Penelope Hobhouse – two influential garden designers whose sense of form is matched by imaginative planting schemes in which shape, texture and colour play an essential role in creating a harmonious whole.

Looking up the main axis towards the house. Visited June 4.

Tintinhull House was built in the sixteenth century with the West Front of mellowed Ham Stone added in 1722. The walled forecourt with its gate piers surmounted by stone eagles and thus known as Eagle Court also dates from this period but although documentation is scarce, it seems that the Azalea Garden, beyond the Eagle Court, did not exist in its present form in 1905. However, it can be seen with its central path lined with clipped box mounds in photographs dated 1931 and sometime between those two dates it is thought that Dr Price, a cultured churchman of ample means with no parish duties who lived at Tintinhull between 1905 and 1920, was responsible for laying out the Azalea Garden and the

The Armillary Sphere.

Fountain Garden, possibly with some helpful advice from Harold Peto (1854–1933) whom he almost certainly knew.

In 1933 Captain and Mrs Reiss bought the property and set about developing the area to the north and north-west of the house. Cedar Court (so called because of the huge cedar of Lebanon that dominated the garden until it was felled in about 1992 owing to disease) was created from a muddy paddock followed, in 1947, by the creation of a Pool Garden in place of the tennis court, to commemorate Mrs Reiss's nephew, Michael Lucas, who was killed in action in the Second World War.

After her husband's death in 1947 Phyllis Reiss continued the development of the garden until her death in 1961. In 1954 she generously donated the property to the National Trust and in her last years she worked closely with the National Trust's Gardens Adviser, Graham Stuart Thomas, to make a definitive inventory of the plants in the garden. In 1979 Penelope Hobhouse, the well-known garden writer and designer, became the National Trust's tenant at Tintinhull and she has taken on the rôle of interpreting how she feels Mrs Reiss would have planted the garden if she were still alive: 'A Hidcote in Miniature; two acres instead of ten,' she feels. Dame Sylvia Crowe in *Garden Design* (1958) wrote: 'The garden as a whole is in the Hidcote tradition because it consists of a series of carefully proportioned spaces, firmly defined within the hedges or walls, within which are free-growing plants'.

These comments made approximately thirty years

From the Fountain Garden looking towards the Kitchen Garden.

apart both summarise its essence. Six main 'garden rooms' formally organised in a rectangular space: three 'rooms' with a central axis running right through them and directly overlooked by the house; the other three larger 'rooms' running parallel to the first three but situated to the north of the building. Each area has been beautifully planted with flowers, trees, shrubs and herbaceous borders that have been carefully designed to give colour and texture to the garden all year round. Each area is arranged to complement and contrast with the other areas.

In 1983 Penelope Hobhouse described her ideal garden as follows:

'I should wish my ideal garden to assume the functions of a sculpture gallery, with plants as well as statues and stonework contributing architectural shape and form. At the same time the whole or each part of the garden should have . . . a strong sense of composition, attained by skilful use of harmony and contrast between shapes of plants, and between colours and textures of leaves and flowers . . . The separate and defined areas within the whole must be held together by planting schemes which entice the visitor on . . .'

It hardly seems surprising that the National Trust allowed her to be custodian of Phyllis Reiss's garden at Tintinhull.

Delicious home-made cakes and teas are available in the courtyard barn – all profits to the upkeep of St Margaret's Church, Tintinhull.

Address: Tintinhull House Garden, Tintinhull, Yeovil, Somerset, England.

The Pool Garden with the Summer House.

Nepeta-lined paths in the Kitchen Garden.

1937–69 EAST LAMBROOK MANOR A cottage garden modelled on the 'garden rooms' concept, described by its creator Margery Fish as 'jungle gardening', which contains a broad collection of rare, unusual and interesting plants.

The front lawn in the shade of the giant maple. Visited June 5.

East Lambrook Manor was purchased by Walter and Margery Fish in 1937. Both the house and gardens were in a very poor state of repair but Margery and Walter set about the job of restoration with energy and enthusiasm, learning as they went. The story of the creation of the lovely garden at East Lambrook is recorded in Margery Fish's book *We Made a Garden*, mistakes and all. Margery came to gardening in her late forties when she married Walter who, as editor of the *Daily Mail*, had been her boss.

Walter knew a surprising amount about gardening and had firm ideas about form and structure so his views probably determined the general layout of the garden. However, his taste in plants was at odds with Margery's. According to Helen Penn in *An Englishwoman's Garden*, Walter was 'a dahlia, delphinium and lupin man' and disliked many of Margery's plants, pulling them up and depositing them on the path like 'a row of dead rats'.

However, after Walter's death in 1947, Margery was able to pursue her passion for rare, unusual and interesting plants unabated. Her enthusiasm was infectious and through her books, broadcasts and lectures she was a highly popular and influential plantswoman and her garden was a source of inspiration to many – Lanning Roper, Esther Merton, Phyllis Reiss and Penelope Hobhouse among them.

After Margery's death in 1969 her sister and nephew maintained the property until 1984. It then stood empty for a year but a loyal staff looked after the garden until it was purchased in 1985 by Mr and Mrs Andrew Norton, the current owners, who are committed to maintaining the garden as a living and developing memorial to its creator.

The garden is rectangular shaped with the house in the bottom left-hand corner if one enters through the main gate (not car park), and the old converted Malt House where one buys entrance tickets is virtually in the middle of the garden. The whole design is really a series of self-contained areas or intimate 'garden rooms' with little paths which lead, in maze-like fashion, from one section to another. Although quite small, the garden actually seems much bigger than it is because there is so much to see and enjoy. The profusion of lavender, geraniums, hellebores and primulas running riot over beds and paths create a delightful, rich cottage garden feel. 'Jungle gardening', Margery called it. One area, the Coliseum with its row of shaped junipers, is particularly charming. Other areas include the White Garden, the Silver Garden, the Green Garden and The Rock Garden. The Nursery has been developed and expanded not only to maintain the garden stock but to supply plants for visitors and to meet the increasing mail order demand.

Overall, this pretty and charming garden shows how a relatively small area can be developed to contain numerous delights – it is like a cross between a traditional cottage garden and a mini-Hidcote.

Address: East Lambrook Manor, Nr South Petherton, Somerset, England.

Shrubs and trees dominate the structure of the garden and obscure the buildings.

The distinctive egg-shaped junipers of the Coliseum.

The path leading from the back of the house.

View from the door of the Malt House.

1697 BARNSLEY HOUSE (Renovated 1951–90s) Family home of Rosemary Verey where the delicate balance of informal cottage planting within a formal framework of crossing axes has created a garden that has become one of the most influential in the late twentieth century.

View from the potager across the lane to the house. Visited June 6.

Barnsley House, a mellow, stone, Queen Anne house built in 1697, has been the family home of David and Rosemary Verey since 1951. In those early days, their four young children used the garden as an open-air playroom but, in the 1960s, the Vereys started to develop the four-acre garden into the delightful place it is today. Rosemary's knowledge of botanical and garden history and of plants, and her husband's experience as an architectural historian, have enabled them to combine their skills in formulating the design, layout and planting of the garden.

Influenced by Hidcote and Sissinghurst, the Vereys were attracted to the idea of a garden with a formal layout based on interconnected axes but at the same time they felt that too rigid an adherence to formality or 'garden rooms' would be at odds with the house and their vision of an ideal garden. The areas of the garden are thus not strictly defined or separated by walls or hedges (except the old Cotswold stone wall that encloses the whole garden) but divided by paths and borders.

The house, which is more or less in the centre of the garden, has a longish, tree-lined driveway on one side but is approached by garden visitors through a gateway in the lane at the back of the house through a yew-lined walk planted in 1948. Crossed at right angles, almost as soon as you enter the gate, by a lime *allée* with a path of large Welsh pebble stones laid by David, it terminates with an intimate, lush, laburnum tunnel. A small,

The lime walk.

The Knot Garden, with the gothic summer house.

The classical temple behind the goldfish pool.

enclosed secret area at the end of the lime walk axis nearest to the greenhouse contains an eighteenth-century classical temple from nearby Fairford Park which was given to the Vereys by the Cook Trust but looks as though it was tailor-made for the lily pool garden.

Another lovely little building lies at the end of a grassy path lined with domed, yellow-foliaged hedges. This is a gothic summer house erected in 1771 by the incumbent rector, the Reverend Charles Coxwell. It was he who also built the stone walls that enclose the whole garden. Known as Mrs Coxwell's Alcove, it houses the family's bicycles (or at least did the day we visited) and is set at an interesting angle which enables anyone within to see not only down the path and across to the knot garden but also to look down across the expanse of the main lawn towards the drive.

Perhaps the most original feature of the Verey's garden is the potager which is situated on the outside of the main garden directly across the lane from the gateway already mentioned. Like a mini-Villandry (see page 56), the vegetable garden is a rectangular shape with a main axis running from the tennis court to the far trellis fence, parallel to the lane, and three main cross axes that divide the area into six sections that symmetrically match each other across the central path. The formal layout, based on a seventeenth-century design, is softened by colour, texture, scent, beauty and usefulness because, it is said, the garden provides a generous proportion of the family's diet.

Helen Penn in *An Englishwoman's Garden* says that Rosemary Verey's style – a combination of informal cottage planting within a formal framework – has been dubbed – 'the look for the 1980s' because it has been so frequently copied by other garden designers. It is so eminently adaptable and suitable for a small-to medium-sized garden, showing as at East Lambrook Manor (see pages 214–215) or Tintinhull, (see pages 212–213) how the general principles of Hidcote (see pages 202–205) can be put into practice on a much smaller scale. However, the disadvantage is that it is very high maintenance gardening – it is a never-ending job to maintain the correct balance of controlled riotousness. Remove the vigilant overseeing eye and it quickly degenerates into a jungle.

One of the most charming things about Barnsley House is the feeling that it is still very much a family home lived in by those who have created its grounds. One of the Vereys' sons, Charles, designs beautiful garden furniture – tables, chairs, sun loungers, etc. – which are dotted around the garden and on display in the antique shop which is in part of the house.

Address: Barnsley House, Barnsley, Nr Cirencester, Gloucestershire, England.

The laburnum tunnel.

1967–90s BETH CHATTO'S GARDEN Natural plant associations in conjunction with soil suitability and low maintenance are the three underlying principles of this eponymous, late twentieth-century garden.

The large dry gravel garden that replaces the old car park. Visited May 2.

Delicate green and yellow euphorbia under the silver birches.

The Nursery.

Beth Chatto's Garden (an area now comprising about 4 acres) was started in 1967 when she and her husband decided to build a house on part of their fruit farm thus enabling them to create a completely new garden from scratch. The garden which evolved and expanded over the next two decades has become one of the most influential modern gardens of the post-war era.

Essex, as Beth Chatto has been quick to point out, is not renowned for its gardens, principally because its climate is one of the driest in England. However, challenged rather than deterred by this regional problem, the Chattos chose a site that was an overgrown, shallow valley running between their farm and their neighbours'. 'Overgrown and neglected . . . the sun-facing slopes consisted of coarse gravel and fine sand. The opposite slope was made of black, water-retaining, acid silt while the lowest levels were wet clay. Here were wildly varying conditions offering homes for a far greater range of plants than we had been able to grow before,' wrote Beth Chatto in her account of the garden in *The Englishwoman's Garden* edited by Alvide Lees-Milne and Rosemary Verey. In that last sentence lies the key to her philosophy of gardening and her importance to the development of gardens in the late twentieth century.

The planting and development of the three main areas in her garden – the Mediterranean Garden, the Woodland garden and the Water Gardens – always take consideration of the natural association of plants and the fact that 'plants grow better and look better if planted as nearly as possible in the kind of conditions to which they have been adapted' (ibid.).

Thus, the area nearest the house which consists of sun-baked gravel slopes has been planted with the kind

Looking down through the series of spring fed ponds in the Damp Garden.

of Mediterranean plants that flourish in such conditions (rosemary, artemesia, santolina and cistus), while plants that thrive in moist conditions are at home on the banks of the five, spring fed ponds that have grown from the initial small lily pond that was gorged out of the ditch bed. Between these two extremes woodland bulbs, plants and shrubs provide throughout the year a succession of interesting flowers and foliage in the lightly shaded, moist areas of the garden.

Busy with writing, running a plant nursery and showing at the Chelsea Flower Show, Beth Chatto has always considered low maintenance in the garden as a top priority. 'I relished those areas that were made trouble free by dense coverings of plants.' She felt that if she could cut down on weeding, there would be more time to create and develop new ideas so planting with a view to controlling weeds has always been at the forefront of her mind.

Although she admits her garden is larger than average, Beth Chatto feels that the many smaller areas into which it divides can provide inspiration for those with less space.

Her emphasis on plant selection and grouping in a naturalistic way, and her recognition of the importance of low maintenance in an area where paid help is both difficult to find and expensive to sustain, has won her a huge audience of admirers and imitators.

Address: Beth Chatto Gardens, Elmstead Market, Colchester, Essex, England.

The Damp Garden.

Simple bark paths match the informal planting.

1932–80 THE SAVILL AND VALLEY GARDENS Famed for its woodland garden and pioneering national collections these gardens were masterminded by Sir Eric Savill on the Windsor Estate with the support and encouragement of the Royal Family.

Azaleas border the Upper Pond in the Savill Garden. Visited May 16.

The Savill Garden is a 35-acre area within Windsor Great Park which itself covers 4500 acres of woodland, ancient hunting forest and parkland adjoining Windsor Castle and owned by the Royal Family.

Windsor Great Park was originally transformed from heathland and bog into magnificent landscaped parkland between 1740 and 1820 under the guidance of William, Duke of Cumberland (1721–65), King George II's third son, and Henry, Duke of Cumberland (1745–90), King George III's brother, who were both Rangers of the Great Park. However, it was not until the twentieth century that the 35-acre Savill Garden and subsequently the 400-acre Valley Gardens were systematically landscaped and planted by Eric Savill (1895–1980), to create the gardens that we see today.

Originally Deputy Surveyor and then Deputy Ranger of the Great Park, Eric Savill first began in 1932 to lay out the area now known as the Willow Garden adjacent to where some sort of nursery garden for the production of park trees already existed and which was subsequently developed into the herbaceous borders and rose gardens. Savill claimed that the Royal couple King George V and Queen Mary gave him 'the green light' for continuing the development of the garden when they praised his efforts on a visit in the very early days, with the following remark: 'It is very small, Mr Savill, but very nice.' From

then on, work continued unabated (except for a hold-up during the Second World War) on, first, the Bog Garden, as it was originally known and then, in 1947, when it was virtually completed, on the Valley Gardens, half a mile away at Virginia Water.

In 1951 the smaller garden known as the Bog Garden was renamed the Savill Garden by the command of King George VI in honour of its creator and in 1955 Eric Savill was knighted by Queen Elizabeth II in recognition of his services and horticultural achievements in the Great Park.

As Director of Gardens from 1959 to 1980 Sir Eric Savill continued to direct and oversee the continuing changes and developments essential to all great gardens if they are to remain flourishing and 'living' spaces, both literally and metaphorically, hence the subsequent additions of a restaurant and gift shop, a Dry Garden, the Jubilee Garden and a new arboretum. He died in 1980 just two years before the garden celebrated its Golden Jubilee and it remains a monument to his landscaping and horticultural genius.

In the history of gardens the Savill Garden stands out for three reasons. Firstly, as an incomparable example of a woodland garden – Savill's original vision remains the overriding concern of the garden today. Secondly, an increasingly important function of both the gardens is to

The Azalea Valley in the Valley Garden.

provide suitable homes for new plants, enabling them to be assessed for general use in British gardens, and thirdly, as a place for conserving our landscape, native and garden plants by developing national collections of interesting or threatened groups. In both gardens the rhododendrons predominate and represent the greatest cultivated planting of wild rhododendrons in the world, now designated the British National Collection, and there are also national collections of hollies, ilex species and cultivars, dwarf and slower growing conifers, magnolias, pieris, mahonia and pernettya.

American skunk weed lining the stream.

The development of the Valley Garden was done in an informal manner, particularly the Heather Garden where the undulations of the soil mounds and walls of the original gravel pits were not levelled but incorporated into the design and planting plan. Everywhere, the aim of planting has been to provide as much variation of colour, flower, fruit and foliage as possible so that there is something of interest for visitors at all times of year. Sadly, huge losses of the biggest trees in the 1987 and 1990 storms have thinned the highest canopy level considerably, thus detracting from the enclosed, woodland feel in some areas, but the extra light has encouraged the development of plants and shrubs in the middle and lower canopies to compensate.

Address: The Savill Garden and the Valley Garden, Windsor Great Park, Wick Lane and Wick Road, Englefield Green, Surrey, England

The Heather Garden.

1550s MOTTISFONT ABBEY GARDEN (Replanted 1957) Home of the National Rose Collection, which has been created in two, walled, Tudor kitchen gardens, re-designed by Graham Stuart Thomas, to display the collection superbly.

A view over the first of Graham Thomas's plantings in the walled kitchen gardens.

Mottisfont Abbey Garden surrounds the Tudor mansion of Mottisfont Abbey which was given to William Sandys, the King's Chamberlain, by Henry VIII after the Dissolution of the Monasteries in 1536. However, Mottisfont's history reaches back to Saxon times whence its name derives. Mottisfont was the moot, or meeting place, by the fountain. The font, or spring, to which the name alludes still throws up clear water (sometimes as much as 300 gallons per minute) in a shaded dell near the old house. The stately front of the mansion which we see today was built in the eighteenth century but remnants of the nave arches of the priory church can still be seen on the north front. Further enlargements of the house and grounds took place in the nineteenth century when magnificent trees were planted and lawns, parkland and three walled gardens were established.

In 1957 the grounds and gardens of Mottisfont were given to the National Trust by Mrs Gilbert Russell though she still retained her tenancy. One walled garden was designated a car park but when, in 1972, Mrs Russell wanted to give up her tenancy on the other two walled gardens, the National Trust asked Graham Stuart Thomas, who was then their Gardens Adviser, to design a rose garden in the old walled garden at Mottisfont. This was opened in 1972 and a second rose garden, in the adjoining old walled kitchen garden, was opened in 1987.

Graham Stuart Thomas had already done a great deal of practical work collecting species roses, old roses and early nineteenth-century hybrids so, as the rose garden at Mottisfont developed and became the greatest collection of old roses in Britain, the National Trust decided to make the rose garden at Mottisfont the home of the National Collections of pre-1900 shrub roses. The National Collections of various plants that exist in gardens all over Britain, designated by the National Council for the Conservation of Plants and Gardens (NCCPG), are an important aspect of garden history. Over the centuries gardens have, of course, specialized in growing particular plants, trees or shrubs. The early monastery herb gardens and the Empress Joséphine's collection of roses at Malmaison are examples of specialized concentrated collections. The importance of such National Collections is that they preserve for posterity plants that might otherwise be lost in the rush to develop new hybrids and they also enable garden or plant historians and visitors to make a study of a particular genus in one spot.

The first rose garden at Mottisfont created a number of practical difficulties related to the fact that the only entrance was an old doorway too small for any modern arm- and back-saving machinery to pass through. All the manure had to be wheelbarrowed in and all the digging had to be done by hand. However, the fact that it had been a well-stocked kitchen garden meant that the soil was in good shape for Thomas to achieve 'the appearance of a collection of roses of the late nineteenth century'.

The squarish garden divides into four, each quarter containing a small lawn with cross paths that meet at a central pool surrounded by eight clipped yews. Gravel paths, hedged with box, run parallel to the old brick walls and the central path leads directly to the doorway in the opposite wall which opens into the second rose garden. The traditional layout of the kitchen garden had provided a perfect setting for an old rose garden with some old apple trees to act as pillars for climbers and the old herbaceous borders to provide colour and contrast to the roses. The disadvantage, though, of this charming compactness has been for the numerous visitors that now come from all over the world. Not so, however, in the second walled garden which had been laid out not as a kitchen garden but as a croquet lawn. Here, there were wide gates which enabled tractors to enter so the plans drawn up for this garden intentionally tried to create a very different atmosphere, despite the fact that the philosophy of planting old roses remained essentially the same.

This garden is much more spacious, lighter and open in feel than the first rose garden. Here the roses are underplanted with grey-leaved perennials and there are no lawns and hedges but wide straight paths that follow the lines of the walls and then gently curving paths that lead to the central octagonal bower up whose supporting chambered oak posts grow alternately the beautiful ramblers Blue Magenta and Debutante.

Two, tiled, corner summer houses are another feature that act not only as bowers on which to grow roses but, as importantly according to Thomas, also act as rain shelters for visitors who get caught out by Britain's notorious climate.

Address: Mottisfont Abbey Garden, Mottisfont, Nr Romsey, Hampshire, England.

The Octagonal Bower in the second rose garden.

The old shrub rose Celsiana.

The Rose Garden at Castle Howard.

Arley Hall.

Sissinghurst.

David Austin Roses.

Rousham House.

The Alhambra Palace.

The Rose Garden at Bagatelle.

Herrenhausen.

Blenheim Palace.

Hever Castle.

Dumbarton Oaks.

Mottisfont Abbey.

225

The still lake at Stourhead in Autumn.

Acer japonicum. (Photographed by Bill Bakaitis)

Maples in Maine. (Photographed by Bill Bakaitis)

Leslie Land's Garden. (Photographed by Bill Bakaitis)

Vitis 'Brant'.

Euonymus alatus.

Japanese maple at Shanagarry Pottery.

Liquidambar styraciflua.

Sugar maples in all their New England glory. (Photographed by Bill Bakaitis)

227

The Hydrangeas in the valley bottom at Trebah.

Trebah Garden in Cornwall (England), like Glendurgan which is only 500 yards away, was owned by the Fox family in the nineteenth century. Charles Fox started planting this stunning ravine garden with hundreds of exotic and tender plants in the 1840s and it now boasts a collection of rare and mature trees, glades of 100-year-old tree ferns and almost 3 acres of the most lovely blue, white and mauve hydrangeas.

A dramatic tor at Eagle's Nest.

Eagle's Nest in Cornwall (England), home of the painter Patrick Heron, was created by the amateur painter and horticulturist W. Arnold Foster who lived there until his death in 1951. His interest in wind tolerant plants (especially those from New Zealand) was put into practice in his planting plans at Eagle's Nest which is built on an exposed hill above Zennor, incorporating the ancient tors into the overall design.

Looking across the Hudson River from Wave Hill.

The Wave Hill estate in New York City (USA), comprising a number of buildings and 28 acres of gardens and woodlands overlooking the Hudson River and New Jersey's Palisades, was used in the middle of the nineteenth century as a residence for famous visitors ranging from Twain to Thackeray to Roosevelt. However, it was brought by the conservationist and banker George Perkins at the beginning of the twentieth century and given by his family to the city in 1960, since which time The Wave Hill Center for Environmental Studies has used its spectacular setting to undertake programmes in horticulture, landscape design and forest restoration and preservation. At the same time, the Curator of the Gardens, Marco Polo Stufano, has made a special feature of the flower garden and the wild garden which he feels are 'perhaps the most interesting [part of the overall gardens] from a plantsman's point of view'.

Looking vertically down from the castle walls into the garden at St Michael's Mount.

St Michael's Mount (England), a tiny island a mile off the Cornish coast, was the site of a Benedictine chapel in the eleventh century. This castle on the mound dates from the fourteenth century and is still inhabited by the St Aubyn family who, over the centuries, have created a unique maritime garden on steep terraces below the castle wall facing out to sea, where sub-tropical species flourish despite their exposure to the elements.

1947 EVERGLADES NATIONAL PARK One of the world's greatest natural botanic 'gardens' of native plants in a unique but fragile ecosystem that is constantly threatened by man's thoughtless overuse of the water that is so essential to the River of Grass's survival.

The viewing platform over Eco Pond near Flamingo Visitor Centre. Visited April 12.

The Everglades National Park was formally established in 1947 by Harry S. Truman to protect an extraordinary and unique ecosystem that Marjorie Stoneman Douglas in her highly acclaimed book on the area, published in the same year, had described so evocatively in its title as *Everglades: River of Grass.*

Covering an area of almost one and a half million acres (in fact most of the south-western tip of Florida, west of Miami), the Everglades National Park is an exceptional environment with a subtropical climate that supports a delicately balanced ecosystem comprising a wide range of flora, fauna and aquatic creatures whose existence is dependent on each other and the natural water cycle of the region, and which has become increasingly threatened by the population expansion and urban growth of the state of Florida.

Named *Pa-Hay Okee*, 'grassy waters' by the native American Indians, this name for the Everglades (which covers an area six times greater than that officially designated as The Everglades National Park) aptly describes the vast, flat area of water-logged sawgrass that extends for miles, relieved only by island hummocks of hardwood trees, occasional stands of cypress and slash pines and clumps of mangroves and a maze of hidden

waterways, no part of which rises more than 10 feet above sea level, the average depth being six inches. The area is home to 300 varieties of birds, 600 kinds of fish, countless mammals and 2000 diverse plant species, about 45 of which are found nowhere else in the world.

Eleven thousand years ago two indigenous groups – the Tequestas and the Calusas – emigrated to the area, establishing permanent villages. They lived in harmony with the environment, hunting and fishing for their survival, and became known as the People of the Glades. The arrival of Spaniards in the sixteenth century gradually reduced the People of the Glades to a handful of survivors by 1800. The Seminole tribes inhabited the area for several decades in the first half of the nineteenth century but after several wars with the US army they were forced out of the area, leaving about 150 Seminoles hiding in the cypress stands and sawgrass prairies. Their descendants still live within the Everglades National Park.

Despite recognition of the Everglades' importance as an International Biosphere Reserve, World Heritage Site and wetland of international importance, the twentieth century has posed numerous threats to the Everglades' environment, wildlife and plant life. For centuries its

Eco Pond, home to numerous alligators.

delicate ecosystem has depended on the annual cycle of summer rains followed by a dry winter season. However, the natural cycle has been interfered with by man. The 60 inches of summer rain that used to cause Lake Okee to overflow, thus flooding the prairie sawgrass in its slow but inexorable journey towards the Florida Bay, are now being diverted into canals and waterways to provide water for the ever-increasing population in the huge urban sprawl of Miami. Attempts to rectify the drought caused in the Everglades by this diversion of water, by opening the canals and falsely flooding the land, have not been successful because it does not always take place at the right time of year. Furthermore, the seepage of agricultural and industrial chemicals and pesticides into the underground water system of Southern Florida is having a profoundly adverse effect on the health of the animals and plants. The whole Everglades system depends on the natural water cycle; the fact that it has constantly been interfered with during this century has

caused a major decline in many animal and bird species, such as crocodiles, manatees, Florida panther, Everglades mink, ospreys, bald eagles, herons and wood storks. These are all threatened and will continue to be while man's rapacious demand for water continues to be met by city planners without due regard for the consequences.

We spent three days in the Everglades National Park in April and found it an extraordinary experience. It is not immediately stunningly beautiful in the way that, say, Grand Canyon or Yosemite National Parks are – there are few dramatic vistas – but there is a great sense of teeming life everywhere if one takes the time to look carefully and slowly. The mosquitoes were horrendous on the trails in the mangrove swamps but out on the waterways the breeze kept them at bay.

Address: Everglades National Park, P.O. Box 279, Homestead, FL 33030, USA.

Mangrove swamp on the edge of Coot Bay Pond.

Boardwalk out to West Lake.

1945–70 THE AUSTRALIAN NATIONAL BOTANIC GARDENS A unique collection of native flora from all the States and Territories including many rare and threatened species and rain forest plants in a special, humidity-controlled environment.

A general view of the native plantings. Visited December 19.

The Australian National Botanic Gardens in Canberra were officially opened in 1970 but their concept and plan had evolved during the previous half century. Walter Burley Griffin's award-winning plan for the Australian National Capital (1911) envisaged an enormous area comprising 800 acres of prime site, from the lower slopes of the Black Mountains to the edge of West Lake, to be set aside for an arboretum and botanical gardens. Like his contemporaries, he was still very much influenced by the ideas on garden and city design then prevalent in Europe and America and his vision was of a large-scale Continental Arboretum comprising areas planted with specimens from different parts of the globe including

The Rainforest Gully.

New Zealand, Australia and the South Sea Islands. For a variety of political and financial reasons, this part of his plan was never executed and the area he had designed for the Continental Arboretum was leased to dairy farms and used for grazing cattle while the important business of building a temporary Parliament House was addressed. The Dickson Report of 1935 urged that work should commence on the Botanic Gardens along the lines of Griffin's original proposal.

Fortunately for the future of the Australian Botanic Garden, the Second World War intervened before the money and expertise had been assembled to begin work under Dickson. It wasn't until 1945 that Lindsay Dixon Pryor, as newly appointed superintendent of Parks and Gardens, put forward his plans for the Botanic Gardens, which he considered his number one post-war project. However, the dairy cows had to be found alternative grazing, surveys had to be conducted and boundaries decided so it wasn't until 1951 that the fencing contractor actually started work.

'Initially, the scheme will concentrate on developing Australian plants, although collections from countries with a similar climate will be included,' Pryor's report stated and this essentially marked the turning point for the development of the Botanic Gardens as we see them today.

As the years passed it became increasingly obvious that the Botanic Gardens should concentrate solely on native Australian flora – the wealth of material to be found all over the continent precluded any necessity or possibility

Natural eucalyptus woodland.

of introducing flora from other continents and it is this concentration of Australia's own plants, shrubs and trees collected from all the states and territories that makes these Botanic Gardens unique.

The gardens occupy 90 hectares on the lower slopes of the Black Mountain, about half of which have already been planted and half of which await development. The overall area is divided into sections where plants are either grouped taxonomically (i.e. species belonging to the same plant group), ecologically (i.e. plants growing in similar climates or soil conditions) or aesthetically (i.e. the most attractive plants are grown near the building and main viewing paths). Throughout there is a strong emphasis on planting rare or threatened species.

The most popular areas for visitors can be seen by following the designated trails: the White Arrow Walk, the Blue Arrow Walk and the Aboriginal Trail. Another popular feature, the Rain Forest Gully, has been transformed from an arid area into a humid, rain-forest type environment by the use of time-switch controlled sprays which regulate moisture levels. This enables rain-forest plants from different latitudes in eastern Australia to be represented in the gardens. Viewing is from specially constructed boardwalks.

The Sydney Flora Basin section has been planted with the rich flora that grows on the sandstone areas of the Sydney Basin and the mallee Shrubland plants from four different communities of mallee (a kind of eucalyptus) thrive in the carefully prepared soil. The Eucalpt Lawn, the Rockery and the Banksia Centre Garden are other attractions. The gardens also contain an extensive herbarium for dried specimens and a nursery for propagating the plants collected on field trips. These areas are not open to the general public.

Address: Australian National Botanic Gardens, GPO Box 1777, Canberra Act 2601, Australia.

Bottlebrush in full flower.

The Rockery.

1926–90s OTARI NATIVE BOTANIC GARDEN One of the largest collections world-wide of native flora and a unique example of virgin bush with some trees nearly 700 years old, only five kilometres from a major conurbation.

The native plant collection just before a dramatic rain storm. Visited December 2.

Otari Native Botanic Garden comprises land that was originally owned by Job Wilton, an early settler who had the foresight to conserve a sizeable area of the native bush forest at Otari when his contemporaries were clearing most of the original forest in the Wellington area. Still called Wilton's Bush by many locals in honour of its first owner, the area was designated a public domain in 1904 and in 1919 the property came solely under the jurisdiction of the Wellington Parks and Reserves Department. By 1926 a four-point plan for the development of the 'Otari Open-Air Native Plant Museum' had been drawn up by Dr L. Cockayne

The Fernery.

(honorary botanist to the parks department) and its acceptance has been the guiding philosophy of the park ever since.

The main aim of the park was to establish a collection of all the New Zealand species it was possible to cultivate in the Museum. This it has done so successfully that there are over 1200 species, hybrids and cultivars at Otari and it is not only the largest single collection of native plants in New Zealand but it is one of the few botanical collections world-wide that concentrates solely on its native flora.

The second aim, to produce artificially various important types of the primitive vegetation of New Zealand, has been so successful that it serves as a storehouse for plants that are becoming increasingly less common and it is an important resource centre for scientists, taxonomists and cytologists.

Its third aim, to illustrate the use of indigenous plants for horticultural purposes and for development in home gardens, has also been very successful as educators, students and home gardeners have been able to come to Otari and see the growth patterns of native plants and how they might effectively be used in domestic or commercial gardening.

The fourth aim of the original development plan, to restore the bush area to its original structure and composition, has also been highly successful. The natural forest, comprising 200 acres of virgin forest and secondary growth is the Museum's most prized asset.

Original lowland forest with emergent trees.

Some trees are estimated to be between 500 and 700 years old and the stand of virgin bush on the north slope is a unique example of its type – existing as it does only five kilometres from a major conurbation. At least 150 species of flowering plants, conifers and ferns are found in the natural bush area including the rare *Elaeocarpus hookerianus*, *Weinmannia racemosa* and *Syzygium maire*. Orchids, climbing epiphytes, passion fruit, supplejack and ratas are just a few of the exotic plants to be seen on the eleven kilometres of walking tracks that criss-cross the forest.

Special features in the 12 acres of cultivated bush include a Rock Garden, a 'look-out' over the main bush area, a wild garden, a fernery and a small alpine garden, each designed both to give visitors greater insight into the wealth of native plants that exists in New Zealand and to encourage them to appreciate and protect the rich plant heritage that is being undervalued and systematically destroyed in many parts of the world.

The plaque on Dr Cockayne's grave is inscribed as follows: 'Will our descendants prize this unique heritage from the dim past and preserve these sanctuaries intact?'

Barely sixty years after his death these words must fill us with a sense of uneasy guilt.

Address: Otari Native Botanic Garden, Wellington City Council, P.O. Box 2199, 7th Floor Anvil House, 138 Wakefield Street, Wellington, New Zealand.

The grass and sedge collection.

Aciphylla squarrosa.

235

1970s THE LIVING DESERT RESERVE Conservation of rare or endangered desert flora by xeriscaping which is the art of landscaping to reduce water consumption by combining drought-tolerant plants with drip irrigation together with the use of sand, rocks and boulders to provide stability and an appropriate environmental setting.

Brittle bush in full flower in the Upper Colorado Desert Garden. Visited April 10.

The Living Desert Reserve began in 1970 when a group of prominent, wealthy and far-sighted citizens, recognizing the rapid encroachment of urban development in the Palm Desert, convinced the Palm Springs Desert Museum to establish an interpretative nature trail and reserve on 360 acres of the Desert. An enthusiastic and ambitious wildlife biology graduate, Karen Sausman, was hired as resident naturalist and her vision and energy have built the Living Desert from a scrubby, rubbish-strewn terrain of 360 acres into an extensive 1200-acre landscape that shows visitors what the desert really is and encourages appreciation and understanding of the desert's plants, animals and landscape. In 1980 the Living Desert was incorporated as an independent, non-profit making organization, no longer part of the Palm Springs Desert Museum, and Karen Sausman is still, in the 1990s, the Living Desert, Executive Director.

The aim of the Living Desert as an education and conservation centre, dedicated to interpreting and preserving the desert, is to show visitors that the desert is not the lifeless wasteland many of us believe but, in fact, an intricate and very fragile eco-system that contains an astonishing variety of plant and animal life. Of the 1200 acres of the Living Desert Preserve, 200 acres have been developed as a zoo, a botanical garden and a natural history museum for interpreting the deserts of the world. The remaining 1000 acres are a natural wilderness preserve accessible by a network of paths and trails.

The importance, in terms of garden history, of places like The Living Desert and Otari Open-Air Native Plant Museum (see page 234) is that they aim to preserve native plants that might become endangered because their natural habitat is under threat from development. Thirty years ago the Palm Desert housed a small, isolated community in what many people thought was an inhospitable environment. However, the last three decades have seen a rapid and seemingly unstoppable expansion, with Palm Springs encroaching right up to the foot of the desert canyons. Such expansion naturally

Yucca and cholla near the Canyon Garden.

Penstemon in the Oasis Garden.

destroys or jeopardizes much of the flora and fauna of the desert.

Planting gardens in The Living Desert (and there are at least ten different ones replicating the plant life of such regions as the Mojave, Sonoran, Baji and Chihuahua deserts) is done so accurately, basing the designs on photographs and drawings of actual desert locations, that within a few years it is impossible to tell that these landscapes are, in fact, man-made because they look as though they have been there forever. Creating these gardens not only preserves native species but enables visitors to see what can be grown in the desert environment thus encouraging them, it is hoped, to grow native plants (which can be bought in the Centre's retail nursery) in their own gardens rather than waste thousands of gallons of water a year trying to imitate European gardens with their ever-thirsty roses and shrubs.

Xeriscape, the art and science of landscaping to reduce consumption of water, involves the use of drought-tolerant plants in combination with controlled drip irrigation. It also combines plants of interesting forms and textures with natural features, such as sand,

rocks and boulders, to provide stability and contrast so that they support each other physically and blend into the environment.

Desert gardens take time to reach maturity. The Curator of Gardens at The Living Desert confesses that they sometimes 'cheat' a little by filling a particular garden with some mature specimens so that the garden doesn't look too barren while smaller plants, or plants grown from seed, establish themselves. However, within three or four years the gardens are ready to be thinned as the important or rarer species establish themselves and the garden starts really to resemble what is found in nature.

The Living Desert gardens are very exciting to visit, particularly for Europeans, not only because they are *so* different from the gardens we are used to but, particularly if you visit between October and the end of March, because they show how amazingly floriflorous, lush and colourful a desert garden can be.

Address: The Living Desert, 47900 Portola Avenue, Palm Desert, California 92260, USA.

Claret cup cactus.

Canyon Garden.

The immaculately maintained rockery at Wisley.

Wisley, The Royal Horticultural Society' Garden in Surrey (England), was built on the site of a woodland garden created by George Fox Wilson in the 1880s and later owned and then donated to the RHS in 1903 by Sir Thomas Hanbury (owner of La Mortola see pages 186–7). Now comprising over 100 hectares this garden is, first and foremost, a centre for scientific research and education, with specialized areas for conducting plant trials and others for exploring what kinds of plants and shrubs will flourish in unpromising or difficult environments. However, the original woodland gardens remain, an alpine rock garden was built in 1911 based on Edward White's designs and the formal gardens were planned by Sir Geoffrey Jellicoe and Lanning Roper in the 1960s. Devastating storms in 1987 and 1990 resulted in the introduction of some innovative planting such as the collection of Mediterranean plants.

Wisley.

Kew Gardens.

ROCKERIES

Chatsworth.

Alton Towers.

St Michael's Mount.

239

1970–90s THE DONALD M. KENDALL SCULPTURE GARDEN Over forty modern sculptures and an enormous arboretum blend harmoniously to create a potentially timeless landscape that combines Art and Nature in perfect counterpoint.

Henry Moore's 'Double Oval' stands on the landscaped lawn that sweeps down to the lake. Visited September 18. (Photographed by Gillian Barlow)

Judith Brown's 'Three Caryatids'. (Photographed by Gillian Barlow)

The Donald M. Kendall Sculpture Gardens at Pepsi Cola's World Headquarters, a site comprising 144 acres in Purchase, New York, was opened in 1970 on 10 acres of land that had originally belonged to the Blind Brook Polo Club. The seven buildings of the corporate campus were designed by Edward Durrell Stone (1902–78) and reflect the influence of his mentor Frank Lloyd Wright. The whole building complex is situated on the top of a knoll and the natural landscape sweeps gracefully down from it to the artificial lake on the south side which provides a focus for the huge lawn that surrounds it.

The seven, three-storey buildings, linked at each corner by a service core, form a circle with an opening on the north side for the main entrance which leads to the formal central courtyard shaped like a Greek Cross. In the centre is a round pool surrounded on three sides by sunken gardens – one is landscaped in a Japanese motif, another is a water garden with two small islands and the third was designed specifically for sculpture.

The original landscape layout was conceived by the architect's son Edward Durrell Stone Jr and he initiated the planting of 6000 trees from thirty-eight species and thousands of flowering bulbs to supplement the existing greenery on the site. In 1981 Russell Page (1903–85), the celebrated English garden designer, was commissioned to initiate a five-year planting programme which would turn the corporate estate into an arboretum able to rival its fame as a sculpture garden. His work has been continued since his death by François Goffinet.

Donald M. Kendall, the Chairman of the Executive Committee of PepsiCo, has a very clear vision of his aims. His goal in creating the sculpture garden was to integrate the three art forms of architecture, landscape architecture and large-scale modern sculpture within the framework of an enlightened, corporate cultural environment. He recognized that 'big business' has a major role to play as patron of the arts and public benefactor. He also believes that a creative atmosphere in the corporate realm stimulates further creative thinking. 'We want our sculpture garden to kindle people's interest as well as offer them something challenging to help them grow.'

The sculptures that Mr Kendall has chosen for the garden (the selection and installation of every piece is undertaken by him personally) are all twentieth-century masterpieces. The collection comprises over forty works by thirty internationally acclaimed artists, starting with Auguste Rodin who is considered the father of modern sculpture and including names such as Calder, Crovello, Dubuffet, Ernst, Giacometti, Maillol, Miro, Moore, Noguchi, Oldenburg, Pomodoro, Salmones, Segal, Smith and Wynne. Together, their work represents every significant historical development in twentieth-century sculpture.

The question that is raised by the existence of a sculpture garden is what comes first? Is it primarily a garden with some sculptures in it to complement or contrast with aspects of the landscape or, is it an open air exhibition space for sculpture and the fact that some trees and lawn surround the pieces is of minor importance?

Parts of the garden (i.e. not the courtyard) were more likely to have been put into the second category if one looks at early photographs of the garden but pictures taken since the maturing of the 1980s' planting programme reveal a fine balance between the two extremes. The trees, lawns and bulb-carpeted, wild-flower areas provide a perfect counterpoint to the many large, dramatic sculptures, whether they are made of 'organic' materials such as stone or marble or whether they are created from 'man-made' materials such as steel or polyester resin.

Perhaps a garden that principally comprises three elements – trees, water and sculptures – will endure as a record of its time better than a 'planted and created', inevitably high maintenance garden that reflects the interests and preoccupations of its creator and which lives while its creator lives but quickly disintegrates into a wilderness once the overseeing eye has disappeared. Trees and sculptures can remain virtually untended for decades or even centuries if not destroyed and exist for future generations to enjoy in much the same way as the current generation enjoys it.

Address: Donald M. Kendall Sculpture Gardens, PepsiCo World Headquarters, Purchase, New York, USA.

Henry Moore's 'Double Oval'. (Photographed by Gillian Barlow)

Alexander Calder's 'Hats Off'. (Photographed by Gillian Barlow)

Jean Dubuffet's 'Kiosque l'Évidé'. (Photographed by Gillian Barlow)

1966–90s LITTLE SPARTA A thought-provoking sculpture garden which is full of symbolism and poetry in the time-honoured tradition of the poet-gardener who explores artistic ideas through shaping his environment.

'The Present Order...' giant stones near Lochan Eck. Visited July 4.

Little Sparta, formerly known as Stonypath, is the home and garden of the poet and sculptor Ian Hamilton Finlay and his wife, Sue. Bought in 1966, the stone house, surrounded by a few old farm buildings and 4 acres of land set on a desolate, windy hillside, was a far cry from the garden that exists today.

Stepping stones across Middle Pool.

During the thirty years that Finlay has lived and worked at Stonypath his artistic output has been prolific and creating the garden there has been part and parcel of that process. Although the Finlays started working on developing the sunken garden at the front of the house and damming the stream to create the pond at the back and the small loch in the field beyond, it was not until the 1970s that the garden began to take on a more coherent shape and Finlay's project for using his garden to express his philosophical and artistic ideals, often referred to as his 'neo-classical rearmament', began.

In 1978 Finlay began a 'Five Year Hellenisation Plan' at Stonypath and subsequently renamed it Little Sparta. During this period a complex series of rows and disagreements with the Scottish Arts Council resulted in one of the farm outbuildings, which had been used as a gallery, being turned into a Garden Temple. On 15 March 1983, Budget Day, the Strathclyde Regional Council seized a number of works of art by Finlay and other artists from the Temple and confiscated them indefinitely. This episode resulted in Little Sparta being closed for a year.

However, in 1984 the garden and Temple reopened to

Grotto of Aeneas and Dido.

View across the moors from the garden.

visitors. The main room of the Temple, a homage to the pastoral and classical values of the French Revolution, is intended to be a sort of extension to the garden and vice versa with the placing of sculpted columns and capitals in the garden. Yves Abrioux in his book on Ian Hamilton Finlay says 'The interpenetration of garden and Temple is now one of the chief features of Little Sparta.'

How does one explain Little Sparta? It is such an intriguing and extraordinary place, particularly if one visits 'cold' without having read anything about its background. What? Why? are the constant questions as one follows the delightful, hand-drawn map that Finlay shyly presents on arrival before giving the visitor free rein around what immediately seems very personal territory. And that is, of course, the point: to provoke thought; to question what it all means. The answers can be found in two ways and on two levels.

You can either do as we did which is to wander round looking at the sculptures and poems and statues and inscriptions, the pools, the boats, and the sundials, laughing at the jokes and puns, puzzling at the classical and unclear references, seeing similarities and contrasts in the images and all the time amazed by the incredible inventiveness of it all. Or you can read Yves Abrioux's book *Ian Hamilton Finlay: A Visual Primer* before you go to visit the garden and steep yourself in the philosophical, intellectual and artistic wavelength on which Finlay operates and then come to the garden able to fit, as it were, all the pieces of the intellectual puzzle into place, understanding every mythical reference and symbol on the numerous levels on which they operate.

In terms of garden history Little Sparta plays a very significant role, continuing a garden tradition that goes back to classical times. There has long been a custom of

Mysterious path.

Pacific Air War Inscribed Stone.

Sailing ships in a window.

243

Memorial stone at Little Sparta.

Huge golden head of Apollo.

Apollo and Daphne.

C. D. Friedrich Pyramid.

the poet as gardener, the poet who seeks to explore artistic ideas through shaping his environment. Two famous poet-gardeners whose work garden historians know a great deal about, although their gardens no longer exist, are Alexander Pope (1688–1744) and William Shenstone (1714–63). Abrioux sums up their work and the work of Hamilton Finlay as follows: 'Within the poet's "kingdom" a counter order has been established with the effect that dedicated poet-gardeners like Pope or Shenstone are rightly viewed not as amateur horticulturists but as social thinkers distilling ethical values from the transformation of their landscape.'

Finlay, who recommended Abrioux's book to us, obviously feels happy with this assessment of his work, having said himself elsewhere that the purpose of his broad allegorical framework is to induce 'a thinking consideration of objects'.

However, I can't stress strongly enough that ignorance of Finlay's philosophical ideas and symbolism is no deterrent to enjoying the garden. It is huge fun and magical for children. If you would like to visit the garden you have to write for an appointment to Ian Hamilton Finlay enclosing a SAE.

Address: Little Sparta, Stonypath, Dunsyre, Nr Lanark, Lanarkshire, Strathclyde, Scotland.

'Certain gardens are described as retreats when they are really attacks.' Ian Hamilton Finley.

'Classic gardens are composed of Glooms and Solitudes and not of plants and trees.' Ian Hamilton Finley.

The Great Wall at Jinlanling.

Introduction

In the *Ye Yuan* (Garden Tempering) 1634, a treatise on Ming dynasty gardening, the author Ji Cheng concludes that although in garden design there are general principles, 'there are no fixed formulae or definite rules for the planning of gardens'. This is why it is so difficult to define a Chinese garden succinctly – there are few hard and fast rules about how a Chinese garden should be laid out or organized yet there is an underlying philosophy to the design of the gardens which has evolved over the centuries as well as a number of essential recognizable elements that have been used to evoke or symbolize the philosophy to both garden designers and garden visitors.

In China a garden is a place where man is transported visually and mentally away from the humdrum cares and vicissitudes of everyday life to 'an eternal moment of suspended time where man and nature seem to be in perfect accord' (Maggie Keswick, *The Chinese Garden*). This belief in the totality of nature has its roots in Taoism and is happily incorporated into the Buddhist philosophy of seeking spiritual enlightenment.

There are four major elements in a Chinese garden that are used to try to create an environment in which this philosophy of the totality or oneness of nature can be achieved. These are used in an evocative not a prescriptive way to suggest an infinite variety of contrasting, parallel and contradicting possibilities. These four components, found in all gardens from the huge Imperial gardens of the north to the private scholar/ poet gardens of Suzhou, are *water, rocks, buildings* and *plants* and, as one of our guides said, they combine together to achieve the final but most important component of all – *peace*, or *harmony*.

The most successful garden makers are thought to be those who achieve a masterly composition of these four components, capturing their essence so that they represent a deeper reality than a mere individual likeness.

The Chinese word for landscape is *shan-shui*, literally 'mountains and water'. This concept has many symbolic associations for the Chinese. Thus *water* is essential to a garden not only because it is physically beautiful in itself but because it evokes the Taoist myth of the Islands in the Eastern Sea where the Immortals dwelt, and the Taoist concept of opposites, of *yin* and *yang*; the soft water (*yin*) in opposition to the hard unyielding rock (*yang*). Therefore *rocks* in a garden (which may represent a single mountain or a whole mountain range) symbolize the wildness of nature and, by sympathetic magic, confer on the owner of the garden and the visitor a kind of immortality and become a substitute for the real thing. By miniaturizing and stylizing rock forms either in *peng jing* landscapes or in rockeries, the mountain wildernesses become more manageable – contemplating them in a confined space like a garden means one can appreciate their symbolic associations without actually having to visit them. Only the most dedicated hermits and Buddhists actually did that.

Buildings in a Chinese garden refer not only to the halls and pavilions (*tings*) constructed as places either for social gatherings or for quiet contemplation, study, painting or writing but also to the winding corridors (*lang*), galleries, bridges and paths that connect the various areas of the garden and also serve to divide space and provide a decorative framework for viewing the garden. The mosaic pebble work on the paths, with its enormous variety of patterns, acts as an indicator of the changing function of one area of the garden from another. The windows in the corridors (*lou chuang*) are often highly decorative in themselves and serve as the 'eyes' of the house, providing an endless number of views both within the garden and out into the world beyond.

The *plants* in a Chinese garden are chosen for their long-standing symbolic associations which explains the general lack of interest in native species 'discovered' by European plant collectors compared to traditional favourites. Flowering plants are popular for creating an expansion of space, a different view, a reminder of the changeability of nature and its cyclic pattern. Totally different moods are evoked by a pond covered in lotus flowers in summer and the same pond in winter with just a few dead-looking stems emerging from the water, yet both are equally admired by the garden-lover.

The two main categories that the Chinese gardens illustrated here fall into are the Imperial Gardens and the Private Gardens. The Imperial Gardens tried to create the image of a garden or park as a microcosm of the world and its riches and as a place so magical that the Immortals might want to live there and in so doing confer immortality on the gardens' owners. The private gardens tried both to express the Taoist philosophy of a man in harmony and unity with nature and to reflect the interconnection between gardening, painting, calligraphy and poetry.

The Main Periods in Chinese Garden History

We can only read about the huge Imperial parks built by the Emperors in the Qin (221–206 BC), Han (206 BC–AD 220), Sui (589–618) and Tang (618–907) dynasties, as nothing remains of these legendary pleasure gardens. However, there are remnants of the great gardening era which flourished under the Northern and Southern Song Emperors (960–1127, 1127–1279) who fled, in 1126, to Xi Hu, West Lake, and built numerous palaces and gardens along the shores and in the hills surrounding this beautiful expanse of water (see page 250). The Song dynasties are often seen as the golden age of gardening because the standards set in those eras in all the art forms – painting, calligraphy and gardening – were so high that they established the standard to which later periods aspired.

The great Imperial Gardens described in this book were mainly built and expanded in the Yuan (1279–1368), Ming (1368–1644) and Qing (1644–1911) dynasties, principally by Emperor Kangxi (1653–1727) and his grandson Emperor Qian Long (1736–95).

The private gardens of Suzhou generally date from the Ming dynasty although some originated earlier and were reconstructed or expanded later.

1044 CANG LANG TING (THE SURGING WAVES PAVILION) Northern Song dynasty.

Looking in towards the garden from the canal side. Visited March 24.

Cang Lang Ting, or the Garden of the Surging Waves Pavilion, was built by the scholar and poet Su Zimei around 1044 on the site of an old Suzhou garden that had been owned by a duke in the tenth century. Su, who gave it its present name, is said to have paid forty strings of coins to buy the 1-acre site which gave rise to the following poem by one of his poet friends, Ouyang, and show how highly thought-of the garden was.

'The fresh breeze and bright moonlight should be priceless yet for forty strings of coins they have been sold.'

A stone at the entrance engraved by Su Zimei in 1044 during the Song dynasty depicts the garden and the landscape beyond as it was then. Remarkably, little has changed about the garden itself in almost nine hundred

The stone which commemorates the Emperor Qian Long's visit.

years although nowadays the countryside beyond the garden bears little resemblance to the early engraving.

The name of the garden refers to the lines of a famous ancient poem which reminds us all that life has its ups and downs and a philosophical acceptance of this fact is essential.

'When the water in the surging waves is clear I clean my hat ribbons in it. If it's dirty I wash my feet in it'.

The garden is important for two principal reasons. Firstly, as mentioned, it survives today very much in the manner in which it was originally designed in the Song dynasty. Obviously things have been added and altered to some extent but the overall concept remains the same. Secondly, two of the most significant features of its early design differentiate it from other Suzhou gardens. It doesn't have a wall surrounding the garden so that not only does the visitor within the garden 'borrow' the views (*jiejing*) of the canal and landscape beyond but those outside the garden can see the landscape of the garden from the city that borders it.

This, and the fact that the garden's central feature is not a pond but a hill, on the top of which is the pavilion that gives the garden its name, distinguishes it from other gardens. The hill was originally made of earth, then Taihu rocks and yellow rocks were added to make it look more 'natural'. As the earth and rocks welded together the effect was very naturalistic and compounded by the fact that trees could grow among the rocks because of the underlying earth. This combination of trees and rocks is a unique one in Suzhou.

The hill is surrounded by single and double *lang* corridors with *lou chuang* windows that frame views of

intricate mass. As lions are not native to China, this interpretation is rather fanciful but the symbolism of the wild mountain landscape, possibly the home of the mythical Immortals, is very real. Creating a wild and picturesque impression by building a rockery with tunnels and grottoes in a garden, particularly one in the middle of a pond reached by a flying bridge, is strongly advocated in the most important Chinese gardening manual, the *Yuan Ye*, by Chi Cheng (1634), because it becomes a fitting place to 'welcome the clouds and the moon'; the book specifically praises the rockery at Shizi Lin.

It is a pity that the large stone boat in one corner of the lake added earlier this century and some rather odd stained-glass windows seem inappropriate but there are many lovely corners in the garden and the building of the pavilions either on the top of the rockery or at high vantage points of the garden gives the visitor marvellous overall views.

Unfortunately, because of its fame, the garden is incredibly crowded (or at least it was when we went) so the harmonious feeling between man and nature which it is the garden's purpose to create is severely reduced in the noise, bustle and crush. Early morning or lunch time is probably the quietest time to experience the garden at its best.

Address: Shizi Lin (Garden of the Lion Grove)
23 Yuanlin Road, Suzhou, China.

Chinese gardens are extremely popular and packed with visitors.

A tunnel through the central Lion Rockery.

On top of the Lion Rockery.

1402–20 THE FORBIDDEN CITY Ming dynasty.

In Yu Hua Yuan, The Imperial Garden, false rock mountains allow the visitor to gain an overview. Visited March 19.

A false rock mountain surrounded by a decorative, tiled wall.

A pebblework mosaic path.

The Imperial Palace, or the Forbidden City (or Palace Museum as it is now called), was built by order of the 3rd Ming Emperor Yongle when he came to power in 1402 and was basically completed by 1420, at which time the Ming dynasty officially moved its capital from Nanjing to Beijing.

Occupying a rectangular area of more than 175 acres and surrounded by a moat wide enough to engage in naval manoeuvres, the Forbidden City (so called because for almost five hundred years ordinary people were not permitted to enter the four main gates that gave access beyond the high walls) was the home of twenty-four successive Qing and Ming dynasty Emperors who lived and ruled their vast territories from within the complex.

The area divides into two main sections: The Front Palace comprising the three huge halls, courtyards and adjoining buildings from which the affairs of state were conducted and which is approached through the south entrance, the Gate of Heavenly Peace at the north end of Tiananmen Square; and the Inner Palace which lies behind the three great halls in the northern half of the complex and was the residential area of the Emperor and the Imperial Household.

The two most renowned gardens of the Forbidden City are in the Inner Palace complex. One is Yu Hua Yuan, the Imperial Garden, which lies due north of the main halls and buildings of the Inner Palace directly inside the North Gate Entrance, which was built in 1417

The Yu Hua Yuan abounds in ancient cypresses and pines planted in the fifteenth century.

but largely remodelled in the Qing Dynasty. The other, in the Palace of Peaceful Longevity is the Qian Long Garden which was remodelled by Emperor Qian Long in the 1770s when, out of respect for his grandfather Kangxi, he planned to retire when he had ruled for sixty years as his grandfather had. So, Qian Long built himself a 'retirement' home in the north east corner of the Forbidden City complex, including within it a long, narrow garden.

Both gardens were at the back of the Inner Palaces and were designed as places where the Emperors could retire and relax after the formalities and ceremonies of court life.

Relative to the vastness of the whole Forbidden City and the Imperial Summer Palaces, these two gardens seem remarkably small yet a great deal is packed into them: rocks, trees, walkways, pavilions, buildings, all have their symbolic associations and serve to remind the Emperor and his courtiers of their relationship with the natural world.

Yu Hua Yuan, the Imperial Garden, seems very formal and controlled compared with, for instance, the lyricism of The Garden of Happy Harmony in Yi He Yuan (see page 272). Its layout is very symmetrical with trees and plants in orderly rows and paths decorated in pebble work mosaic. The ancient cypresses and pines planted in the fifteenth century, many of which have had to be propped to sustain their great weight and unusual

Prunus glandulosa 'Alba Plena'.

255

The Gate of Peaceful Longevity, Ning Shou Gong, in Qian Long's Garden in the Forbidden City.

View through to Qian Long's Garden.

The cup-floating stream in Xi Shang.

growth, are very impressive and imposing and provide much coolness and shade in the arid summer heat. Grotesquely shaped, lake-washed rocks and miniature trees are placed on plinths around the garden and three 'false' rock mountains enable the visitor to climb above the beautiful pavilions and look down on the garden.

Qian Long's Garden, in the Palace of Peaceful Longevity, is a 60-metre-long area arranged in five sections or courtyards with each courtyard separated by halls. Here Qian Long's love of the landscape and gardens of southern China is again reflected as in Yi He Yuan (see page 272). Although it was impossible to build around water, as at the Imperial Summer Palace, long walkways, rockeries, highly decorative pavilions and 'false' mountains create an atmosphere redolent of the private gardens of Suzhou so admired by Qian Long.

One particularly striking symbolic feature in the Xishang (Pavilion of the Ceremony of Purification) is the cup-floating stream. Here the floor is curved to resemble a running brook, in honour of the famous calligrapher and poet Wang Xi Zhi (fourth century), who together with friends and other poets composed the poems in the *Anthology on Orchard Pavilion* beside a 'wine-cup stream' In Lan Tin, a garden near Shaoxing which was visited and admired by Qian Long.

If the Imperial Gardens within the Forbidden City seem remarkably small in comparison with the overall

The Nine Dragon Wall in the Palace of Peaceful Longevity in the Forbidden City.

size of the complex, this is because the Emperors, from the time of Kublai Khan (1214–94) onwards, had been landscaping the area immediately to the north and north-west of the Forbidden City for their use as Imperial Pleasure Grounds.

Jin Shan Park, immediately opposite the northern gate, was created from earth excavated to make the moat around the Forbidden City. Beihai Park to the north-west comprises one of a series of lakes originally dug in the twelfth century and still fed from the Jade Fountain Spring in the Western Hills. Now a large public park, it was originally the site of an Imperial Hunting Lodge which was enlarged and extended first by Kublai Khan and then by subsequent Qing and Ming dynasty Emperors. However, most of what remains today was built in the time of Qian Long. The main features are the island in the middle of the lake dominated by the great

White Dagoba and the elegant white marble bridge that connects the island to the shore. Other pavilions, gardens-within-gardens and religious courtyard buildings are dotted around the island and lake.

The Imperial Gardens within the Forbidden City are hard to appreciate. The buildings are so dominant and the crowds so numerous that it is difficult to imagine how they could have provided much peace or rest for the Imperial Household after their ceremonial duties were over. If only one could visit at dawn or dusk when no one else is around, or in the middle of an ice-bound winter, then the peacefulness and calm they were supposed to engender could be captured.

Address: Yu Hua Yuan (Imperial Garden) and Emperor Qian Long's Garden, The Forbidden City (Palace Museum), Northern Gate, Beijing, China.

A tranquil, shady courtyard in Qian Long's Garden.

The White Dagoba in Jin Shan Park.

1506–20 JI CHANG YUAN (THE GARDEN FOR EASING THE MIND) Ming dynasty.

The garden 'borrows' the distant misty view of Tin Hill and the Dragon Light Pagoda.

View down from the complex rockery showing the wonderful pebble walkways.

The engraved tablet by Qian Long - and the rock called The Lady Combing Her Hair.   *Intricate paving patterns.*

Ji Chang Yuan, literally translated as The Garden for Easing the Mind, is sometimes known as The Garden of Ecstasy. It was originally built in the middle of the Ming dynasty, reputedly between 1506 and 1520, on the site of an early, well-known Buddhist monastery which later became the country house of a Finance Minister in the early Ming dynasty.

Destroyed in 1860, Ji Chang Yuan was accurately rebuilt according to the original plans so that what we see today is very much as it would have looked three to four hundred years ago.

Although only about a hectare in size, the garden's construction and imaginative use of space creates the impression that it is much larger than that. This has been achieved in the choice of the site which, set in a valley surrounded by hills, enables the Chinese passion for *jiejing* (borrowed views) to come into play by 'borrowing' Tin Hill and the Dragon Light Pagoda into the view as well as 'borrowing' the reflections of the landscape and sky. The garden's complex rockery, built by the rock craftsman Zhang Shi, is cleverly arranged so that it looks like a natural rocky spur on the western hill beyond.

Fed by a natural spring, the stream that bubbles musically down the long gully known as Music Box Ravine into the long narrow pool in the eastern part of the garden represents the vicissitudes of life. Around the pond, corridors (*lang*) lead from one pavilion (*ting*) to another and divide the space by providing enticing views into other sections of the garden through the latticed windows (*lou chang*).

One of the pavilions that juts out into the pond is known as 'Trying to Understand the Fish' pavilion. A well-known and ancient Chinese traditional story tells of how two philosophers were sitting by a pond one day looking at the fish.

'How happy those fish must be,' said one to the other.

'How do you know they are happy?' said the second philosopher. 'You are not a fish and cannot tell what a fish feels.'

'How do you know that I am not right? You are not me and cannot tell what I feel. You cannot know whether I understand the fish's feelings,' argued the first sage.

Ji Chang Yuan was reputedly visited by the gardening Emperor Qian Long seven times and several tablets are said to have been engraved by him. One stone with a drawing and poem on it imitates the rock in front of which it stands, which resembles a lady combing her hair.

It was to remember his visits to the south and to this garden in particular that Emperor Qian Long built Hsieh Chu Yuan, the Garden of Harmonious Interest at the Yi He Yuan, the Imperial Summer Palace in Beijing (see page 272). Hsieh Chu Yuan's plans are reminiscent of Ji Chang Yuan but it lacks the highly lyrical quality of its southern counterpart.

Address: Ji Chang Yuan, Wuxi, China.

The Trying to Understand the Fish Pavilion.   *The Music Box Ravine.*

259

1506–21 ZHOU ZHENG YUAN (THE HUMBLE ADMINISTRATOR'S GARDEN) Ming dynasty.

There is nothing humble about The Humble Administrator's Garden; it is one of the biggest gardens in Suzhou.

Zhou Zheng Yuan, the Unsuccessful Politician's Garden or the Humble Administrator's Garden, is the largest private garden in Suzhou and was built between 1506 and 1521 in the Ming dynasty (1368–1644) on a site that had previously been the house of a Confucian Scholar in the Tang dynasty (618–907) and was subsequently a monastery in the Yuan dynasty (1279–1368).

Wang Xian Chen, the eponymous builder of the garden was a high court administrator who, it is said, had the job of touring the country to ascertain and punish corrupt practices among minor officials and was then discovered to be accepting bribes himself. He lost his job but doesn't appear to have forfeited the wealth he had accumulated for, the story goes, he brought three or four boat loads of silver to Suzhou where he had come to live the quiet retired life of a humble man in accordance with the philosophy of the 2000-year-old poem which propounds: 'It is the greatest pleasure in life for a man to grow some vegetables and flowers in his own garden'.

Wang Xian Chen's 16-acre garden is reputed to have cost one boat load of silver and taken sixteen years to build. Wang enlisted the services of a 'scholar without office', the famous painter/poet Wen Cheng-ming renowned for his austerity, cool intellectual restraint and high ethical standards. Surprisingly these qualities were of no account in the official job market so, penniless, he took up the offer of a studio in Zhou Zheng Yuan and captured his love of the changing moods of the garden in two series of little album leaves, thus ensuring fame for himself, his patron and the garden they both loved.

Perhaps Wang Xian Chen was not as corrupt as contemporary history claims. Perhaps another possible translation of the garden's name is more accurate. The Garden of the Stupid Officials could refer to those who put the Humble Administrator or Unsuccessful Politician out of office.

When Wang Xian Chen died, his son lost the entire garden in one night paying off gambling debts to three different families and thus the garden was divided into three sections by walls. Xu Shi Tai (the original builder of Liu Yuan, the Lingering Garden) acquired one of the sections (see page 262).

Over the next three centuries the garden changed hands many times, repeatedly falling into disrepair and then being renovated. In the early part of this century photographs show the garden in a very sorry state but a programme of intensive restoration since the 1950s has opened it once more to the public and conferred on it the status of Key Place of National, Historical and Cultural Importance.

Wen Cheng-ming's paintings depict a garden very much simpler and more rustic than the one seen today. They show a house set in the countryside with chickens, vegetables and fruit trees and within the garden the pond has been expanded into a lake that stretches to distant hills. The Confucian ideal of the simple scholar's hut (though on a larger scale) is the impression he creates but the reality is, in fact, very different. The complexity of buildings, the intricate workmanship, the numerous changing views, the labyrinth of water and corridors make it fit far more easily into the elaborate garden tradition similar to that seen in the Imperial Summer Palace (see page 272).

Looking down from the central mountain.

The central and western sections of the garden are the most interesting, being composed as much of water as of land. More than half of the central area is taken up by an interconnecting series of pools dividing islands surrounded by corridors and buildings and crossed by bridges. The pools wind into secret backwaters which, together, create the impression of the famous water villages of the southern Yangtze River area in which Suzhou lies and which had been so much admired by successive Emperors.

The overall impression of this Ming style garden is that, although elaborate, it is more open and spacious than the intricate compactness of the smaller Qing gardens. Trees and flowers are planted to reflect the different seasons and celebrate the changes that take place throughout the year.

A long walk to the Moon Gate.

The western garden, developed as a separate garden in its own right, was built at the end of the Qing dynasty and is called Bu Yuan. A water garden, like the central garden, its style reflects and imitates that of the main, original section of Zhou Zheng Yuan garden. The smaller eastern section has been newly laid out since the 1950s in a Western-inspired style with grassy lawns and numerous trees. It was at this time, too, that the wonderful *peng jing* (miniature trees) garden was established to commemorate and continue a tradition that dates back to at least the Han dynasty (206 BC – AD 220 when archaeological finds of paintings in the ancient Emperors' tombs in central China depict a woman holding a *peng jing* in her hand).

This garden is not only important for revealing a different style from that of the smaller gardens in Suzhou but, because its spaciousness and interesting use of views provides a much larger landscape, it invites comparison with some of the garden ideals being explored in Europe during the eighteenth century, although the overall atmosphere still remains singularly different.

Address: Zhou Zheng Yuan (The Humble Administrator's Garden), 178 Dongbei Street, Suzhou, China.

A lang corridor winds between two of the sections.

Geometric pebblework.

1550 LIU YUAN (THE LINGERING GARDEN) Ming dynasty.

The biggest Taihu rock in Suzhou.

Animal-shaped rocks in the garden.

The calm waters of the pond are used as mirrors.

Liu Yuan, the Lingering Garden, originally built in the Ming dynasty (*c.*1550) by Xu Shi Tai, was first known as the East Garden to distinguish it from another garden he owned which was called the West Garden. Later his son turned it into a Buddhist temple. It was Xu Shi Tai who won a part of the Zhou Zheng Yuan (The Humble Administrator's Garden) in settlement of a gambling debt (see page 260).

In 1798 the garden was brought by Mr Liu who called it Han Bi Shan Zhuang (the Chilly Green Manor) but he was such a popular and well-known character in Suzhou that it was always known by the family name, thus Liu Yuan – Mr Liu's garden.

Miraculously untouched in the Taiping Rebellion (1851–64), Liu Yuan was bought by a new owner Liu Yung-Fent in 1876. Irritated by the fact that it was referred to as Liu's garden when that was not his family name, the new owner cleverly changed the Chinese character for Liu into a character that had the same pronunciation but a different meaning. The new character meant 'to linger in' and thus it became known as The Lingering Garden.

Although the large, cedar wood hall had been used for stabling horses under the rule of the Kuomintang in the early part of the twentieth century it has, since the mid-

twentieth century, undergone a programme of extensive renovation and is now designated a Key Site of National and Historic Importance.

Arranged in four sections, the garden is such a complex labyrinth of corridors (*lang*), buildings and rocks built around a central pond that it seems much larger than it actually is, which is the object of course, and it is hard to describe systematically.

The main entrance into the garden is small and unassuming. The purpose of this is to retain the feeling of privacy and mystery that is an important element in private gardens. A long, narrow passage twists and turns past tiny spaces, offering tantalizing views, into an open corridor that zigzags around the large pond and leads the visitor to the various halls, *tings* (pavilions) and highly acclaimed rockeries. To the north-west of the garden, in the outer section, an enclosed area houses a wonderful collection of *peng jing* (miniature trees), some individual and some incorporated into a miniature landscape with water and rocks (*shan-shui peng jing*). This area was developed after 1953 and is acclaimed as one of the best collections of *peng jing* in China (see page 264).

To the garden historian, Liu Yuan has some of the finest examples of garden features that symbolize the philosophy of Chinese gardens as a whole. These individual features all harmonize beautifully to create the essential atmosphere that a garden should provide, captured in Qian Long's immortal phrase: 'a place to relax the heart and refresh the mind'. It is a place where man and nature seem to be in perfect accord.

As Maggie Keswick explains in her marvellous book *The Chinese Garden*, a successful garden must have a *double* vital spirit or *ch'i*. Firstly, that which is supplied by nature itself i.e. water, rocks, trees, stones; and secondly, the harmonious vibration which is a result of the masterful selection and composition of the natural and man-made elements in a garden.

In Liu Yuan the four important and symbolic elements in a garden – water, rocks, plants and buildings – combine to create the fifth essential element – peace. This was how one of our guides, Jamie, succinctly expressed it and I think it is hard to improve on.

In Liu Yuan the elegant Mandarin Duck Hall, for instance, symbolizing conjugal fidelity, has two sections back to back. The dignified but less ornate south-facing part was used by the men to entertain their guests; the more ornate north-facing section was the women's quarters. Views from the two sides of the hall and from the numerous *lang* that connect the buildings and lead the visitor around the pond past numerous small 'space-cells' which are viewed through the lattice work windows (no two are alike in this garden) give the impression of a scroll painting unfolding. The aims of the Chinese landscape painter and the garden designer are inextricably linked. Both are trying to recreate the essence of Taoist philosophy which emphasizes the totality of nature, by presenting numerous different experiences in a relatively small space.

The 'cloud-crowned rock' weighing five tons and standing 6.5 metres high is considered one of the most beautiful Taihu rocks in Suzhou and is one of the largest. It is admired for exhibiting all the characteristics most sought after in rocks from Lake Tai. It is slim with wrinkles on its surface which emphasize the fact that it is formed by nature not by human hand. The many horizontal holes in it suggest transparency in the midst of solidity, and its numerous vertical holes mean that it doesn't hold water after rain but retains its beautifully clean and dry appearance. Other rocks in the gardens are thought to resemble the shapes of animals – an elephant, eagle or dog – and these grotesque shapes confuse the viewer's sense of time and space and thus lead to that state of 'suspended time' which makes us aware of our oneness with nature.

Finally, the reflections of rocks, buildings, trees and corridors in the luminous surface of the pond help to create a mood of harmony, delight and refreshment.

The pebble mosaic work in Liu Yuan is also designed to indicate changes of mood or function in a particular part of the garden as well as to portray actual patterns denoting recognized symbols. Thus goldfish represent gold in abundance, the lotus symbolizes the spirit of an intellectual scholar, a deer symbolizes propriety, and so on.

Lastly Liu Yuan contains numerous engraved stones in the halls and corridors. These beautiful tablets of calligraphy are common in Suzhou gardens because writing was considered an essential part of civilized intellectual pursuits. It is one of the things a person would do while in a garden – compose poems, study historical figures and write about them. Stone calligraphy added authority and importance to a garden, authenticating its owner as a scholar and man of letters and sometimes suggesting his high connections if a tablet was engraved by a friend or visitor who was also a person of rank or importance.

Liu Yuan justly deserves its name. There is so much to see and absorb that one should allow plenty of time to 'linger' otherwise much of the subtlety of the composition is lost.

Address: Liu Yuan (The Lingering Garden), 79 Liu Yuan Road, Suzhou, China.

A lang corridor, open on both sides, zigzags round the pond linking tings and rockeries.

Shansui peng jing (Chinese landscape bonsai) in which rocks, moss, water and plants are used to make a miniature landscape, in The Lingering Garden.

Rock, moss and pine shansui peng jing in The Lingering Garden.

The Lingering Garden.

The Humble Administrator's Garden.

Peng jing (Chinese bonsai) concentrates on the miniature plants alone, in The Humble Administrator's Garden.

The Humble Administrator's Garden.

The Humble Administrator's Garden.

1703–92 BI SHU SHUAN ZHUANG (MOUNTAIN HAMLET FOR ESCAPING THE HEAT) Qing dynasty.

The Emperors Kangxi and Qian Long spent 89 years building this enormous and complex Imperial garden. Visited March 24.

The frozen lake.

Barges take visitors across the lake.

Bi Shu Shuan Zhuang, the Imperial Mountain Resort, is literally translated as Mountain Hamlet for Escaping the Heat and it was because of its delightfully cool and pleasant landscape set in the valley and hills around the town of Chengde (formerly known as Rehe) that in 1703 Emperor Kangzi initiated the construction of the Imperial Mountain Resort so that the Court could spend the hot summer months 256 kilometres away from the claustrophobic heat of the Forbidden City.

Emperor Kangxi and his grandson Emperor Qian Long after him together spent eighty-nine years building the enormous complex of palaces, halls, towers, courtyards, pagodas, temples, lakes, islands and causeways that make up the Imperial Mountain Resort which covers over five million square metres and is twice the size of the Summer Palace in Beijing.

The Imperial Mountain Resort can be divided into two distinct parts – the enormous walled area in which the Imperial Family lived, worked and played and the equally enormous hilly area outside the walls, dotted around which, in the shape of a crescent moon, twelve temples were built that reflected the cultural diversity of the Chinese people. The enormous scale of the entire project was designed, of course, to reflect the power and wealth of the Qing dynasty.

It is impossible to view this garden in detail in one or even two days as the complex is so vast, so we confined ourselves to looking at certain areas in some detail in order to appreciate the particular distinguishing qualities of this, the largest surviving Imperial Garden in China.

What differentiates Bi Shu Shuan Zhuang from other Qing Imperial gardens is that it is enclosed by a wall ten kilometres in circumference, in which the 110 or so buildings on the complex are grouped in relatively independent clusters dotted around the landscape devoid of the extravagant ornamentation characteristic of other Imperial Palaces. The Hall of Frugality and Sincerity, the main hall of the Front Palace, the equivalent of the lavish Hall of Supreme Harmony in the Forbidden City, is built of *nanmu* wood which, on rainy or misty days, emits a fragrant aromatic odour that permeates the Hall. The beams, rafters and columns of this wooden structure are not lavishly painted although some partitions are engraved with patterns symbolizing good luck and longevity.

The natural elegance and simplicity of these buildings is very much in keeping with the overall design of the resort which aimed to retain the rich pastoral feel of the northern hamlets and Mongolian grasslands beyond as well as preserving and protecting the natural environment of hills, crags, waters, woods and wildlife, in the midst of which the resort is situated.

To the north of the Front Palace buildings and overlooked from it is the lake area, covering more than 30 hectares and dotted with eight islands of varying sizes, joined or reached by bridges, causeways and boats. Qian Long himself declared that the best views of the resort were from the lake area and one of the Emperor's favourite viewing areas was reported to be from Yan Yu Lou (the Tower of the Mist and Rain) on the Green Lotus Isle on the north of Ruyi Island. Here the 'borrowed' views (*jiejing*) of the strange pestle-shaped rock silhouetted on the mountains beyond, create an extraordinary sense of space and timelessness. The stairway to the Ming Pavilion on top of the rockeries and caves next to the two other pavilions around the tower on the islet gives wonderfully scenic views across the lake.

The ideas behind the creation of islands on water go back to the Taoist myth of the Islands in the Eastern Sea inhabited by the Immortals. The Emperors hoped that by creating such beautiful and dream-like scenery the Immortals would be diverted from their real home to visit these islands and thus confer immortality on the Emperors who created them.

Not generally visited by foreign visitors, probably because of shortage of time, is the western part of the garden. Here the remains of about forty buildings are dotted around the hillside and a few of them have gradually been reconstructed. One building well worth visiting in the north-eastern area is the Wen Jin Je Hall, the Emperor's Library, which was one of the four major book repositories of the Qing dynasty. Surrounded by a wall, this secluded hall has, in front of it, a huge rockery reflecting into a small pool between its base and the platform of the Library Hall. In the pool can be seen the reflection of the sun and moon simultaneously. This scientific 'miracle' came about because Emperor Qian Long, who considered himself the ruler of the entire universe, wanted to view all elements of his empire (earth, sun and moon) at the same time. So, a sycophantic but brilliant courtier devised the idea of cutting a crescent moon shape in a certain part of the

View across the lake from The Golden Hill Pavilion.

Wen Jin Je Hall. Note the tiny moon reflection in the foreground.

The extraordinary pestle-shaped rock on the horizon is a superb example of jiejing (borrowed views) at Bi Shu Shuan Zhuang.

Pu Tuo Zong Sheng Zhi Miao, Temple of Potaraka Doctrine, is modelled on the Potala Palace in Lhasa, Tibet.

View from the Grand Red Terrace over the Temple of Potaraka Doctrine shows that many of the buildings at Bi Shu Shuan Zhuang are just shells built for effect (follies).

rockery with the result that when the sun shone a crescent moon reflection could be seen in the pool as well as the sun's own reflection. Thus the Emperor achieved his heart's desire and, no doubt, the courtier received his too!

The vast tract of grassland to the north of the lake comprises the Wan Shu Yuan (Garden of Ten Thousand Trees) and the Shi Ma Dai (Horse-Testing Ground). Here there are no large-scale buildings as this was the area where the Qing Government concentrated on cementing friendly relationships with the national minority tribes by holding grand banquets, firework displays and equestrian shows. Qian Long erected twenty-eight yurts in the Wan Shu Yuan which were used for meeting and housing ethnic minority dignitaries and envoys from foreign countries, including the first British ambassador to China, George MacCartney, in 1792 (the meeting was not a success), and the 6th Biangen Lama from Tibet.

In contrast to the austere simplicity of the buildings within the walls of the Mountain Resort, the buildings in the foothills outside the walls are renowned for their magnificent ornamentation. The contrast of the two styles is felt to offset and complement each other and together form a single harmonious entity.

The twelve temples originally built around the Bi Shu

Shuan Zhuang were designed to reflect the different ethnic nationalities of the borderland. Of the original twelve, three are no longer extant and two are totally dilapidated. Known as the Eight Outer Temples, they are very different in style but have one feature in common – Lamaism: they all represent the architecture of both inland and borderland temples and 'embody the civilization created jointly by Chinese ethnic nationalities and show that China is a multinational country', according to the guide book.

Because it is rather less accessible than Beijing, the Bi Shu Shuan Zhuang at Chengde is not overwhelmed by crowds of tourists – either Chinese or European – which makes it much more rewarding to visit. Wandering around the virtually empty garden (although there was a Chinese film crew filming the latest episode of a popular historical 'soap' in the hall of the Green Lotus Isle!) the incredible wealth, power and culture attained by the Qing Emperors, who every year were carried in sedan chairs the 256 kilometres from Beijing, can be felt in the complex combination of artificial and natural landscape that has been incorporated into the Imperial Mountain Resort.

Address: Bi Shu Shuan Zhuang (Mountain Hamlet for Escaping the Heat), Chengde, China.

1750 WANG SHI YUAN (MASTER OF THE FISHING NETS' GARDEN) Qing dynasty.

This view of The Master of the Fishing Nets' Garden shows how a single specimen tree can be used to great effect. Visited April 2.

View of the Library Courtyard.

Wang Shi Yuan, Master of the Fishing Nets' Garden, was first built in 1140 by Shi Zhenghi, a cultivated scholar-official, to house his private library of 10,000 books and was called Yu Yin, or Fisherman's Retreat. After a period of obscurity the garden was redesigned in about 1750 by another famous scholar-official Song Zenghuan, Vice-Director of Imperial Entertainment at the Court of Emperor Qian Long. It was he who gave the garden its present name Wang Shi, which alluded not only to his own pen name which meant Master of the Fishing Nets but also to the garden's earlier name. Falling into disrepair again by the end of the eighteenth century it was redesigned by Qu Yuancun. He named many of the halls and pavilions after famous literary works and subsequent owners have fine-honed the complicated series of buildings, gardens and courtyards that make up this tightly packed and complex 1-acre garden.

Wang Shi Yuan is different from most of the other Suzhou gardens because it has living quarters attached to the garden (many gardens were completely separate from the owner's house) and these buildings are open to the public along with the rest of the garden. Indeed the house was lived in until 1958.

Access to the garden is from the north-east corner through an entrance in a high white-washed wall off a jostling alley selling silk shirts and *chops* (carved soapstone stamps). The screen in front of the entrance to the house was designed not only to keep evil spirits away

A Chinese garden can be compared to a scroll painting with composition after composition being created at every turn.

by preventing them turning around and escaping (therefore they avoided the place altogether) but also to block the view into the garden and thus heighten our anticipation of what was to come. Once through the first small, rectangular courtyard, the visitor is confronted by a choice of directions, which all lead to the lake and Pavilion of the Clouds and Moon.

All the paths take the visitor by different routes, around the complex series of halls, courtyards, corridors, engraved tablets, rockeries, pavilions and galleries that fit together so intricately and compactly, just like a Chinese puzzle. If there is a little sliver of extra space, it is used to create another view, another scene, so that the whole tour is like the slow unrolling of a scroll of landscape painting. Layer upon layer of images can be unpeeled, each adding to the series of contrasts and counterpoints (*yin* and *yang*) with which the garden abounds. Hard rocks, silky fronds of bamboo, light, shade, water, sky, dark halls, tight framed views, open spacious courtyards, single rocks, rock piles, views from upper storeys accessed only from the winding rockery at its side, views on the level of the water from dark, wooden screened halls – the list is endless, the density unparalleled in other gardens.

Even though the area of the house and garden is so small (relatively) and the layout when studied on paper so logical (the overall plot is virtually square and the buildings are more or less built around the central pond) the experience of actually going round the garden is one of great mystery and complexity. It's like a maze – one catches numerous glimpses of the lake and the central pavilion but it is impossible to go to either of them directly.

Wang Shi Yuan deserves its reputation and status as one of the most important gardens preserved by the State for it epitomizes all the attributes and characteristics most admired by the Chinese in their gardens and, despite its smallness and popularity, there always seems to be a quiet, secluded corner in which to enjoy and achieve harmony.

In the evening it is possible to go to Wang Shi Yuan and watch snippets of traditional art forms being performed in the garden. It is a charming experience because not only do you see and hear some interesting pieces of music, opera, theatre and dance but the garden has far fewer people in it than during the day and captures the magical peaceful quality, the aura of transporting one's soul into a harmonious relationship with the natural world, so central to Chinese garden philosophy.

Address: Wang Shi Yuan (Master of the Fishing Nets' Garden), 11 Kuojia Lane, Suzhou, China.

A view across the lake towards the Pavilion of the Clouds and Moon.

1750–65 YI HE YUAN (THE GARDEN OF HAPPY HARMONY) Qing dynasty.

The Seventeen Arch Bridge on Kunming Lake. Visited March 26.

Yi He Yuan (I Ho Yuan), The Garden of Happy Harmony, is the Imperial Summer Palace on the north-western outskirts of Beijing designed by the great garden-building Emperor of the Qing Dynasty (1644–1911), Qian Long (1736–95). In the area in which Yi He Yuan is situated, around Wengshan Hill and Lake, Qian Long had already built one famous garden called Yuan Ming Yuan, whose purpose was to 'refresh the mind and regulate the emotions' by providing an Imperial retreat from the Forbidden City, but he couldn't resist creating another garden.

Although this area seemed a totally wild and natural site when Qian Long began landscaping it, in fact, the contours of the land had already been shaped and adapted by earlier Emperors. In the twelfth century Wengshan Hill had been known as Golden Hill and at that time it was only 60 metres high. However, an Imperial order was made to divert water from the Jade Mountain Hill into the Golden Water Pond at the foot of Golden Hill and it is said that in the following century an old man found a jar or Golden Hill so the name was changed to Wengshan Hill (Jar Hill).

Around this time Emperor Shizu (1260–94) ordered the dredging of the Golden Water Pond and by diverting the springs of the Sheshan and Jade Mountain Hill into it, the pond was expanded into a lake known as Dabo Lake which acted as a conduit for water into the capital and as a reservoir for watering the fertile paddy fields of the area. These grew rice so wonderfully flavoured by the Jade Spring water that it was reputedly reserved exclusively for the Emperor's consumption.

Over the next couple of centuries successive Emperors, recognizing the great beauty of the area which, with its fertile paddy-fields, was reminiscent of the scenery in southern China, built various temples and residences around the lake. However, it was during Qian Long's reign that the area was systematically developed into what still remains the largest Imperial Garden in China, covering an area of 290 hectares of which about 220 hectares are water.

When Qian Long came to the throne he asserted that he would bring no shame upon himself and his ancestors by indulging in any form of excess, yet he could not resist the urge to create yet another Imperial Garden right next to the far-famed one he had just built at Yuan Ming Yuan.

'When I had this beautiful hill and beautiful lake, how could I refrain from building the terrace and buildings suitable to it?'

So, as 1750 saw his mother's sixtieth birthday, he decided to build the new garden in her honour taking as his model one of her favourite areas Xi Hu, West Lake in Hangzhou (see page 250).

Originally named Qing Yi Yuan (The Garden of Clear Ripples), the relandscaping and building of the garden took fifteen years to complete. The lake was expanded and dredged, dikes were built to divide it and its name was changed to Kunming Lake. The hill was enlarged, the old Ming dynasty temple was removed and the Temple of Gratitude for Longervity was built on its site. The hill itself was renamed Longevity Hill in honour of Qian Long's mother Empress Xiaosheng.

Qian Long didn't stop there. During the rest of his reign he continued to create gardens in the north-western suburbs of Beijing. In all, he built what were known as The Three Hills and Five Parks in the area but, it was said Qing Yi Yuan (the Garden of Clear Ripples) was his favourite.

A hundred years later, in 1860, the Three Hills and Five Parks were reduced to ashes when the Anglo-French

Jade Fountain Hill and Pagoda overlooking Kunming Lake.

The Boat of Purity and Ease, known as the Marble Boat.

forces invaded Beijing. Six years later the Empress Dowager Cixi, under the pretext of developing a naval training academy on Kunming Lake, directed funds given for that project into secretly rebuilding the garden buildings on the front part of Longevity Hill which on its completion in 1888 was renamed Yi He Yuan, The Garden of Happy Harmony, and declared to be the Imperial Summer Palace – both names by which it is still known today.

Devastated for a second time in 1900 by the Allied Forces after the Boxer Rebellion, the ruined buildings were rebuilt by the Empress Dowager Cixi immediately on her return in 1902 and from then until her death in 1908 she spent the greater part of each year at the Summer Palace, living and conducting state business in the numerous buildings that form the complex.

In the mid-twentieth century funds were allocated for the restoration of Yi He Yuan but during the Cultural Revolution most of the original paintings on the *lang* walkway were slashed with knives and it was not until the 1980s that full-scale renovation of the dilapidated buildings on Longevity Hill commenced.

The enormous complex of Imperial Gardens – the Three Hills and Five Parks – that existed around this area between 1760 and 1860 were famed throughout

China and known about in the West from the descriptions written by Père Attiret (1760–68), a Christian missionary who worked as a court painter for Qian Long. Yet today we can only get a feel of its magnificence from what remains, namely the Yi He Yuan, which incorporates most of the important philosophical ideas about gardens which had developed over the centuries both from the north and the south.

Qian Long visited the area south of the Yangtze six times in his life and ordered his court painters to make references sketches of ideas and scenes that appealed to him for use in his landscaping plans. Thus the Yi He Yuan combines elements of the restraint and refinement typical of southern gardens with the grandeur and space more typical of northern traditions.

The Imperial Summer Palace is composed of two main elements: the lake with its islands and bridges and the hill with its complex buildings.

Kunming Lake, which covers three-quarters of the total Summer Palace area, is divided into three sections by a forking dike and each section has a small island in the centre. This pattern of 'one pool, three hills', which the lake and islands represent, was a traditional one based on the Taoist myth of the Immortals.

The largest island, South Lake Island, is linked to the

The Tower of the Fragrance of Buddha.

Blue Iris Hill. A huge boulder found by Emperor Qian Long.

Giant rocks in the courtyard of the Hall of Benevolence and Longevity.

Details within the Garden of Harmonious Pleasures, a garden within a garden.

The lang corridor.

A lotus door.

Bronze lion.

The Garden of Harmonious Pleasures.

dike by the Seventeen Arch Bridge and views from here, of the lake and the islands, 'borrow' (*jiejing*) the landscape of the Western Hills beyond and seemingly increase the dimensions of the overall landscape, in a way that is very reminiscent of Xi Hu, West Lake, in Hangzhou (see page 250).

Another striking feature around the lake is the marble boat at the bottom of Longevity Hill at the far end of the lake from the eastern entrance through which visitors enter. This boat, built in 1755 and symbolizing the solidity of the Qing dynasty, can be reached by walking along the *lang* (walkway) or Long Promenade. Corridors are very important in Chinese gardens as a way of linking or dividing space and providing viewing points for looking at scenic spots. This walkway is reputed to be the best in China because its open sides offer views both across the lake and up the hillside. Seven hundred and fifty metres in length, it has four large octagonal pavilions along it and is divided into 273 sections, each beautifully decorated on the eaves and beams by little scenes of gardens, flowers and landscape, many of which were destructively scraped by knives during the Cultural Revolution but have been renovated in the last two decades.

The complex of buildings on both sides of Longevity Hill has been greatly reduced since Qian Long's time but the dominating features are the huge Tower of the Fragrance of Buddha and the Hall that Dispels the Clouds, both of which offer spectacular views out across the lake. Numerous other buildings grouped around these two main features are dotted around the hillside.

One of the most famous and beloved sections of Yi He Yuan is the Xie Qu Yuan, the Garden of Harmonious Pleasures or the Garden within a Garden which is based on Ji Chang Yuan, the Garden for Easing the Mind (see page 258), a famous southern garden in Wuxi. Its five halls, seven pavilions and numerous walkways and bridges are all built around a lotus pond and the overall

impression and atmosphere is very reminiscent, though on a larger scale, of the southern Chinese Gardens.

Continuing around the Back Hill area from Xie Qu Yuan to the northern slope of the hill, one comes to the area where in Qian Long's time, according to the old records, there were eight gardens of different sizes. Recent renovations have included the rebuilding of the massive temples of the four Great Regions and the restoration of the Suzhou Street, a typical riverside street where, in Qian Long's time, his concubines would go shopping in the little stores to get a flavour of 'real' life. Today, the Back Hill area remains a quiet and relatively unvisited section of the park.

Contemplating the immensity of this garden, and realizing that it is only a part of what was once a much larger area landscaped and shaped to give pleasure to the Emperor and his court, makes Versailles (see pages 78–80) seem relatively small and self-contained. Here, despite the shaping of the landscape and the symmetry within the building complexes, the overall impression is one of great naturalness; like the great landscaped parks in Britain, the artifice has been designed to appear 'a natural and wild view of the country; a rural retirement, and not a Palace formed according to the rules of Art' as Père Attiret wrote in 1749.

Yi He Yuan is so huge and there is so much to see that you should try to allow a day to visit it all. It's easy to get bogged down in the building complexes and architectural features whereas viewing them from the lake, and vice versa, is really the purpose of the garden and seeing the interplay of light and shade of the whole landscape is the way to achieve the mental relaxation Qian Long declared was essential for moral health: 'Every Emperor . . . must have a garden in which he may stroll, look around and relax his heart'.

Address: Yi He Yuan (Imperial Summer Palace), Beijing, China.

19TH Century OU YUAN (THE COUPLE'S RETREAT) Qing dynasty.

Prunus glandulosa 'Plena' on the rock mountain. Visited April 5.

Ou Yuan means Garden of the Couple's Retreat and is so called because it comprises two gardens, an east garden and a west garden, which were built on either side of a residential house by Lu Jin, a magistrate, in the late-seventeenth century (early Qing dynasty) but completely redesigned in its present form in the nineteenth century, by Shen Bingcheng.

The west garden has two courtyards divided by a studio building and an interesting rockery. However, this section of the garden is closed to the public and although we were told by our guide that it is undergoing renovation at the moment and was due to open in June 1994 we didn't see or hear any evidence of restoration work.

The east garden, which is open to the public, has an open courtyard inside the entrance which is bounded by a white wall with several *lou chuang* (latticed windows) set into it and a beautiful round moon gate framing the garden beyond and enticing one in. Through this the two-storeyed main hall is obscured from view by a large artificial 'hill' or rockery made of yellow stone which is admired for the craftsmanship of its composition. To the east of the rockery is a narrow reflecting pool which runs southwards to a summer house with numerous lattice-worked windows alongside the water. There are wonderful views across the garden to the city beyond from the double-storeyed *lou* (building).

This is one of the best gardens to visit in Suzhou. Not because its individual features are necessarily better than those of the city's other famous gardens but because it, above all the others, has that essential quality of being 'a place to relax and beat the heart' and 'refresh the mind'. Being ten minutes' walk along canalside streets, away from anywhere accessible by coach, it is rarely visited by tourists and even more rarely by Europeans. We had to insist to our guide that we were capable of walking for a whole ten minutes and definitely wanted to see the garden. It was well worth it. Our guide said she had only visited it once before in 1981 (and she was the China International Travel Service garden specialist) so that gives one some idea of how quiet and peaceful it is.

The only other people there were two lads sword fighting with bamboo poles. When I asked why they weren't at school, I was told that the caretaker had given them special permission to come in and study peacefully. Boys and caretaker alike were subscribing to the age-old tradition of a garden as a place for quiet study and contemplation but the boys obviously also subscribed to the view that a garden was a place for frivolity and play!

Address: Ou Yuan (Garden of the Couple's Retreat), 8 Xiaoxinqiao Lane, Suzhou, China.

The Moon Gate.

Stalactite-shaped rocks known as Bamboo Shoot Rocks.

1918 LI YUAN (LI'S GARDEN) Republic era.

A labyrinth of rocks make up the Lake Tai Rockery. Visited April 2.

Pond of the Four Seasons with tings on the causway which separate it from the lake.

The One Thousand Step Corridor features 80 latticed windows, no two the same.

Li Yuan, literally Li's Garden, was built in 1918 to commemorate the work of Fan Li, an eminent prime minister who, reputedly, lived 3000 years ago and is credited with introducing Wuxi to the four major industries on which the city still thrives: silk manufacture, fish farming, freshwater pearl culture and tea growing. Xi Hu, West Lake, (see page 250) was named after Fan Li's favourite concubine, so his importance to this part of China is undisputed.

Li Yuan covers about 15 hectares of which approximately 7 hectares are water. The garden is arranged in four main sections: the pavilions and fountains in and around the Pond of the Four Seasons, the promenade or causeway across the lake, the One Thousand Step Corridor and the Lake Tai Rockery.

Despite the fact that it is a twentieth-century garden, it has been landscaped to reflect the centuries-old traditional characteristics and symbolic features of Chinese gardens. The causeway or promenade has enabled part of the landscape of the lake (Lake Li, which is connected to Lake Tai) to be 'borrowed' (*jiejing*) into the garden to provide the harmonious water setting so essential to the Chinese philosophy of landscape. In addition to this, the planting of trees and the positioning of pavilions (*tings*) on the causeway add foreground and variety to the views of the lake and the hills beyond, thus 'borrowing' that further landscape into the garden.

The principal kinds of trees planted in the garden symbolize the seasons and ensure that something is blooming throughout the year to emphasize the cyclical aspect of nature. Thus plum trees for spring, oleanders for summer, sweet osmanthus for autumn and chimanthus for winter.

The provision of constantly changing views, which is such an important feature of Chinese gardens, is facilitated by the building of corridors (*lang*). The Thousand Step Corridor, which joins the two parts of Li Yuan that run along the shore of the lake, is open on the side nearest to the water to enable the wide vistas across the lake to be enjoyed and is walled on the other side. However, the walled side has eighty different latticed windows that provide tantalizing and charmingly framed views of the inland fields outside the garden.

The Great Rockery, constructed from contorted lumps of rock dredged up from Lake Tai and highly acclaimed for their grotesque and fantastic shapes, seems rather coarsely and crudely made when viewed from close-up. Size and quantity seem to have become more important than the dignity and strangeness of form which can be seen in the smaller or individual rocks found in the private gardens in Suzhou.

Address: Li Yuan (Li's Garden), Wuxi, China.

One of the 80 latticed windows.

Plum blossom symbolizes spring.

The symbolic cherry in the reconstructed Heian Shrine.

Introduction

Japanese gardens, like Chinese ones, fascinate and intrigue the Western visitor and garden historian because, particularly on first encounter, they seem so different from European gardens. The religious and philosophical ideas that have shaped the cultures of the East – Shintoism, Hinduism, Taoism and Buddhism – are very different from the classical mythologies, Christianity and Islam, that have shaped Western thought in general and influenced European garden traditions in particular.

Having visited some of Japan's most renowned gardens and done some reading around the subject to write this book, it was interesting to observe the reaction of two European children, who had been dragged round many famous gardens in Britain, France, Italy and Germany, to some of the dominant recurring themes in a Japanese garden.

'Why can't we walk on it?' and 'This isn't a garden – there are no flowers,' were frequent observations yet one of the fundamental philosophies underlying the making of gardens in any culture is essentially the same – namely man's attempt, in his garden, to search for his place within nature and, by extension, his search for himself. Gardens reflect man's view of the world.

In the middle of the sixth century AD Chinese culture began to permeate all aspects of Japanese life but before that time Shintoism was the prevailing religion and its fundamental emphasis on the parity between man and nature, including stones and plants as well as animals, meant that any remarkable feature in nature could be worshipped and had its own divinity. This gave rise to the importance of the *genius loci* – the spirit of the place – which has, over the centuries, remained an important element in Japanese garden design. Seeing, maintaining and emphasizing the essential spirit of nature in the garden is always a priority.

From Shintoism, then, arose a number of archetypes that have remained characteristic of Japanese gardens throughout the centuries. One is the appreciation of the beauty of natural rock which probably stems from the fact that rock formations were considered sacred. Another is the common occurrence of pebble beaches or pebble areas that hark back to the areas of hallowed ground in ancient and modern Shinto shrines.

Other archetypal features arose from the arrival of Buddhism via China. For example, the representation of a mountain, referring to Mount Meru, the cosmic mountain at the centre of the universe in Buddhist philosophy, is a recurrent image that has been interpreted in various ways throughout the history of Japanese gardening. From Taoist mythology comes the belief in the existence of an island of immortality. The Chinese believed that there were five islands inhabited by the Blessed who had obtained immortality (see page 247) but the Japanese condensed this to just one, the island of P'eng-lai or Horai-zan, which was symbolized in garden architecture as a Horai mountain, island or rock or sometimes as a crane or turtle island.

Another archetype, that of the pond islands in Buddhist temples, reflects the popular belief in the Pure Land attained by those who devote their life to the Amida Buddha. Like the other religious influences, this one offers man what he craves above all else, namely to outwit nature, defy death and achieve immortality.

The arrangement of rocks in groups of three also appears frequently. The significance here is more aesthetic than religious but, for example, the use of three elements, one large, one medium and one small in dynamic juxtaposition or balance, sometimes alone or as part of a larger sequence (often beside a waterfall or on the banks of a pond), is also found in other Japanese art forms such as Noh theatre or the art of flower arranging. The three elements have been defined in gardening texts as representing three forces – the horizontal, the diagonal and the vertical – corresponding to the tripartite structure of the universe: Heaven, Earth and Mankind.

All these archetypes are at the heart of Japanese gardening history but, as Günter Nitschke points out in his book *Japanese Gardens*, the role assigned to rocks and plants by garden designers has evolved over the centuries reflecting the religious, social and artistic changes in the nation's culture. Each generation has taken the traditional archetypes and then superimposed its own ideas on top of these to create a new prototype – old and new ideas fusing together to form a dynamic reinterpretation of the fundamental elements. Sometimes, of course, a hackneyed cliché is produced and then the archetypal concepts are reduced, in later generations, to repetitious stereotypes.

The Heian Period (794–1185)

The first great era of Japanese garden history is the Heian period (794–1185) which began when the capital of Japan was moved in 794 to Heian-kyo, Capital of Peace and Tranquillity (present day Kyoto), where it remained until 1868. This period reflects the second great phase of Chinese influence on Japanese culture which can be clearly identified in the design of the palaces and gardens. Sadly, no gardens of this period survive but descriptions in the *Tale of Prince Genji* by Lady Murasaki Shikibu (*c*.987–1031) (translated by Arthur Waley) and other literary and historical sources have given the modern garden historian quite a clear picture of what gardens of this period were like. The oldest surviving text on garden architecture is the eleventh-century *Sakutei-ki* by Tachibana no Toshitsuna. It describes in detail the first major prototype of the Japanese garden, incorporating the important Chinese geomantic principle of *feng shui* (see page 250) which the Japanese thought essential to the design of palaces and gardens: 'to ensure good fortune, water must flow in from the east, pass beneath the floor of the house and flow out to the south-west.

As well as discussing design principles that were imported from China, the *Sakutei-ki* also describes other design principles, namely that gardens should be recreated in the likeness of real nature; that rocks already on the site should be respected for their own inner stillness and personality; that rocks, islands and ponds should always be placed asymmetrically within the symmetrical Shinden style, i.e. the asymmetry of nature should be placed in opposition to the symmetry of the man-made object, and lastly, it stresses the importance of the paradox that exists between the instinctual spirit of the garden and the highly personal taste of the garden architect.

Nothing remains of the great Imperial Palace pleasure gardens of the eighth century, known as *dai-dairi* 'the great inner interior', based on the Chinese model (The Forbidden City, see page 254), but we know it was composed of symmetrically arranged buildings on a central axis around a main hall or Shinden. Gardens in the palace were of two types: the south garden reserved for political and religious ceremonial occasions which was carpeted with white sand and contained two trees, a cherry and a mandarin fenced off and symmetrically positioned within the courtyard; and, in stark contrast, the inner courtyard garden which was small and intimate, often concentrating on one plant or plant type and providing views for the ladies whose rooms overlooked them.

The Heian nobility, like the Emperor's household, modelled their homes and gardens on Chinese fashions. But the south garden in houses of the nobility became much more elaborate than the stark empty sandy surfaces of the Imperial Palace's south garden. Their residential halls were connected by covered corridors that wound round the edges of large ponds with islands linked by arched bridges.

In the later Heian period symmetry was abandoned in favour of asymmetrically constructed palace complexes in which buildings no longer stood isolated but flowed from one to the next. The gardens featured a pond, with one or more islands, fed by a stream entering and leaving the garden as prescribed by ancient geomantic principles.

Sadly, we only know of these great Fujiwara palaces from historical reconstructions based on scroll paintings, not from any extant buildings.

The Kamakura and Muromachi Period (1185–1333–1568)

These two periods of Japanese garden history show how, over a period of nearly four hundred years, the political, social and religious changes that took place in Japan were reflected in the types of gardens constructed and admired in these eras.

The twelfth century saw another great wave of Chinese cultural influence on its neighbour; the most important elements being the rise of Zen Buddhism and the effect of Chinese landscape painting of the Song and Yuan dynasties. These created an emphasis on a new garden prototype – *kare-sansui*, literally 'withered mountain-water'. This was the small dry landscape garden attached to or bordered by a *shoin*-style building (see glossary) which was designed not as a pleasure garden but as an object to be contemplated, like a painting, from several fixed vantage points. Although the materials used in the construction of these gardens were natural (i.e. rock, stone, moss, etc.), the abstract composition of the garden was such that the aim was to suggest the inner essence of nature, not to reproduce its outward forms in a naturalistic landscape.

It was during the Kamakura period that the important Rinzai sect of Zen Buddhism was founded in Japan by the monk Eisai (1141–1215) and understanding something of the essential philosophy behind Zen Buddhism is important for the westerner trying to grasp the meaning of Japanese gardens. The word Zen is derived from a Sanskrit word meaning meditation and the importance of Zen Meditation is that it is based on the belief that meditation is the route to enlightenment, not as in Pure Land Buddhism where salvation is by the means of *ta-riki* 'power from outside', but by *ji-riki* 'power from oneself'. Zen Meditation means passing beyond the limits of the mind to a state of *mu-shin*, 'no mind'. This is not mindlessness but full awareness; by distancing oneself from the questioning, thinking and judging aspects of the mind, one is able to 'experience' enlightenment. This achievement of *mu-shin* that is unknown to the West and yet is at the heart of Eastern/Asian spirituality is the East's greatest contribution to the development of human consciousness.

The importance of this to the history of gardens is not that contemplating *kare-sansui* gardens made Zen disciples achieve enlightenment, but rather that these gardens are the products of minds that have experienced enlightenment and have tried to express that experience in the design of their gardens.

During the Kamakura and early Muromachi eras, gardens of the Old Heian prototype with their ponds and islands were still constructed. Kinkaku-ji, the Golden Pavilion (see page 290) and Ginkaku-ji, the Silver Pavilion (see page 292) are two examples although there were also new variations, such as pond-spring-strolling gardens, which were designed to be enjoyed on foot rather than by boat as was previously the case.

However, it was the *kare-sansui* landscape that became the prototype for these eras. Shigemori, one of the most renowned scholars of Japanese gardens, sees the development of *kare-sansui* into the new prototype for Japanese gardens as having four stages.

The first, prehistoric stage was the worship of huge rocks and boulders by Shinto followers believing them to be the homes of the gods. The second stage, in the Heian period, when the word first appeared in the *Sakutei-ki*, was when rock formations were very occasionally incorporated into the pond-and-island gardens as a small integral component not having any importance in their own right. The third stage, in the Kamakura era, shows the dry garden still appearing in conjunction with the pond garden but no longer being relegated to a secondary role, and the fourth and final stage, starting from the end of the Kamakura era and continuing until the present day, being when some gardens were laid out exclusively in the *kare-sansui* style.

Shigemori propounds that the *kare-sansui* garden reflects two ideals essential to Muromachi thought: one, a deep and austere elegance that conceals layers of symbolic meaning and two, the beauty of empty space. So, while the Heian garden tries to imitate nature with a carefully selected and composed collection of natural features, the Muromachi garden is attempting to capture the inner forms of nature by making abstract compositions out of natural materials.

Kodai-ji.

The Momoyama Period (1568–1603)

The Momoyama period is probably best known for its development of a new garden prototype. The *roji*, the 'path' or 'dewy ground' which is the tea garden, that leads to the *so-an* 'the grass-thatched hut' where the *wabi-cha*, the 'tea ceremony', is performed.

Unlike other contemporaneous gardens the *roji* was not designed to be viewed from a building but was a path which led to the tea arbour and, in due course, came to be seen as a rite of passage and an essential component in preparing oneself for the tea ceremony. Tea-drinking and tea ceremonies of various kinds had been popular in earlier centuries, the belief in the medicinal, religious and moral, aesthetic and social properties of tea having originally come from China.

It is thought that the Zen monk Muratoshuko (1422–1502) probably originated the *wabi*, tea ceremony. He built a little tea hut in the middle of Kyoto and furnished it with simple utensils which reflected his ascetic tastes. Other tea masters took this ideal of simplicity and austerity a step further. Takenojoo (1502–55) was the first to use the word *wabi*, meaning 'poverty' or

'restraint', to describe his tea ceremony and he, like his follower Sen no Rikyu who was also a Zen adept, felt that 'Zen and tea have the same taste'.

Thus the tea ceremony is designed to elevate our consciousness of our daily activities and in so doing to heighten our consciousness of ourselves. Similarly, every element in the tea garden has not only a functional but also an aesthetic and metaphorical purpose. For example, the *naka-kuguri* 'the middle crawl-through gate', because it is so small, forces the visitor to crouch which not only raises one's consciousness about one's body but also emphasizes the humility that is a necessary mental attribute when participating in a tea ceremony, as all social rank is suspended for the duration of the ceremony.

The main features of a tea garden are the *tobi-ishi*, the stepping-stones which physically guide visitors to the tea house, prevent them from trampling on the beautiful moss and dictate the views they see while, at the same time, slowing them down to prepare them mentally for what lies ahead. Stone lanterns to light the way at night and simple stone basins for cleansing oneself physically and spiritually are common features. The actual tea arbour usually resembles a small rustic retreat based on the traditional Japanese farmhouse. From inside the hut no view of the garden is visible, a marked contrast to previous eras in which the view from the house basically determined the garden's design.

The simplicity of the tea house was very influential in subsequent architectural design, giving rise to a break with the rigid traditional style of *shinden-zukuri* and *shoin-zukuri* and allowing a much freer and more functional kind of layout to become popular in all types of houses. This style, known as *Sukiya* 'a building of refined taste' is best seen in the Katsura Imperial Villa (see page 304).

The aesthetic ideal of the simple, common, modest rusticity implicit in the *wabi* tea ceremony is reflected in the design of the garden – it is not dry and austere like a *kare-sansui* dry landscape garden, nor are there large or dramatic rock formations or brightly coloured flowering trees and shrubs; instead there are muted colours, a great deal of moss, kept damp and green by water sprinkled on the paths, and stepping-stones. Everything appears totally natural. Hence the lovely story told of Sen no Rikyu going into the *roji* and finding that all the beautiful leaves that had shed on the moss early in the morning had been swept up by a fastidious host. Sen no Rikyu spent several minutes shaking the tree so that leaves would fall again and henceforth he told his disciples to sweep the *roji* several hours before the tea ceremony so that a natural effect of fallen leaves would be seen.

Although the pond gardens of the Momoyama period are based on the pond gardens of the earlier Muromachi era, they are much more complex in their overall design. The ponds' shores twist and wind about with jutting peninsulas and craggy inlets. Rocks had become a symbol of power and individuality and larger and more impressive rock formations became a garden feature.

Gardens were no longer designed mainly for strolling in but were increasingly constructed with the view from the *shoin* in mind. Ponds were sunk below the level of the buildings and shored up by rocks so that a dramatic overview was presented to those inside or on the veranda of the building.

Unfortunately, the main example of this type of Momoyama gardens, Tokushima Castle on the island of Shikoku, no longer exists. However, one garden that combines the qualities of a 'strolling' garden with those of a 'picture' garden – the winding paths constantly revealing a new vista – in the manner favoured by Hideyoshi, is the Daigo Sambo-in (see page 298).

In the *kare-sansui* dry gardens of the Momoyama period several features are noted. One, the fondness for larger rocks; two, the less abstract quality of the composition; and three, the decline in influence of the Chinese landscape painting style. The use, too, in some gardens of hewn stone, is something that would never have been found in the *kare-sansui* gardens of the Muromachi era.

Another feature of the Momoyama period is the use of *o-karikomi*, i.e. shrubs and bushes clipped into shapes suggestive of, for instance, Mount Horai, a treasure-laden ship or a storm-tossed sea, in junction with *kare-sansui*. It had existed before in garden design but under the great master of the art, Kobori Enshu (1579–1647), it became an important feature in gardens such as Konchi-in (see page 302). When he died so, too, largely did the fashion for this type of work.

The Edo Period
(1603–1868)

The Edo era was one of peace, stability and isolationism under the successful rule of the Tokugawa shoguns who established Edo (modern day Tokyo) as the capital and maintained control by imposing a rigid social structure on Japanese society and closing their doors to any outside influences from China and the West.

The Edo epoch, being one of great prosperity, saw a flowering of the creative arts, particularly in painting and woodcut printing, which was to have an influential impact on the development of gardens during the period. Many of the gardens of the Edo era are imitations of the prototypes of earlier times, i.e. the pond-and-island garden and the *kare-sansui* dry landscape garden. Yet what both types of garden benefited from was the clever use of *shakkei* 'borrowed landscape' in which distant views were incorporated into the overall design of the garden. Although *shakkei* had been a garden design technique for centuries, it became very popular in all types of gardens (except tea arbours) during the Edo period.

However, the new garden prototype for the Edo era was the large strolling garden. Although it is not an original prototype in the sense in which the original pond-and-island gardens or the *kare-sansui* gardens were, it is original in the sense that it makes use of numerous popular garden features such as ponds, islands, winding streams, waterfalls and rocks, in a completely new kind of way.

The object of a strolling garden is to take visitors around the whole site in a pre-ordained way in order that they may see the various changing vistas and set views that have been designed around the garden for that purpose. There is no climax to this process and the sequence of views which the visitor sees while strolling around are not a set of symbolic objects, but are perceived differently by different individuals with their own cultural perspectives. Some of the vistas are known as *shakkei* because they replicate, in miniature, natural scenery and, often, famous views. Strolling gardens were not, however, conceived of as one big master plan but rather worked on and added to over several generations.

The main components of the Edo period strolling garden were artificial hills (useful for an overview of the garden), artificial ponds, broad winding streams and waterfalls, islands (smaller than previously and often found singly, breaking with the earlier tradition of islands in pairs); rocks (fewer in number and less formal in composition than before) often erected as *yin/yang* stones to stress the male/female principle; plants, with an increase in topiary, groves of plum or cherry trees and sometimes small rice paddies to emphasize the rustic ideal; paths and bridges in greater number and variety to enable the visitor to traverse the irregular edges of the pond or to pass through groves or over hills; and tea arbours tucked away in small rustic tea gardens of their own, within the bigger strolling garden.

Another type of garden which is characteristic of the Edo period is the Hermitage garden. It combines elements of the strolling garden, tea garden, dry landscape garden and *shakkei* garden but scales it all down to a domestic size and, by manipulation of space and our experiences of it, creates an illusion of size in a confined area, rather in the manner of Sen no Rikyu's ritual for proceeding to the rustic tea hut. Shisen-do (see page 310) is one of the most famous examples of this type.

The Meiji Period
(1868–1912–Present)

When, in 1854, a friendship treaty between America and Japan was signed, followed twelve years later by a royalist coup that finally swept power away from the Tokugawa shoguns and restored it to the newly enthroned Emperor Meiji Tenno (1852–1912), Japan embarked on a policy of *bummei kaika*, the adoption of Western civilization and enlightenment.

This new receptiveness to the previously banned culture and values of the West had an immediate impact on architecture, literature and painting although it also brought with it a problem that continues to perplex the nation to this day: namely, how to enjoy the benefits of Western culture with its emphasis on the individual's needs and desires, with the centuries-old Japanese ethics of loyalty to the family, conformity to the social group and allegiance to the Emperor.

In 1871 a large number of the temples and *daimyo* gardens of the Momayama and Edo eras were declared public parks and those that had fallen into disrepair underwent an extensive restoration programme. Unfortunately, European influences crept in resulting in some very strange juxtapositions of styles. Sadly, too, many of the traditional architectural features such as stone lanterns and rocks were sold. The emphasis on the natural, the concept of gardens as true copies of nature, which had a worldwide following at this time, turned Japanese landscape and garden designers away from the 'nature as art' principles that had always been so dominant.

The idea of gardens being shaped and moulded by man into abstract landscapes only regained popularity in the Showa era (1926–89) with the result that there has been a revival of interest not only in the history of Japanese gardens owing to the extensive work of Mirei Shigemori, the great Japanese garden designer and historian, but also in the *kare-sansui* dry landscape garden.

Shugakuin Imperial Villa.

1337 TENJUAN in the NANZEN-JI COMPLEX Early Muromachi Period.

The pathway through the front garden of the Main Hall. Visited April 7.

Binding trees both protects and helps to shape them.

Originally constructed in 1337 to commemorate Daimin Kokushi, the great Zen master to whom Emperor Kameyama had dedicated the temple of Nanzen-ji, Tenjuan was ravaged by fires both before and during the Onin Wars (1467–77) and it was not until the end of the sixteenth century (Momoyama period) that it was reconstructed.

Tenjuan has two gardens – one on the front, or eastern side of the *shoin*, the other on the southern side, near the Study. Although the present buildings date from the Momoyama period, it is thought that much of the garden's design dates back to the early or middle Muromachi era. The eastern *kare-sansui* dry rock garden, with its geometrically designed stone footpath embedded in white sand and moss which connects the Main Hall with the Main Gate, was constructed in 1338 although the shorter stone footpath to Yusai's mausoleum dates from 1610.

The southern garden, based on the pond-and-island prototype with its rock waterfall, also has its origin in the mid-fourteenth century although other features such as the island in the western pond and the bridge connecting the island with the shore are representative of the Meiji era when some remodelling of the garden was undertaken. However, the overall feel of the garden remains rooted in the Muromachi era.

Address: Tenjuan, Nanzen-ji Fukuchi-cho, Sakyo-ku, Kyoto, Japan.

The southern pond-and-island stroll garden.

Ancient rocks around the waterfall.

The ponds are full of carp.

The gateway to the stroll garden.

1399 SAIHO-JI (THE TEMPLE OF WESTERN FRAGRANCES) Early Muromachi
Period.

The covering of moss dries out in summer so the garden is best visited in wet periods of the cooler seasons. Visited April 8.

Moss-covered bridges link the islands.

The main garden consists of a series of three pools.

An early example of 'kare-sansui', dry landscape garden, representing a stream and waterfall.

Shitoan, a small temple in the upper garden, built by Muso Kokushi.

One of the most interesting extant gardens of the Muromachi era is Saiho-ji Temple, the Temple of Western Fragrances (1399) in Kyoto, also commonly called Kokedera, the Moss Temple, because of later plantings of moss which carpet much of the garden. Saiho-ji is a garden whose composition reflects the transition from the Heian period Pure Land Buddhism 'paradise garden' to the new *kare-sansui* prototype of the early Muromachi period.

The lower half of Saiho-ji is a strolling and pond garden with several islands and peninsulas, while the upper half consists of a series of rock arrangements representing a waterfall in deep mountains which many garden historians believe to be the first example of *kare-sansui* and the influence of Zen Buddhism. Others argue that *kare-sansui* is no more than the logical extension of ideas propounded in the *Sakutei-ki* which mentions a type of garden in which there is no water – either literally or metaphorically – and rocks are placed where part of the hill has been shaped like a cliff or undulating landscape.

There is considerable debate as to whether the rock arrangement in the upper half of the Saiho-ji Temple is the work of Zen master Muso Kokushi (Soseki), who took over the temple in 1338 and turned it into a Zen monastery, or whether it existed before his arrival. This question will probably remain unresolved but it is important as a reflection of the changes that were taking place in gardens between the eleventh and fourteenth centuries.

Address: Saiho-ji (The Temple of Western Fragrances), Matsuo Kamigaya-cho 56, Japan.

A forest of bamboo on the slopes.

Camellia blossoms are left where they drop.

1220 and 1390 KINKAKU-JI (THE GOLDEN PAVILION) Kamakura and Muromachi Periods.

The Golden Pavilion seen across Kyoko-chi, the Mirror Pond. Visited April 3.

Another important garden of the Kamakura and Muromachi eras is the Kinkaku-ji or Golden Pavilion. This was originally known as Kitayana dono, The Villa of the Northern Hills, and dates back to approximately 1220 when it was the villa garden of Saionji Kitsune, in the Heian style of a Shinden hall with a pond-and-island garden. By 1390 it had been converted into the personal retreat of Shogun Ashikaga Yoshimitsu who renamed it Rokuon-ji, Temple of the Deer Park, which remains its official name although it is now more popularly known by the name Kinkaku-ji, inspired by the gilded roof of one of the pavilions. On Yoshimitsu's death the Rokuon-ji was made into a Zen temple, in accordance with his will. Although not in the grounds of Shokoku-ji, it is affiliated to the Shokoku-ji branch of the Rinzai sect of Zen Buddhism.

The Ashikaga shoguns saw themselves as cultural patrons as well as political leaders and as a result they took great interest in the Chinese landscape painting of the Song period (960–1280) and in the newly arrived Zen Buddhism. The garden at Kinkaku-ji reflects both the historical influence of the Heian garden as well as the new wave of Chinese influence.

The garden can be experienced by strolling around the pond called Kyoko-chi, the Mirror Pond, but it was obviously originally designed to be enjoyed principally from the water, as is shown by historical records of festivities and boating parties organized for the Emperor Gokoma-tsu's visit in 1408. The pond is divided into an inner zone – the section in front of the pavilion – and an outer zone which is separated from it to some extent by a peninsula on the western edge and the pond's main island. In the inner zone lie small-scale versions of the traditional turtle and crane islands and two larger turtle islands one of which faces towards the pavilion – 'the arriving turtle' – and the other which faces away from it – 'the departing turtle'. Behind the Mirror Pond is a small pond An-min-taku, and at the top of the garden is a classic tea house called Sekka-tei.

The three-storeyed pavilion which dominates the garden shows evidence of influences from Southern China. The ground floor in the Shinden style comprises a reception hall; the second storey is a study; the top floor with bell-shaped windows in the Zen style provides a peaceful temple for meditation. The original Golden Pavilion was destroyed by a fire in 1950 but reconstructed and renovated in the following decades. The restoration of artwork and gold leaf was a huge undertaking but the present gold leaf is five times thicker then the original.

At the foot of the hills behind the Golden Pavilion two springs are marked by rock formations and at the Dragon Gate waterfall a small shrine houses the legendary carp stone inherited from the original garden built by Kitsune.

Address: Kinkaku-ji (The Golden Pavilion), Kinkaku-ji-cho 1, Kita-ku, Kyoto, Japan.

The turtle islands in the inner zone of the Mirror Pond.

The pathway up from the Mirror Lake.

The grotto.

Wonderfully trained and shaped trees in front of the main buildings inside the entrance.

1450–90 GINKAKU-JI (THE SILVER PAVILION) Muromachi Period.

The Kare-sansui garden in which both mountain and ocean are symbolized in silver sand. Visited April 3.

The kogetsudai (platform facing the moon) is sculpted to look like Mount Fuji.

Another important garden of the Muromachi period is Ginkaku-ji, 'The Silver Pavilion'. Built by the eighth Ashikaga Shogun, Yoshimasa (1435–90), the grandson of Yoshimitsu (who built the Golden Pavilion), Ginkaku-ji was originally called Higashiyama dono, Villa of the Eastern Hills, and was, during Yoshimasa's lifetime, the cultural centre of Japan in an era when political infighting and the Onin Wars (1467–77) were causing havoc in Kyoto culminating in the destruction of the city and its villa-palaces. On the death of Yoshimasa, the villa was converted into a Zen temple called Jisho-ji but it is more popularly known as Ginkaku-ji although it is not silver at all. Whether in fact it ever was silver plated to emulate, but not compete with, that of its gilded counterpart is not known.

Like the Golden Temple, the Silver Temple was inspired by the gardens at Saiho-ji and, in particular, the division of the garden into two sections reflects the design of the earlier Zen temple. It is difficult to be sure how the gardens at the Silver Pavilion in the past looked because only two of the twelve buildings originally on the site remain today.

However, it is clear that the lower part of the garden with its pond and islands, winding paths and stone bridges and its *shoin*-style Hall of the Eastern Quest was designated as a strolling garden in the manner of the pleasure garden prototype of the Heian period. The steep slopes of the upper section, however, contain a dry rock arrangement similar to that at Saiho-ji which would have been highly unusual for a villa palace garden of the earlier period.

The other outstanding feature at The Silver Pavilion is the raked and sculptured sand garden. For the first time in Japanese garden history the natural elements of mountain and ocean are represented symbolically in sand. The *ginshanada*, silver sand open sea, is raked to represent rippling waves and the *kogetsudai*, platform facing the moon, is a cone of sand sculptured to look like Mount Fuji.

What is not known is whether Yoshimasa planned and designed these two features of the garden himself (much of the work at the villa was still not completed when he died in 1490) because the first recorded reference to it is in a poem written by a Zen monk in 1578.

Address: Ginkaku-ji (The Silver Pavilion), Ginkaku-ji-cho 2, Sakyo-ku, Kyoto, Japan.

Ginkaku-ji, The Silver Pavilion.

Looking down at the Pavilion complex from the hillside.

Raked sand and clipped hedges.

Tiny stone bridge.

293

1450–88 RYOAN-JI (TEMPLE OF THE PEACEFUL DRAGON) Muromachi Period.

The rectangular Zen garden from the hojo, surrounded by the wall made of clay boiled in oil. Visited April 2.

The Kyoyochi Pond in the lower part of the garden.

Turtles on Kyoyochi.

Ryoan-ji, The Temple of the Peaceful Dragon, is part of a complex that was first built at the beginning of the eleventh century by Fujiwara Saneyoshui who created the Kyoyochi pond in the lower part of the garden where the main temple Daiju-in still exists today.

The site was purchased by Hosokawa Katsumoto, a powerful member of the Buke Clan, in 1450, as his principal residence and it was he who built the Zen temple of Ryoan-ji in the upper part of the complex. This first temple was destroyed during the Onin Wars (1467–77) and Katsumoto died in 1473 but his son Masamoto rebuilt the temple in 1488 and it is generally acknowledged that the *kare-sansui* garden in front of the *hojo*, the abbot's quarters, dates from this time, probably being completed by 1499. The literature distributed at the temple claims that the garden was laid out by the painter and gardener Soami but Günter Nitschke in *Japanese Gardens* asserts that the designer of this masterpiece is unknown, although several theories exist. One of the most interesting is that it was built by *sensui-karawamona* 'river-bank workers turned gardeners', supervised by Zen monks; two *kawaramona* signatures have been found carved into the back of one of the rocks.

Early engravings and literary references to Ryoan-ji reveal that it was not always experienced in quite the same way as it is today. A woodcut of 1799 indicates that visitors could walk through the garden; the porch and wall to the east of the garden were probably built as part of the reconstruction that took place following the great fire of 1797; the view from the *hojo* verandah was almost certainly more panoramic, borrowing views – *shakkei* – from the garden and distant landscape beyond.

Whatever its past, this garden remains today one of the most compelling and influential gardens in the world. Almost anyone who is remotely interested in gardens or gardening will have seen a picture of this extraordinary place that has no trees, no plants (except a little moss at the base of the rocks) and no flowers. The thirty-by-ten-metre area contains fifteen rocks in three groups (seven, five and three respectively) set in perfectly raked sand and surrounded on three sides by a wall made of clay boiled in oil and, on the fourth side, by the viewing verandah of the *hojo*.

Numerous suggestions about the 'meaning' of the garden have been advanced ranging from the view that the garden symbolizes an ocean dotted with islands or represents tiger cubs crossing the sea, to more abstract theories such as that the positioning of the rocks reflects 'secret geometry' or obeys 'the rules of balance by odd number'. But probably the garden should just be enjoyed and experienced for itself or as an aid to meditation. The simplicity of the composition enables the visitor to concentrate on the inner self and thus, it is hoped, to achieve the state of void, of nothingness, of *mu-shin* so essential to achieving 'enlightenment'. *Ryoan-ji*, says Nitschke, is 'an abstract composition of "natural" objects in space which is intended to induce meditation. It belongs to the art of the void.'

Address: Ryoan-ji (The Temple of the Peaceful Dragon), Ryoan-ji Goryo Shitamachi 13, Ukyo-ku, Kyoto, Japan.

Detail of the rock garden.

Detail of the rock garden.

The rocks have been variously described as symbolizing islands in an ocean, tiger cubs crossing the sea or reflecting secret geometry.

1509–13 DAISEN-IN (THE GREAT HERMIT'S TEMPLE) Muromachi Period.

Looking from the Stone of Experience and the Turtle Island towards Mount Horai. Visited April 9.

The white gravel symbolizes the river of life impeded by rocks representing difficulties to be surmounted.

Daisen-in, The Great Hermit's Temple, is part of an enormous temple complex belonging to the Rinzai sect of Zen Buddhism called Daitoku-ji which comprises a *hondo* (administrative headquarters) and twenty-four subtemples of which, both historically and culturally, Daisen-in is the most important.

Daitoku-ji was founded in 1319 by Daito-Kokushi, a contemporary of Muso Kokushi who developed Saiho-ji (see page 288), but it was largely destroyed during the Onin Wars (1467–77). The whole temple complex was rebuilt in the following years and the Daisen-in Temple was built within the complex in 1509 by Kogaku Soko; the garden was probably completed by 1513.

The *kare-sansui* dry landscape garden at Daisen-in, built around the *hojo*, remains in its original form and is renowned as an exceptional example of Zen gardening combining, as it does, the earlier Chinese myth of Mount Horai and the crane and turtle islands with the more austere rock symbols of a dry landscape garden.

The garden at Daisen-in is built around the four sides of the *hojo*, though to break up the obvious symmetry one of the four sections of the garden is L-shaped and goes around the north-east corner of the building. It is in this north-east corner that the visitor should start because the garden is designed to be viewed and understood symbolically from this point.

Here the abstract composition of a clipped camellia represents Mount Horai and the 'spring' of white gravel which plunges over the imaginary waterfall branches into two symbolic rivers. The vigour of the waterfall shows the impetuous energy of man coursing through life. One river flows west into the north garden whose raked white gravel interspersed with three rocks represents the central sea; the other flows east past many rocks which represent the difficulties of life. Swirling about, the soul is confronted by the eternal question: Why do I exist?

Doubt and contradiction are represented by the corridor that crosses the garden at this point. However, the river crosses the dam and broadens out, symbolizing the broadening of human understanding and the inevitability of life's continual movement onwards, until at last the large south garden, named The Great Ocean, is reached. Here, raked white gravel, two hills of sand and one tree symbolize the ocean of nothingness, the achievement of purity and enlightenment, the abandonment of avarice and greed. To the Zen Buddhist this is the ultimate achievement – the large gravel garden represents the life of meditation while the rock garden represents the material side of life.

One of the things that Nitschke in *Japanese Gardens* feels makes Daisen-in exceptional is the physical juxtaposition of 'built' and 'painted' landscape: 'the visitor is surrounded on all sides by a garden which is both painting and architecture at once'.

Address: Daisen-in (The Great Hermit's Temple), Murasakino Daitoku-ji-cho 54–1, Kitaku, Kyoto, Japan.

A single camellia dominates this seascape.

A much less formal area in the complex.

The treasure boat and small turtle stones.

The two gravel hills symbolize purity and enlightenment.

1598 SAMBO-IN in DIAGO-JI TEMPLE Momoyama Period.

Behind the old wall you can see the intricate bamboo structure used to train a weeping cherry. Visited April 5.

A giant weeping cherry, one of hundreds in the Daigo-ji Temple complex.

The Sambo-in Pond Garden.

Although it is now part of a much bigger temple and garden complex, Sambo-in still has much of the feel of a palace garden combining the contradictory elements of wealth and extravagance typical of the Momoyama shoguns with the simplicity and rusticity of the *roji*, the dewy path that leads to the tea arbour which they also encouraged and supported in their palaces.

In 1598 Toyotami Hideyoshi (1536–98) decided to redesign a garden on the grounds of an existing one, as a setting for one of his extravagant cherry blossoming parties. Work commenced in April; the design of the area (covering 1.5 hectares) was based on the pond-and-islands theme and about seven hundred rocks and innumerable rare tree varieties (some from his palace at Juraku-dai, now destroyed) were transported to Sambo-in and used in the creation of its garden.

Whether Hideyoshi saw the work completed is unknown as he died unexpectedly later that same year but for the garden historian it remains one of the finest examples of the garden ideals of the Momoyama period.

Although early records indicate that boating parties took place on the pond and although paths meander around the islands and pond, with numerous stone, moss and earth bridges, it is clear that the best views of the garden are seen from the *shoin*.

The rock grouping represents the Horai islands, bridges connect the crane and turtle islands. The *kare-sansui* garden between the building and the pond is narrow compared with earlier eras and the tea arbour set mysteriously at the end of the pond contrasts with the wide expansiveness of the pond garden. Another *roji* set on one side of the building as one exits also makes a marked contrast to the pond garden at the front.

This garden is immensely popular with Japanese tourists and, probably to preserve the garden as much as anything, visitors are only allowed to view it from the veranda – there is no possibility of strolling around the pond as would have originally been intended. Also, the taking of photographs is forbidden although we managed to sneak a couple to illustrate this important era.

Address: Daigo-ji Temple, Daigo, Kyoto, Japan.

A moss covered bridge.

299

1605 **KODAI-JI TEMPLE** Late Momoyama to early Edo Period.

The renowned landscape architect Kobori Enshu laid out this garden, famed for its use of stone. Visited April 9.

Carefully shaped trees add to the harmony.

The Garyoro (Reclining Dragon) Corridor.

Kodai-ji Temple was established in 1605 by Kita no Mandokora, the widow of Toyotami Hideyoshi (1536–98) one of the great shoguns of the Momoyama epoch. Largely financed by his successor Tokugawa Ieyasu (1542–1616), the temple was renowned for its exquisite craftsmanship and in 1624 (when Kita no Mandokora died) Sanko Joeki, Abbot of Kennin-ji was appointed founding priest; Kodai-ji has remained an important subtemple of Kennin-ji ever since.

Despite being ravaged in a series of fires at the end of the eighteenth century, the founder's hall, Kaisan-do, the moon-viewing pavilion, Kangetsu-dai, and the two tea houses Kasa-tei, umbrella house, and Shiguretei, rainshower house, survived.

These two tea houses were moved to their present location from Fushimi Castle on the death of Hideyoshi because it was he who had employed the great tea master Sen no Rikyu (see page 283) at his palace castle to show that despite his flamboyance and extravagance he was also a man of taste who could appreciate the simplicity and restraint that Sen no Rikyu advocated.

The garden built by Kobori Enshu (1579–1647) at Kodai-ji is an excellent example of the pond-island-rock garden of the Edo period.

Address: Kodai-ji, Simo Kawaramachi Jovi Yasaka Torrii Mae Sagaru, Higashiyama-ku, Kyoto, Japan.

An excellent example of the pond-island-rock garden typical of the era.

The kare-sansui dry landscape garden with spectacular cherry blossom.

1628–32 KONCHI-IN, in the NANZEN-JI COMPLEX Early Edo Period.

O-karikomi, clipped shrubs, form a massive bank beyond the gravel ocean. Visited April 8.

The roji or pathway to the Tea House.

Originally founded in about 1400 by Shogun Yoshimoshi Ashikaga, Konchi-in is part of the temple complex of the Zen monastery of Nanzen-ji.

The *hojo*, the *roji* tea house and the Toshogu shrine were designed by Kobori Enshu (1579–1647) for the Zen priest Suden (1569–1633) in accordance with the will of Shogun Tokugawa Ieyasu (1542–1616). Its construction by *kawaramono*, river-bank workers (who became highly respected gardeners), was overseen by Enshu between 1628 and 1632.

The area of garden in front of the *hojo* (raked into the shape of a boat) represents a vast ocean and parallel with each end of the veranda lie a turtle and crane island. In the middle, opposite the viewing platform, lies a large, flat, worshipping stone and behind it rises layer upon layer of *o-karikomi* – well trimmed shrubbery – which conceals the sharp fall of the land beyond. Unlike other *o-karikomi* these do not represent anything specific and are more decorative than symbolic.

Address: Kochi-in, Nanzen-ji Fukuchi-cho, Sakyo-ku, Kyoto, Japan.

A detail of the o-karikomi.

Across the corner of the gravel ocean a path that is becoming submerged in the sea.

1615–60 KATSURA IMPERIAL VILLA Early Edo Period.

A stroll garden. A large pond in the centre has five islands connected by bridges. Visited April 4.

Katsura Imperial Villa and Garden, on the western banks of the Katsura river, was constructed in stages by Prince Toshihito and subsequently his son Noritada between 1615 and 1660.

Principally a strolling garden around the pond-and-island theme, Katsura consists of three *shoin*, constructed in a staggered or zigzag arrangement to create the maximum number of views, and four tea arbours which are strategically placed around the complicatedly designed pond with its five islets connected by wooden, earthen and stone bridges. One thousand seven hundred and sixty stepping-stones lead one past scenes that depict a sea shore, a mountain pass and a mountain hamlet and

A view of a moss-covered bridge.

a pebble peninsula representing some of Japan's most famous natural sights.

The overall size of the garden is reminiscent of the palace pleasure gardens of Heian times but the attention to minute detail reflects the influence of Tea House architecture which came to be known as the *Sukiya* style. The *roji*, the dewy path, to the Tea House, is a series of stepping stones which lead the visitor from one beautiful view to the next, but here the difference is that it is all much more open and expansive than the earlier *roji* which was small, private, enclosed and mysterious. What the *Sukiya* style has in common with the tea house style is a passion for diagonals, presenting views from an oblique angle, contrasting the man-made, right-angled buildings with the complexity of the natural forms to be viewed from them.

Although there are no records to prove that Kobori Enshu (1579–1647) worked on the design of this garden, it is generally thought that either he or his close disciples were involved as, for instance, the straight lines in paving and bridges which characterize his work are to be found in Katsura.

It is extremely hard to get tickets to visit Katsura which is why many Japanese themselves have never been there. Tourists and visitors must apply for tickets at least one month before they wish to visit. Persons under twenty are not admitted.

Address: Katsura Imperial Villa, Katsura, Kyoto, Japan.

A detail of the moss-covered bridge with the Imperial Villa in the background.

A view of the Tea Pavilion.

An unassuming path leads to the Villa.

Looking towards the tree-covered Tea House.

1655–59 SHUGAKUIN IMPERIAL VILLA Edo Period.

Looking out at the mist-covered hills from the Upper Villa complex. Visited April 4.

A bridge to the island on which Kyusui-tei is situated.

The name Shugakuin is derived from the temple Shugahuji which existed on the site in the eleventh century but had long disappeared when the ex-Emperor Gomino-o (nephew of Prince Toshihito who built Katsura Imperial Villa) decided, in 1655, to construct a retirement villa at the foot of Mount Hiei, in north-east Kyoto. By 1659 the Upper and Lower Villas were completed (the Middle Villa was not built until ten years later) and the 133 acres of the site had been reshaped and designed to create a unique landscape garden that, with its different elevations, is one of the finest examples of *shakkei* 'borrowed scenery' in Japanese garden history.

Although constructed at roughly the same period, the overall feel of Shugakuin Imperial Villa is very different from that at Katsura Imperial Villa. Shugakuin has a much freer, more naturalistic, landscape feel with views of the distant hills incorporated into the overall setting; at Katsura the environment is more controlled, the landscape is more 'designed' with the building complex forming an integral part of the whole experience. At Shugakuin the main villas are not so integrated with the scenery; in fact, our guide did not offer a tour of the main buildings, but concentrated on visiting the various areas of the garden and the small garden buildings dotted around the lake. Shugakuin is very reminiscent of an English landscape garden in the Stourhead tradition with its waterfalls (one male, one female), its streams, its dam (constructed to make the lake and concealed with *o-karikomi*, clipped trees and shrubs of many varieties, along its 200 metre length and 15 metre width), its stone lanterns, its rills, stepping stones and stone bridges, its lake and old boating house.

As at Katsura, tickets to view Shugakuin Imperial Villa cannot be obtained on the spot – application must be made to the Imperial Household at least one month in advance of your intended visit. Persons under twenty are not admitted.

Address: Shugakuin Imperial Villa, Shugakuin, Kyoto, Japan.

Chitose-bashi, Bridge of a Thousand Years, a bridge between two islands.

O-taki, the Male Waterfall.

The Upper Garden lake.

17TH **CENTURY NANZEN-JI TEMPLE** Early to middle Edo Period.

The Leaping Tiger Garden made by Kobori Enshu. Visited April 6.

A crooked path. The kinks and curves designed to confuse evil spirits.

A more distant view of the Leaping Tiger Garden with its naturalistic plants and rocks shown to advantage against a plain white wall.

Although Nanzen-ji, one of the most famous temples of the Rinzai sect of Zen Bhuddhism, was originally built in 1264 as a palace for the Emperor Kameyama, he dedicated it as a Zen temple in 1291 in honour of the Zen master Daimin Kokoshi.

Several fires in the following centuries razed the original buildings to the ground and the present Nanzen-ji Temple was built after the Momoyama period. The garden in front of the *hojo* was built in the early seventeenth century by Kobori Enshu (1579–1647) and is a superb example of a *kare-sansui* garden. However, unlike its predecessors, the rocks are not dotted around the raked gravel in abstract compositions but grouped together in one corner in a more naturalistic setting, leaving the rest of the space virtually empty.

Because of the shape of one of the rocks, the garden is sometimes called the 'Leaping Tiger Garden'.

Address: Nanzen-ji, Nanzen-ji Fukuchi-cho, Sakyo-ku, Kyoto, Japan.

The gravel sea and rocks resemble Ryoan-ji but are much more stark and simple.

Carved stone.

309

1641 SHISEN-DO (THE POETS' HERMITAGE) Edo Period.

The tranquil garden of o-karikomi shrubs merges into the natural woodland.

Shisen-do, The Poets' Hermitage, was built in 1641 by Ishikawa Jozan (1583–1672) as a retreat where he could pursue his scholarly interests in the Chinese classics and garden design, after the death of his mother with whom he had previously lived. The name of his house and garden, which literally translates as The House of the Poet Hermits, arose from the thirty-six portraits of Chinese poets that decorated his study.

Retreat or hermitage gardens like Shisen-do incorporate many traditional garden elements favoured in the Edo period – the tea garden, the strolling garden, the *kare-sansui* garden, the *shakkei* garden and the *o-karikomi* garden – but all on a much smaller scale than the palace gardens of the Daimyo lords.

Slippers for visitors to wear in the garden.

Here, all kinds of devices are used to make the most of the limited amount of space available on the site so that it seems as though it is actually much bigger than it is. The tunnel-like uphill entrance creates the impression of distance and the second gate with raked white gravel inside is reminiscent of a Buddhist temple. The house itself is compact, comprising small living quarters, a study, a main room, a Buddhist sanctuary and a moon-viewing room.

From the main room the view across the garden stretches to a hill on the right and beyond that the city can be seen in the distance. Stepping off the veranda onto more raked gravel the visitor follows a path leading past the clipped azalea bushes (*o-karikomi*), a trickling stream and waterfall, and a bamboo *sozu* – a kind of waterwork scarecrow whose gravitation principle causes a clunking noise every few minutes. *Sozus* used to be commonplace in seventeenth-century Japan, employed by farmers in the fields to scare deer or boar away from the crops.

Although some way from the centre of Kyoto, Shisen-do is well worth a visit as it is not only an excellent example of an Edo era hermitage but it is also refreshingly different and more acceptable to children because the gravel can be walked on using the slippers provided. The intriguing *sozu* and overall greenness, quaintness and mazelike quality of the garden made it a great favourite with our daughters.

Address: Shisen-do, (The Poets' Hermitage), Ichijo-ji Monguchi-cho 27, Sakyo-ku, Kyoto, Japan.

The small pond in the o-karikomi garden.

Sozu, a sort of water-work scarecrow.

The kare-sansui garden.

Decorative bamboo and rice straw screen.

1895 THE HEIAN SHRINE GARDEN Meiji Period.

The long covered bridge in this huge stroll garden behind the Heian Shrine. Visited April 7.

A naturalistic planting of trees and shrubs, designed to give colour all year round.

Stepping-stones made from the pier stones of Gojo Bridge in Kyoto.

Cool clean water with which to cleanse oneself.

The Heian Shrine was constructed in 1895 to commemorate the 1100th anniversary of the founding of Heian-Kyo (now Kyoto) by the Emperor Kammu Tenno (737–806) and to console the citizens of Kyoto for the demise of their city as the nation's capital which would, henceforth, be Tokyo.

The original plan had been to construct a replica of Chodo-in, the main Hall of State situated within the original Heian Palace complex. Unfortunately there were two problems. Firstly, there was the paradox of creating a religious Shinto temple in the manner of a secular building such as a Hall of State and, secondly, there was the fact that the Meiji architects did not know enough about the history of Heian architecture to construct an accurate imitation. Similarly, in the garden, the large pond-and-island prototype of the Heian period was abandoned by the designers in favour of the more recent Edo models of the strolling garden.

Nevertheless the Heian shrine and garden are an impressive sight. The startling orange-red paintwork on the pillars and buildings and the green tile work on the roofs boldly insist on a visit.

The garden, which covers 5 acres, has three sections – western, central and eastern – which enclose the buildings on three sides. Famous features of the garden are its all-year-round flowering trees and shrubs, a six-foot-high waterfall, a pond with several rock islands reached by stepping-stones made from the pier stones of Gojo Bridge in Kyoto, and a long, covered bridge that enables visitors to get a panoramic view of the garden and, incidentally, feed the numerous fish that loiter beneath in anticipation.

Many colourful festivals take place at the Heian Shrine throughout the year as the area within the building provides an excellent open space for such displays.

Address: Heian Jingu Shrine, Okazaki, Kyoto, Japan.

The approach from Otenmon Gate.

Bibliography

Alcosser, Murray, *America in Bloom*, Rizzoli, New York, 1991

Balmori, Diana, McGuire, Diane Kostial, McPeck, Eleanor M., *Beatrix Farrand's American Landscapes*, Sagapress, Inc., Sagaponack, New York, 1985

Beard, Geoffrey, *John Vanbrugh*, B.T. Batsford Ltd., London, 1986

Brown, Jane, *The English Garden in our Time*, Antique Collectors' Club, Suffolk, 1986

Carita, Helder, Cardosa, Miguel Esteves, *Portuguese Gardens*, Antique Collectors' Club, 1990

Chatto, Beth, *Beth Chatto's Garden Notebook*, J. M. Dent & Sons Ltd, London, 1988

Chatto, Beth, *The Damp Garden*, J.M.Dent & Sons Ltd, London, 1986

Clarke, Ethne & Wright, George, *English Topiary Gardens*, Weidenfeld and Nicolson, London, 1988

Clarke, Ethne, & Bencini, Raffaello, *The Gardens of Tuscany*, Weidenfeld and Nicolson, London, 1990

Clarke, Ethne, *Hidcote*, Michael Joseph, London, 1989

Clarke, Ethne, & Perry, Clay, *English Country Gardens*, Weidenfeld and Nicolson, London, 1985

Elliot, Brent, *Victorian Gardens*, B.T. Batsford Ltd, London, 1986

Fearnley-Whittingstall, Jane, *Historic Gardens*, Webb & Bower, Devon, 1990

Fleming, Laurence, & Gore, Alan, *The English Garden*, Spring Books, London, 1988

Guest, Sarah, & Harpur, Jerry, *Private Gardens of Australia*, Weidenfeld and Nicolson, London, 1990

Gunn, Fenja, *Lost Gardens of Gertrude Jekyll*, Charles Letts, London, 1991

Hadfield, Miles, *A History of British Gardening*, Penguin Books, England, 1985

Harvey, John, *Medieval Gardens*, B.T. Batsford Ltd, London, 1990

Hobhouse, Penelope & Taylor, Patrick, eds., *The Gardens of Europe*, George Philip, London, 1990

Hunt, John Dixon, *William Kent Landscape Garden Designer*, A. Zwemmer Ltd, 1987

Jacob, Irene & Walter, *Gardens of North America and Hawaii*, Timber Press, Oregon, 1985

Jacques, David, *Georgian Gardens: The Reign of Nature*, B.T. Batsford Ltd, London, 1983

Jellicoe, Geoffrey & Susan, Goode, Patrick, & Lancaster, Michael, eds., *The Oxford Companion to Gardens*, Oxford University Press, 1991

Jellicoe, Geoffrey & Susan, *The Landscape of Man*, Thames & Hudson, London, 1987

Joyce, David, ed., *Garden Styles* Pyramid Books, London, 1986

Katsuhiko, Mizuno, *Masterpieces of Japanese Garden Art*, Kyoto Shoin, Japan, 1992

Keswick, Maggie, *The Chinese Garden*, Academy Editions, London, St. Martin's Press, New York, 1986

King, Ronald, *Tresco: England's Island of Flowers*, Constable, London, 1985

Lees-Milne, Alvide, & Verey, Rosemary, eds., *The Englishwoman's Garden*, Chatto & Windus, London, 1983

Levick, Melba, & Prentice, Helaine Kaplan, *The Gardens of Southern California*, Chronicle Books, San Francisco, 1990

Logan, Harry Britton, *North American Gardens*, Charles Scribner's Sons, New York, 1974

Loxton, Howard, ed., *The Garden*, Thames & Hudson, London, 1991

McGuire, Diane Kostial, ed., *Beatrix Farrand's Plant book For Dumbarton Oaks*, Dumbarton Oaks, Washington DC, 1980

McLean, Teresa, *Medieval English Gardens*, Barrie & Jenkins, London, 1989

McRae, Alison, *Gardens to Visit in New Zealand*, David Bateman Ltd, New Zealand, 1989

Mosser, Monique, Teyssot, *The History of Garden Design*, Thames & Hudson, London, 1991

Nitschke, Gunter, *Japanese Gardens*, Benedikt Taschen, Köln, 1993

Ohashi, Haruzo, *Japanese Gardens of the Modern Era*, Graphic-sha, Japan, 1988

Page, Russell, *The Education of a Gardener*, Penguin Books, London, 1985

Pearson, Robert, Mitchell, Susanne, & Hunt, Candida, *The Ordnance Survey Guide to Gardens in Britain*, Ordnance Survey, Newnes, Country Life Books, 1986

Penn, Helen, *An Englishwoman's Garden*, BBC Books, London, 1993

Racine, Michel, *Les Guide des Jardins de France*, Guides Hachette, France 1990

Ramsay, Alex, Attlee, Helena, *Italian Gardens*, Robertson McCarta, London, 1989

Rix, Martyn & Alison, *Wisley*, Julian Holland Publishing Ltd, England, 1989

Robinson, William, *The English Flower Garden*, The Amaryllis Press, New York, 1984

Rose, Graham, & King, Peter, eds., *Good Gardens Guide 1994*, Vermilion, London, 1994

Scott-James, Anne, *Sissinghurst*, Michael Joseph, London, 1987

Thacker, Christopher, *The Genius of Gardening*, Weidenfeld and Nicolson, London, 1994

Thacker, Christopher, *The History of Gardens*, Croom Helm, London, 1979

Thorpe, Patricia, & Sonneman, Eve, *America's Cottage Gardens*, Random House, New York, 1990

Valdés, Marquesa de Casa, *Spanish Gardens*, Antique Collectors' Club, 1987

Wedda, John, *Gardens of the American South*, Galahad Books, New York, 1971

Wharton, Edith, *Ville Italiane e Loro Giardini*, Passigli Editori, Firenze 1991

Wright, Tom, & Katsuhiko, Mizuno *Zen Gardens*, Suiko Books, Kyoto, Japan, 1990

Glossary

Allée A sand or gravel walkway or passage, bordered with trees or clipped hedges; in French formal gardens the allée is an important feature of the garden's framework.

Ambulatio A place for walking, a promenade.

Amida-Buddhism A form of Buddhism in which the followers believe that if they devote their lives to the Amida-Buddha they will attain the Pure Land and thus achieve immortality.

Arboretum A botanical garden or section of a garden devoted to a collection of living trees to show the variety of species and forms.

Atrium The central court of a Roman house.

Azulejo A glazed, decorated tile, based on a technique introduced by the Moors in about the tenth century, it was usually blue on white but not always so; characteristically used in decorating Spanish and Portuguese gardens and houses.

Bassin An ornamental, formal pool, tank or reservoir usually lined and edged with stone; often found in French formal gardens.

Bedding plants Plants raised elsewhere and planted in beds to create attractive floral displays at different times of year; first popularized in Victorian times.

Belvedere A summer house, look-out tower or turret that is either part of a house or a separate building which has a commanding view over the surrounding countryside.

Berceau A vault-shaped trellis on which climbing plants are trained to create a cool, shady bower.

Bian A calligraphic board in Chinese gardens which usually records the name of the garden's owner or the name of an important visitor such as the Emperor.

Borrowed views This is the translation of the Chinese term *jiejing* which refers to places in the garden where views of the scenery outside the garden can be seen and thus become 'borrowed' and incorporated into the overall design or atmosphere of the garden that the visitor experiences.

Bosco In Italian gardens this is an ornamental grove or thicket of trees that either provides a reinforcement or contrast to the formal geometry of the garden.

Bosquet A grove, plantation or thicket of trees intersected by paths or rides, often with ornamental statuary placed at strategic points; frequently associated with French formal gardens

Box parterre A formal, ornamental bed with low, clipped box hedges; see **Parterre**

Buddhism Asian religion or philosophy, founded by Gautama Buddha in India in the fifth century BC, which teaches that elimination of the self and earthly desires is the highest goal man can achieve.

Canal In gardens this refers to a formal stretch of ornamental water, usually rectangular, which is not part of any communications system.

Carpet bedding Using foliage, plants and flowers raised elsewhere to make patterned, uniform, ornamental display beds, trimmed to resemble a carpet.

Casino In Italian this literally means a small house and refers to a small, ornamental pavilion, lodge or house usually, but not always, within the grounds of a large villa. Frequently associated with Italian gardens between the sixteenth and eighteenth centuries.

Chahar-bagh An Islamic term which literally translated means 'fourfold garden' and describes the motif of a square or rectangle divided into four equal parts by intersecting water channels with a central gazebo, platform or fountain.

GLOSSARY

Chinoiserie This literally means 'in the Chinese manner' and refers to the fashion, prevalent in the eighteenth and nineteenth centuries, for imitating Chinese garden motifs and techniques.

Clairvoyée An opening in a wall or hedge or at the end of an allée that provides a view of the countryside beyond.

Congruity The harmonious juxtapositioning of plants, buildings and design of the garden in order to create a unified whole.

Daimyo A Japanese word for the powerful clan lords of the Edo era.

Dairi A Japanese word that refers to the residential quarters within the Imperial Palace.

Daoism More commonly known as Taoism, it is the Chinese philosophy based on the writings of Laoze (c. 500 BC), which advocates humility and religious piety.

Edo period The period of Japanese garden history from 1603 to 1868.

English Landscape Movement This influential period of garden history occurred in the eighteenth century initially as a reaction against the rigid formality of French and Dutch gardens but also reflecting the overall change in philosophy that took place at this time. Seminal in the change of attitude was the idea expressed by Pope in his *Epistle to Burlington* 'In all, let Nature never be forgot. . . . Consult the Genius of the Place.' Although we know how artificial the creation of sweeping lawns, flowing water and woodlands that so characterized this movement actually was, the idea of Nature as an ideal to be imitated, albeit Nature improved by Art, which is at the heart of the landscape tradition, started from a very different premise than that behind the French formal movement of a century earlier.

Espalier A lattice-work along which the branches of ornamental shrubs or fruit trees are trained to grow flat against a wall.

Exedra Popular in eighteenth-century English gardens, the exedra is an ornamental, open garden building based on classical architecture which is usually semicircular with a seat or bench inside from which to view the garden.

Feng shui A Chinese word meaning geomancy which is the divination of the good and evil properties that emanate from a particular site that enable one to determine whether it is an auspicious place to build a house or garden.

Ferme ornée A term invented by Philip Southcote to describe a garden which includes an ornamental farm where animals graze up to and around the buildings.

Fluorspar A mineral which is a natural deposit of fluoride of calcium.

Folly An ornamental building, often a tower or mock Gothic ruin, characterized by its eccentricity, excessive cost or general uselessness; popular in Victorian times.

French Formal Movement This is the term used to describe the period of French gardening popular in the seventeenth and early eighteenth centuries. It reflected the prevailing philosophy that Man dominated the universe and in garden terms this took the form of Man imposing his will over Nature by creating highly structured and excessively formal gardens which were best viewed from the house so that the owner could constantly remind himself of the fact that he was master of all he surveyed, including Nature itself.

Garden rooms A term used to describe the compartmentalizing of spaces or areas within a garden so that each section seems to be a room.

Gardenesque This was originally a term coined by J.C. Loudon (1783-1843) which referred to a planting design in which each plant was allowed to develop its individual character as much as possible , in contrast to the **Picturesque** style where plants were chosen for their ability to be shaped into suiting the imagination of the painter or landscape designer who wanted to create a picturesque effect. Later, **gardenesque** came to be used as a term to describe eclectic Victorian gardens which combined a great mixture of styles, often with a noticeable lack of unity.

Gazebo A small building or structure such as a summer house or turret, designed to give a wide view over the garden.

Genius loci A Latin phrase meaning 'the spirit of place'.

Geomancy This is the divination of the good and evil properties which emanate from a particular site that enable one to determine whether it is an auspicious place to build a house or garden.

Giardino segreto An Italian phrase meaning a secret or secluded garden which refers to the intimate walled garden popular in some gardens of the Italian Renaissance.

Giochi d'acqua An Italian expression meaning 'water jokes' which refers to trick jets that squirt water on unwary visitors.

Grotto A small, natural, picturesque recess or an artificial ornamental cave in a park or large garden.

Grove A small group of trees, usually of one species, either growing naturally or artificially planted, which creates an atmosphere suitable for quiet reflection.

Ha-ha A ditch with a wall on its inner side below ground level which forms a boundary to a park or garden without interrupting the view.

Hameau A French word meaning hamlet that refers, in gardening terms, to a group of rustic buildings constructed in a park or garden where the wealthy landowner could play at leading the simple peasant life.

Heian Period The period of Japanese garden history from 794 to 1185.

Herbaceous border A long flowerbed usually set along a wall or bordering either side of a central path, planted with perennials and low, flowering shrubs.

Herm A squared stone pillar on a tapering base with a head (originally of Hermes but later of any god or important person) on top, used as a boundary-marker.

Hinduism The main religious and social system of India, including belief in reincarnation, the worship of several gods, and a caste system which forms the basis of society.

Horai-zan A Japanese word that refers to the use of a rock or stone formation to recreate the image of Mount Horai, the mountain or island where the Immortals lived.

Hortus A garden.

Hortus conclusus A medieval Latin term for a small, enclosed or secret garden.

Impluvium A Latin word for a cistern or square basin in the floor of the atrium to catch rain water from the roof.

Islands of the Immortals In Taoist mythology these were the five Isles of the Blessed far out in the ocean east of the China coast, where the Immortals lived in perfect harmony.

Jiejing A Chinese term meaning 'borrowed views' i.e. creating spaces in the garden where views of the scenery outside the garden can be seen and thus become 'borrowed' and incorporated into the design and atmosphere that the visitor experiences

Karesansui A Japanese word that literally translates as 'withered mountain water' and refers to the dry landscape gardens of rocks and raked sand or stone, typical of the Kamakura and Muromachi eras.

Kamakura period The period of Japanese garden history from 1185 to 1333.

Kawaramono A Japanese term meaning 'riverbank workers' who rose from being social outcasts to professional garden designers and architects during the Muromachi era.

Knot garden This originally referred to a garden or part of a garden which was designed in the form of a knot with a continuous pattern of interlacing bands. Nowadays, the term is used more loosely to refer to any flowerbed planted in an intricate, decorative pattern or design.

Lang A Chinese word meaning a covered walkway or corridor with either one or two open sides.

Lou A Chinese word meaning a building.

Lou chuang A Chinese word meaning latticed windows.

Meiji period The period of Japanese garden history from 1868 to 1912.

Middenallée A Dutch word meaning a middle allée or walkway.

Ming dynasty The period of Chinese garden history from 1368 to 1644.

Mirador A Spanish term which means a turret, tower or belvedere attached to a building, and commanding an excellent view.

Momoyama period The period of Japanese garden history from 1568 to 1603.

Moon gate In Chinese gardens a decorative, circular doorway (hence the name moon gate) in either an outer or inner wall of the garden heralding the transition from one space to another.

Mount Meru The cosmic mountain at the centre of the universe, in Buddhist philosophy.

Muromachi period The period of Japanese garden history from 1134 to 1568.

Naka-kuguri A Japanese word that literally translates as 'middle crawl through gate' and refers to one of the gates a visitor has to crawl through on his hands and knees to get to the tea house and tea ceremony in a sufficiently humble frame of mind.

NCCPG The National Council for the Conservation of Plants & Gardens.

NGS The National Garden Scheme. A charity that raises money for numerous good causes by organising the opening of private gardens for one or two days a year for a small charge.

GLOSSARY

Northern Song dynasty The period of Chinese garden history from 960 to 1127.

Nymphaeum A grotto or shrine, usually composed of fountains, supposedly the home of the nymphs.

O-karikomi The Japanese art of topiary.

Orangery A special heated building for protecting oranges and other tender plants during the winter months. Orangeries were sometimes used as venues for musical and theatrical concerts during the summer months.

P'eng-lai In Japan, the Chinese belief in the five islands of the blessed where the immortals lived, was condensed to one island called p'eng-lai or horai-zan.

Parterre A French word that literally means 'on the ground' which refers to a level space in a garden occupied by ornamental flower-beds arranged formally and usually bordered with low, clipped hedges.

Parterre de broderies A particular kind of parterre which literally means embroidered parterre and refers to the circling, arabesque patterns of the trimmed hedges and flowers which look like embroidery.

Parterre de compartiments de fleurs A specific French term meaning a parterre with flowers in each of the compartments or sections.

Peng jing The Chinese term for bonsai in which trees and shrubs are cultivated in miniaturized form and are either planted on their own or with rocks, moss and water to create miniature landscapes.

Peristyle gardens Roman town gardens in which a wall or row of columns surrounds a courtyard or cloister containing a fountain, some plants and statuary creating a cool, enclosed space away from the bustle of the streets.

Picturesque A landscape that is deliberately designed to look like a painting.

Plates bandes These are beds bordered by low, trimmed boxwood hedges which contain flowering plants. Each plant in the bed is separated from the next by a controlling piece of string and trimmed shrubs.

Pleached limes Branches of lime trees that are entwined or interlaced to form a hedge.

Pleasance or Pleasaunce Originally this meant an enclosed medieval hunting park but now more generally refers to a secluded enclosure or part of a garden, attached to a large house.

Portico A colonnade; a roof supported by columns at regular intervals and usually attached as a porch to a building.

Potager A French word meaning kitchen garden. A potager is usually arranged formally with fruit, flowers and vegetables laid out in decorative patterns.

Pure Land Buddhism This is the belief in Amida, a transhistorical Buddha of light and life who governs a Pure Land in the West.

Qing dynasty The period of Chinese garden history from 1644 to 1911.

Red books These were the 'before' and 'after' books produced by Humphrey Repton for his clients so that they could see what their gardens would look like once he had carried out his proposed changes.

Rocaille A French word for the kind of decorative rock and shell work found lining the inside of grottoes and fountains.

Roji A Japanese word that translates as 'path' or 'passageway' and means the tea garden that leads to the tea house or arbour where the tea ceremony takes place.

Sacro bosco This means sacred wood.

Sakutei-ki The Japanese title of the oldest surviving garden book that dates back to the eleventh century.

Shakkei The Japanese word for 'borrowed landscape' equivalent to the Chinese word Jiejing, referring to the technique of incorporating the landscape outside the garden into the overall composition of the garden.

Shan-shui A Chinese term that literally translates as 'mountains and water' but is used to describe what in the West is called landscape.

Shan-shui peng jing This is the Chinese term for Bonsai and refers specifically to the art of creating a Lilliputian landscape with the use of miniaturized trees and shrubs, water and rocks.

Shinden A Japanese word meaning the main hall in a building.

Shinden-zukuri A Japanese word referring to the palace and garden architecture of the Heian period.

Shintoism The official religion of Japan which incorporates the worship of ancestors and nature-spirits.

Shoin A Japanese word for the most sophisticated room within the residential quarters of Zen priests.

Shoin-zukuri A Japanese word for the architectural style of the Kamakura and Muromachi eras.

So-an A Japanese word that literally means 'the grass-thatched hut' and refers to a simple rustic tea arbour where the tea ceremony takes place.

Southern Song dynasty The period of Chinese garden history from 1127 to 1279.

Stroll garden This is the type of Japanese garden that is primarily designed for walking around and admiring the different vistas and aspects of the garden that are presented or revealed as one does so.

Sukiya A Japanese word for the new kind of architecture that evolved out of the tea house arbours and roji of the Momoyama era.

Taihu rock A kind of rock dredged up from Lake Taihu, near Suzhou in eastern China, that is highly prized in the construction of Chinese gardens for its interesting and symbolically evocative shapes.

Taoism .The Chinese philosophy based on the writings of Laoze (c.500 BC), which advocates humility and religious piety. Also known as Daoism.

Tea garden A Japanese term for the kind of gardens where tea ceremonies where performed, which first became popular in the Momoyama era.

Term A statue or bust of the upper part of the body usually emerging from a pillar-like plinth, originally representing the Roman god Terminus, guardian of boundaries, but often used in a more general sense.

Ting A Chinese word meaning an open-sided pavilion in a garden used for rest or viewing.

Tobi-ishi A Japanese word referring to the stepping stones in a garden.

Topiary The art of clipping, shaping and training shrubs and trees to grow into ornamental shapes.

Triclinium A Latin word to describe an open-air dining-room.

Trompe l'oeil A French expression that literally means 'to deceive the eye' which refers to the technique of doing a painting on a wall, ceiling or piece of garden furniture in such a way that an illusion of reality is created; for instance, something will appear much nearer or further away than it actually is.

Tufa A porous rock composed of calcium carbonate and formed round mineral springs which is frequently used to decorate fountains and grottoes.

Vista A long, narrow view as between rows of trees or a closely framed view that opens out onto a panoramic prospect.

Wabi-cha A Japanese word meaning tea ceremony.

Xeriscaping The art of landscaping to reduce water consumption by combining drought-tolerant plants and drip irrigation together with the use of sand, rocks and boulders to provide an appropriate and stable environment.

Yuan dynasty The period of Chinese garden history from 1280 to 1368.

Zen Buddhism A form of Buddhism which emphasizes the value of meditation and intuition, based on the belief that the path to enlightenment is through power over the self.

Index

The numbers set in bold face indicate the major entry for this garden. The entries in italic type refer to important people mentioned in the text.

INDEX